Rowan Allen Greer III is Walter H. Gray Professor of Anglican Studies and Fellow of Jonathan Edwards College, Yale University Divinity School. His previous books include *Broken Lights and Mended Lives: Theology and Common Life in the Early Church; Theodore of Mopsuestia: Exegete and Theologian; The Captain of Our Salvation: A Study in the Patristic Exegesis of Hebrews; The Sermon on the Mount;* and *Origen: An Exhortation to Martyrdom, Prayer, and Selected Works.*

D1549542

THE FEAR OF FREEDOM

A Study of Miracles in the Roman Imperial Church

THE FEAR OF FREEDOM

A Study of Miracles in the
Roman Imperial Church

Rowan A. Greer

The Pennsylvania State University Press
University Park and London

Library of Congress Cataloging-in-Publication Data

Greer, Rowan A.
The fear of freedom.

Bibliography: p.
Includes index.
1. Miracles—History of doctrines—Early church,
ca. 30–600. 2. Christianity—Early church, ca. 30–600.
3. Freedom (Theology) I. Title.
BT97.2'.G73 1988   231.7'3   88–17947
ISBN 0-271-00648-X

Copyright © 1989 The Pennsylvania State University

Printed in the United States of America

Contents

	Abbreviations	vii
	Introduction	1
1	The Wonderworker in the Gospels	8
2	The Wonderworker Proclaimed from the Pulpit	35
3	Christ the Wonderworker in Context	62
4	Wonderworkers in the Church	88
5	Hope in the Community	117
6	Divine and Human Freedom	150
	Epilogue	180
	Notes	183
	Bibliography	201
	Index	205
	Index of Biblical Citations	209

Abbreviations Used
in Citing Primary Texts

AC	Prosper of Aquitaine, *Against Cassian* (see ACW 32)
ACW	Ancient Christian Writers

    31   John Chrysostom, *Baptismal Instructions*, English trans. and ed. Paul W. Harkins (Westminster, Md.: Newman Press, 1963)

    32   Prosper of Aquitaine, *Defense of St. Augustine*, English trans. and ed. P. DeLetter (Westminster, Md.: Newman Press, 1963)

    34   Palladius, *The Lausiac History*, English trans. and ed. Robert T. Meyer (Westminster, Md.: Newman Press, 1965)

    35   *Letters of St. Paulinus of Nola, Volume 1*, English trans. and ed. P. G. Walsh (Westminster, Md.: Newman Press, 1967)

    36   *Letters of St. Paulinus of Nola, Volume 2*, English trans. and ed. P. G. Walsh (Westminster, Md.: Newman Press, 1968)

    40   *The Poems of St. Paulinus of Nola*, English trans. and ed. P. G. Walsh (New York and Ramsey, N.J.: Newman Press, 1975)

    45   Palladius, *Dialogue on the Life of St. John Chrysostom*, English trans. and ed. Robert T.

	Meyer (New York and Ramsey, N.J.: Newman Press, 1985)
AJ	Augustine, *Homilies on the Gospel of John* (*NPNF* 1.7)
AJJ	Jerome, *Against John of Jerusalem* (*NPNF* 2.6)
AL	Ambrose, *Homilies on Luke* (see SC 45 and 52)
Amm. Marc.	Ammianus Marcellinus, *History*, English trans. and ed. John C. Rolfe, Loeb Classical Library, 3 volumes (Cambridge, Mass.: Harvard University Press; first printed 1935–40; revised and reprinted 1948–52)
ARI	Gregory of Nyssa, *Address on Religious Instruction* (see LCC 3)
AV	Jerome, *Against Vigilantius* (*NPNF* 2.6)
Burns	J. P. Burns, *Theological Anthropology*, Sources of Early Christian Thought (Philadelphia: Fortress Press, 1981)
CD	Augustine, *The Care to be Taken for the Dead* (see FC 27)
CG	Augustine, *City of God* (see PC)
CM	Prudentius, *Crowns of Martyrdom*, in Loeb Classical Library, Prudentius, 2 volumes, English trans. and ed. H. J. Thomson (Cambridge, Mass.: Harvard University Press, 1949 & 1953)
CS	Cistercian Studies 88, Theodoret of Cyrrhus, *A History of the Monks in Syria*, English trans. and ed. R. M. Price (Kalamazoo, Mich.: Cistercian Publications, 1985)
ChJ	John Chrysostom, *Homilies on John* (*NPNF* 1.14)
ChM	John Chrysostom, *Homilies on Matthew* (*NPNF* 1.10)
Conf.	Augustine, *Confessions* (see PC)
Cure	Theodoret of Cyrrhus, *The Cure of Pagan Maladies* (see SC 57)
Cureton	W. Cureton, *Eusebius: The Martyrs of Palestine* (London: Williams & Norgate, 1861)
CWS	Classics of Western Spirituality
	Athanasius, *The Life of Antony and the Letter to Marcellinus*, English trans. and ed. Robert C. Gregg (New York, Ramsey, and Toronto: Paulist Press, 1980)
	Gregory of Nyssa, *The Life of Moses*, English trans. and ed. Abraham J. Malherbe (New York, Ramsey, and Toronto: Paulist Press, 1978)
D	Eusebius of Caesarea, *Demonstration of the Gospel*, English trans. and ed. W. J. Ferrar, *Eusebius: The Proof of the Gospel* (Grand Rapids, Mich.: Baker Book House, 1981; reprint of 1920)

Dial.	Palladius, *Dialogue on the Life of St. John Chrysostom* (see ACW 45)
Dials.	Sulpicius Severus, *Dialogues* (*NPNF* 2.11)
DIC	Gregory of Nyssa, *De instituto Christiano*, ed. W. Jaeger, *Gregorii Nysseni Opera*, volume 8.1 (Leiden: E. J. Brill, 1963)
DP	Gregory of Nyssa, *De perfectione*, ed. W. Jaeger, volume 8.1
DPC	Gregory of Nyssa, *De professione Christiana*, ed. W. Jaeger, volume 8.1.
EH	Ecclesiastical History (Eusebius and Theodoret)
FC	Fathers of the Church
	27 Augustine, *Treatises on Marriage and Other Subjects*, English trans. C. T. Wilcox et al., ed. R. J. Deferrari (New York: Fathers of the Church, Inc., 1955)
	65 Ambrose, *Seven Exegetical Works*, English trans. and ed. Michael P. McHugh (Washington, D.C.: The Catholic University of America Press, 1972)
FM	Gregory of Nyssa, *Homilies on the Forty Martyrs of Sebaste* (*PG* 46)
GT	Gregory of Nyssa, *Panegyric on Gregory Thaumaturgus* (*PG* 46)
HM	Hilary of Poitiers, *Commentary on Matthew* (see SC 254 and 258)
HSD	Basil of Caesarea, *Homilies on the Six Days of Creation* (see SC 26)
I	Ambrose, *Isaac, or the Soul* (see FC 65)
J	Ambrose, *Jacob and the Happy Life* (see FC 65)
JM	Jerome, *Commentary on Matthew* (SC 242 and 259)
LA	Athanasius, *Life of Antony* (see CWS)
LC	Eusebius, *Life of Constantine* (*NPNF* 2.1)
LCC	Library of Christian Classics
	3 *Christology of the Later Fathers*, English trans. and ed. E. R. Hardy (Philadelphia: Westminster Press, 1954)
	4 *Cyril of Jerusalem and Nemesius of Emesa*, English trans. and ed. William Telfer (Philadelphia: Westminster Press, 1955)
	6 *Augustine: Earlier Writings*, English trans. and ed. John S. Burleigh (Philadelphia: Westminster Press, 1953)

	12 *Western Asceticism*, English trans. and ed. Owen Chadwick (Philadelphia: Westminster Press, 1958)
LH	Palladius, *The Lausiac History* (see ACW 34)
LM	Gregory of Nyssa, *Life of Macrina* (see SC 178)
LMar	Sulpicius Severus, *Life of St. Martin* (*NPNF* 2.11)
LMo	Gregory of Nyssa, *Life of Moses* (see CWS)
LMY	*Life of Melania the Younger*, English trans. and ed. Elizabeth A. Clark, Studies in Women and Religion 14 (New York and Toronto: The Edwin Mellen Press, 1984)
Mart. Pal.	Eusebius, *The Martyrs of Palestine* (see Cureton)
MS	Theodoret of Cyrrhus, *A History of the Monks in Syria* (see CS)
NPNF	A Select Library of Nicene and Post-Nicene Fathers of the Christian Church, English trans. and ed. Philip Schaff and Henry Wace (Buffalo and New York, 1886–1900). Volumes are cited by series (1 or 2) and volume number.
OI	Athanasius, *On the Incarnation* (see LCC 3)
OP	John Chrysostom, *On Providence* (see SC 79)
OSR	Gregory of Nyssa, *On the Soul and the Resurrection* (*NPNF* 2.5)
OT	Augustine, *On the Trinity* (*NPNF* 1.3)
OTR	Augustine, *Of True Religion* (see LCC 6)
P	Philip E. Pusey, *Sancti Patris Nostri Cyrilli Archiepiscopi Alexandrini in D. Joannis Evangelium*, 3 volumes (Brussels: Impression anastaltique, culture, et civilisation, 1965; reprint of 1872 edition). Numbers refer to volume and page.
PC	Penguin Classics
	Augustine, *Confessions*, English trans. and ed. R. S. Pine-Coffin (Harmondsworth: Penguin Books, 1961)
	Augustine, *City of God*, English trans. Henry Bettenson, intro. and ed. David Knowles (Harmondsworth: Penguin Books, 1972)
PG	J. P. Migne, *Patrologia Graeca*, 161 volumes (Paris, 1857–66)
R	Joseph Reuss, *Lukas-Kommentare aus der griechischen Kirche*, TU 130 (Berlin: Akademie-Verlag, 1984)
SC	Sources chrétiennes
	25 *bis* Ambroise de Milan, *Des Sacrements, Des Mystères, Explication du Symbole*, French trans. and ed. Bernard Botte (Paris: Editions du cerf, 1980)

26 Basile de Cesarée, *Homélies sur l'Hexaéméron*, French trans. and ed. Stanislas Giet (Paris: Editions du cerf, 1949)

45 and 52 Ambroise de Milan, *Traité sur l'évangile de s. Luc*, French trans. and ed. Gabriel Tissot (Paris: Editions du cerf, 1956 and 1958)

57 Théodoret de Cyr, *Thérapeutique des Maladies Helléniques*, 2 volumes, French trans. and ed. Pierre Canivet (Paris: Editions du cerf, 1958)

79 Jean Chrysostome, *Sur la Providence de Dieu*, French trans. and ed. Anne-Marie Malingrey (Paris: Editions du cerf, 1961)

178 Grégoire de Nysse, *Vie de sainte Macrine*, French trans. and ed. Pierre Marraval (Paris: Editions de cerf, 1971)

242 and 259 Saint Jérôme, *Commentaire sur s. Matthieu*, French trans. and ed. Emile Bonnard (Paris: Editions du cerf, 1977 and 1979)

254 and 258 Hilaire de Poitiers, *Sur Matthieu*, French trans. and ed. Jean Doignon (Paris: Editions du cerf, 1978 and 1979)

SF   *The Sayings of the Fathers* (see LCC 12)

SH   Sulpicius Severus, *Sacred History* (*NPNF* 2.11)

Soc.   Socrates, *Ecclesiastical History* (*NPNF* 2.2)

Soz   Sozomen, *Ecclesiastical History* (*NPNF* 2.2)

T   R. M. Tonneau, *S. Cyrilli Alexandrini Commentarii in Lucam*, Script. Syri 70 (Louvain: CSCO 140, 1954)

TM   Gregory of Nyssa, *Praise of Theodore the Martyr* (PG 46)

UB   Augustine, *The Usefulness of Belief* (see LCC 6)

V   J.-M. Vosté, *Theodori Mopsuesteni Commentarius in Evangelium Iohannis Apostoli*, Script. Syri 4.3 (Louvain: CSCO, 1940)

WS   Woodbrooke Studies

5 A. Mingana, *Commentary of Theodore of Mopsuestia on the Nicene Creed* (Cambridge: W. Heffer & Sons, 1932)

6 A. Mingana, *Commentary of Theodore of Mopsuestia on the Lord's Prayer and on the Sacraments of Baptism and the Eucharist* (Cambridge: W. Heffer & Sons, 1933)

Introduction

I have chosen as the title for this study the words E. R. Dodds uses to describe the last chapter of his book, *The Greeks and the Irrational*. His argument in that chapter is that by the third century B.C. it looked as though Greek rationalism was about to usher in an Age of Reason. Instead, "Greek civilisation was entering . . . on a period of slow intellectual decline which was to last, with some deceptive rallies and some brilliant rearguard actions, down to the capture of Byzantium by the Turks" (p. 244). This change in "the intellectual climate of the Mediterranean world" marks the background for the rise of Christianity. Indeed, "it made the triumph of the new religion possible, and it left its mark on Christian teaching; but it was not created by Christians" (p. 248f.).

Dodds tackles the problem of explaining this shift of sensibility and does so with our modern predicament in mind. Without denying the complexity of the problem and explanations that involve intellectual and economic factors, he suggests that we must reckon with "another sort of motive, less conscious and less tidily rational." What he means is "the fear of freedom—the unconscious flight from the heavy burden of individual choice which an open society lays upon its members" (p. 252). In this Dodds finds the shadow of our own problems (p. 254):

> We too have witnessed the slow disintegration of an inherited conglomerate, starting among the educated class but now affecting the

masses almost everywhere, yet still very far from complete. We too
have experienced a great age of rationalism, marked by scientific
advances beyond anything that earlier times had thought possible,
and confronting mankind with the prospect of a society more open
than any it has ever known. And in the last forty years we have also
experienced something else—the unmistakable symptoms of a re-
coil from that prospect.

In antiquity, says Dodds, the horseman refused to jump the fence and to
establish an open society. We are on the brink of the same sort of failure;
but there is hope in suspecting that the problem lies in the horse and not
the rider, that is, in "those irrational elements in human nature which
govern without our knowledge so much of our behaviour and so much of
what we think is our thinking" (p. 254).

There can be no doubt that Dodds's conclusions are open to question in
many ways.[1] Is the contrast between rational and irrational the best way
of defining the problem he is studying? Can we be satisfied with implying
that the rational is purely human and liberates us from any reliance on the
divine? Can freedom be understood adequately by defining it in terms of
choice? Has Dodds freed himself from assumptions made by the Enlightenment and no longer congruent with a post-Newtonian science? Does his
view take account of the community as the locus in which individuals seek
virtue in common? Obviously, to attempt answers to these questions goes
beyond both my aim and my competence. What interests me is not so
much Dodds's answers as his questions. And the reason for this attitude is
that much of what he says finds an analogue in the way the early church
has often been treated. To read studies of the theological development of
the early church is to find oneself supposing that the church fathers not
only Hellenized the Gospel but also rationalized it. For the Christian
Platonists of the early church the Gospel became largely an appeal to
human freedom. Granted that our capacity to choose the good is a gift of
God and that we can exercise that capacity fully only by trusting in God's
love, nonetheless, the Christian life for most of the church fathers before
Augustine was primarily a quest for moral and spiritual virtue.

On the other hand, when we turn from the theologians to Christianity as
a social phenomenon in late antiquity, we find what Dodds would describe as the triumph of the irrational. More particularly, after Constantine we find the development and organization of the cult of the saints and
the rise of monasticism as a movement in early Christianity. These two
developments build upon earlier precedents; but their importance is, I
think, novel and revolves around treating special places and special people
as sources of divine power. Ramsay MacMullen in his *Christianizing the*

Roman Empire has usefully reminded us of the importance of the miraculous in the early church. A gap begins to appear in the literature that studies ancient Christianity. Historians of doctrine virtually ignore the miraculous, while social historians increasingly see it as a central dimension of the church. If the gap corresponds, as I think it does, to what was really the case, and if I am correct in arguing that the miraculous only occupies center stage after the Constantinian revolution, then it looks as though Dodds's scenario has played itself out in the history of the church. By the end of the third century Christian Platonism commanded the way the Gospel was proclaimed, but in the fourth century an emphasis upon miracles developed that scarcely harmonized with the way the Christian message was being proclaimed.

The first part of my argument, then, is the suggestion that in the fourth and fifth centuries we discover a dissociation between the theological interpretation of the Gospel and the way the Christian community lived it. In trying to understand this dissociation there are, I think, a number of blocks that must be overcome and that derive from our own assumptions and prejudices. The first of these is a view deriving largely from Hume and Gibbon that contrasts official and popular piety and that treats popular piety as superstitious and irrational. Peter Brown in *The Cult of the Saints* (p. 13ff.) has exposed this block and persuasively argued that, however much we may distinguish how Christianity appeared to different people in the ancient world, all Christians were responding to a single phenomenon. As we shall see, Gregory of Nyssa was both a Christian Platonist who wholeheartedly embraced a Gospel of freedom and also a Christian deeply committed to the cult of the saints, including the miraculous help their relics supplied. The gap of which I have spoken, in other words, runs through the sensibilities of individual figures. It is not one that divides official from popular piety.

A more difficult set of blocks to our understanding attaches to what we mean by the miraculous. We can, of course, use the word in a way that appeals to its root meaning as something that evokes our wonder. We speak of the "miracles" of modern science. And Arm & Hammer baking soda is a "miracle" because it "does so many things." On the whole, however, I suspect that we think of the miraculous as something that violates the order of nature.[2] It may be that the roots of this understanding are to be found in late antiquity, and especially in the thought of Augustine.[3] But it is, more exactly, a Western medieval and scholastic one. For example, Aquinas can say:

> God operates through secondary causes, but beyond shadow of doubt is quite able to manage without them. He can break the

common and customary rhythm of nature by producing natural
effects or fresh effects of a different kind.

Prodigies are of two kinds, relative and absolute. Prodigies are
relative when their cause is hidden only to this man or that. . . .
Prodigies are absolute when their causes are quite hidden and they
run counter to all the natural factors in the situation. . . . Only
those effects which are wrought solely by divine power are called
miracles in the narrow technical sense.[4]

This view, of course, opposes God to nature and in this sense treats miracles as "supernatural."

Even though it is difficult to do so, understanding how miracles were
perceived in late antiquity requires us to put aside the notion of a miracle
as the violation of the natural order. It does not seem to me going too far to
suggest that "miracle" for the church fathers refers to anything that evokes
our wonder. And we can take one further step by arguing that whereas we
always look for a scientific and empirical explanation of the wonderful,
the ancients tended in the opposite direction. The wonderful always suggested the presence of the divine. Let me illustrate this sharp difference in
sensibility by appealing to a brief passage from the second-century writer
Pausanias.[5] He makes the astonishing claim: "I myself have seen Niobe
when I was climbing up the mountains to Sipylos." But he goes on to
explain: "Niobe from close up is a rock and a stream, and nothing like a
woman either grieving or otherwise; but if you go further off you seem to
see a woman downcast and in tears." For us there would be little to see but
a remarkable natural spot; for Pausanias, the divine presence of Niobe is
obvious. By making a distinction between what really happened and the
explanation given to an event, we can sometimes see that an ancient
miracle is not necessarily something totally beyond our experience.[6]

Let me say, however, that my concern with the issue of defining the
miraculous is negative rather than positive. That is, it seems to me important that we recognize how very different ancient attitudes were from our
own. But I do not wish to seek for an explanation of miracles that will be
true to the evidence and congruent with modern sensibilities. I am not
really interested in conclusions about the truth or falsity of the miracles
reported in the ancient sources. This is partly because I am skeptical that
we can often penetrate beyond the explanation given to what really happened. But it is partly because what seems far more interesting to me is
how the miracle stories function in the way people understood Christianity
in the fourth and fifth centuries. Few people in late antiquity would have
correlated the miraculous with the irrational and the superstitious. As a

result, we can better understand their point of view by setting to one side the modern problem of miracles and by examining how the miracles that are told us by ancient Christians function.

What has struck me most forcibly in this study is the way in which miracles are constantly associated with the community life of Christians. I shall suggest that this phenomenon needs to be seen as part of the Constantinian revolution. That is, once the church gained predominance in the Empire, most Christians thought that a new Christian commonwealth was in the making. Their enterprise was the sacralization of the Roman order. Heaven had come down to earth, and Christ was transforming the kingdom of this world into his own realm. The miracles associated with the cult of the saints and with holy people in the Christian Empire were part of this sacralization. The power of heaven and of the age to come was, in a sense, domesticated and made available here and now. No longer did Christian pilgrims restrict their longing to the heavenly Jerusalem; instead, they also found its power in the actual holy places of the earthly Jerusalem. No longer were martyrs and saints merely exemplars of the Christian life; on the contrary, they assumed importance as sources of potent patronage for the Christian people. The sacralization of the Empire, then, was accompanied by a burgeoning of the miraculous. And this new emphasis in the church pulled in a slightly different direction from the Christian Platonist theology that remained dominant but that had its roots in the thought of people like Origen for whom the Christian message had to do with freedom and virtue rather than with power.

If the first part of my argument is to agree that a gap appears between the Christian message and Christianity as a social phenomenon, the second part of it is to suggest that what we discover is a tension between the theology of the Roman imperial church that appealed primarily to the individual and the corporate piety that characterized the life of that church. It occurs to me that an analogy from our own time helps make the issue vivid. At the risk of oversimplification, let me say that in our generation a strong tension has developed between our commitment to self-fulfillment and our longing for community. It seldom occurs to us that these two desiderata are in possible conflict with one another. Part of the argument of Robert N. Bellah's *Habits of the Heart* concerns this issue. Bellah and his associates point out that in some respects the framers of the American Constitution agreed with Montesquieu that "the virtuous citizen was one who understood that personal welfare is dependent on the general welfare and could be expected to act accordingly. Forming such character requires the context of practices in which the coincidence of personal concern and the common welfare can be experienced."[7] Our modern dilemma springs largely from the loss of any sense of our common welfare.

We are apt "to treat normative commitments as so many alternative strate-
gies of self-fulfillment. What has dropped out are the old normative expectations of what makes life worth living. With the freedom to define oneself
anew in a plethora of identities has also come an attenuation of those
common understandings that enable us to recognize the virtues of the
other."[8]

The freedom of the individual right to "life, liberty, and the pursuit of
happiness" correlates, I suggest, with the message of Christian Platonism
that treated the Gospel as a Christianized version of the late antique quest
for virtue. People like Origen and Gregory of Nyssa assumed, like our
Founding Fathers, that the individual's quest for virtue, far from being
incompatible with the community, actually helped constitute it. With
God's grace the Christian associated himself with a common commitment
that led to his participation in the fellowship of saints who shared a
common goal. In late antiquity, unlike our own time, it was not the
erosion of a sense of community that rendered the individual quest for ˙
virtue problematic. On the contrary, a new understanding of community
caused the problem. After Constantine the church tended to become less a
by-product of common commitments and more a prior reality that, at
least in principle, was meant to urge Christians toward virtue. Perhaps
more important, attention shifted from the fellowship of saints that was
primarily a heavenly and future reality anticipated by the church to the
church itself. In these ways the church took on an importance it had not
really had before. Power became more significant than virtue; and the
miracles of the saints, dead and living, tended to eclipse an emphasis upon
the right use of human freedom in choosing the good.

Perhaps I have exaggerated, but I have done so with the hope of clarify-
ing the issue that primarily emerges from a study of miracles in the
Roman imperial church. Of course, the predominant theology did not
ignore the corporate character of the Christian life any more than it excluded the absolute necessity of belief in the decisiveness of what God had
done in Christ. But its emphasis was upon the importance of human and
even individual freedom. Similarly, the community piety of the fourth-
and fifth-century church did not obliterate the individual any more than it
did away with the moral and spiritual character of the Christian faith. But
it did emphasize God's power acting in the community as prior to and
determinitive of the Christian life. In what I have said I may seem to have
chosen sides. And, I must confess to a predilection for the Christian
Platonist insistence upon human freedom as our God-given capacity to
move towards the good. At the same time, I should be reluctant to claim
that the other side is undeserving of a hearing.

One can put the point in terms of freedom. What does it really mean?

E. B. White faced the issue when he was asked early in 1942 to be on a government committee charged with writing a pamphlet on the "Four Freedoms" enunciated by President Roosevelt in his State of the Union address the year before. He found himself confused at the time, and eleven years later he returns to his perplexity in order to respond to a reader who had protested one of his editorials on human rights. White's words are worth citing:

> *The New Yorker* isn't against freedom from want and didn't attack it or minimize it as a goal. But we're against associating freedom from want (which is an economic goal) with freedom of speech (which is an exact political principle). . . . I do not think it safe or wise to confuse, or combine, the principle of freedom of religion or the principle of freedom of the press with any economic goal whatsoever, because of the likelihood that in guaranteeing the goal, you abandon the principle. This has happened over and over again. Eva Peron was a great freedom-from-want girl (specially at Christmas time), but it also happened that *La Prensa* died and the Argentinians were left with nothing to read but government handouts.[9]

Modern circumstances, of course, differ in many ways from those of the Roman imperial church. Nevertheless, the tension that White sees between a freedom that encourages free expression and free activity by individuals and a freedom designed to empower the masses by supplying them with basic needs corresponds in some degree to the tension between freedom as virtue and freedom as power that we find in late antique Christianity. With these introductory reflections in mind, let me turn in the following three chapters to the ways in which the predominant theology of the period interpreted Christ's miracles.

1

The Wonderworker in the Gospels

Eusebius of Caesarea's *Life of Constantine* remains a chief source for what we can know of the watershed between the pagan Roman Empire and what had become by the end of the fourth century a Christian Roman Empire. In some respects this watershed was as much a transition as a revolution. The church had already become a highly visible and important part of late antique society; and Eusebius's own account of the state of the church on the eve of the Diocletian persecution (*EH* 8.1), however exaggerated, suggests a degree of success and prosperity for Christianity that would argue against any absolute shift from rags to riches when Constantine decided to become the church's patron. Christianity had spread through all the classes of the Empire, and congregations had expanded to such an extent that large buildings were required for the public worship of the church. On the other hand, pagans clearly represented the majority of the Empire's population; even for them the Constantinian revolution did not bring any absolute discontinuity with the past. The public and pagan rites associated with Rome, for example, were carefully protected by Constantine. In many respects Constantine's work needs to be seen as the completion of the imperial revival begun by Aurelian and, above all, by Diocletian; and he put the seal on the establishment of a totalitarian autocracy that had already begun to transform the principate of the earlier Empire. Despite these continuities, there can be no doubt that the church experienced a great change by becoming public and prosperous beyond what could have been imagined before the battle of the Milvian Bridge.

It is beyond my purpose to enter upon a discussion of this mixture of continuity and discontinuity in the Constantinian revolution. Instead, let me suggest that the same mixture attaches to the Bible and its use by the church. In his *Life of Constantine* Eusebius tells how Constantine wrote him of his plans to increase the number of churches in his newly founded capital, Constantinople. The Emperor requested Eusebius to supply fifty copies of the Scriptures for use in these churches. Continuity is implied by Constantine's recognition that the Bible was central to the church; discontinuity, by the extraordinary fashion in which the Bibles are to be procured. Eusebius will have the help of professional transcribers and will be given two of the public carriages to bring them to the new capital. The copies, according to Eusebius, were at length sent "in magnificent and elaborately bound volumes" (*LC* 4.36–37; *NPNF* 2.1, p. 549).

We can presume that the same continuity and discontinuity characterized the use made of Scripture in the post-Constantinian church. Of course, my chief interest is in the Gospels and in the miracles of Christ. My task in this and the next chapter is to describe how those miracles were interpreted, and I wish to accomplish this task by examining what survives of Gospel commentaries and homilies in the fourth and fifth centuries. Hilary of Poitiers and Jerome both wrote commentaries on Matthew that survive; Theodore of Mopsuestia and Cyril of Alexandria have left us their commentaries on John. We possess homilies on Luke delivered by Ambrose and Cyril, homilies on Matthew by Chrysostom, and homilies on John by Chrysostom and Augustine. I shall examine the commentaries in this chapter and reserve discussion of the homilies for the next. The distinction, let me admit, is in some degree an artificial one for the simple reason that the church fathers make no fundamental distinction between theology and exegesis or between an erudite exposition of the Biblical text and a popular adaptation of that exposition. At the same time, a difference is made by the audience envisaged. The commentators tend to be writing for learned Christians and seldom seem very much concerned with the life of the ordinary Christian. The preachers, on the other hand, take more account of popular piety and do so in the interest of keeping piety in touch with their rather more sophisticated understanding of the Christian faith.

In both contexts the writers I shall be studying are concerned to place their interpretation of Christ's miracles in relation to a coherent account of Christianity, in other words to a theological framework. One way of suggesting what I mean by this is to employ an analogy. In the last decade of the fourth century a large bath hall in Rome was transformed into the

Church of Santa Pudenziana. The apse mosaic may still be seen, and it depicts what can be regarded as an iconographical representation of the central meaning of Christianity. Christ is enthroned in the center of the mosaic, dressed in a senatorial toga. On both sides of him stand the apostles. Behind Peter stands a female figure representing the church from the synagogue and holding a floral crown; behind Paul, a similar figure representing the church from the Gentiles. In the background we see an architectural depiction of Jerusalem. Above everything else is a jeweled cross with the four symbols of the evangelists on both sides of it.[1] It is difficult to escape the fact that we are in the presence of a depiction of a new commonwealth, a heavenly Jerusalem that finds its analogue in the church on earth.

In one way or another all the writers I shall be examining think of Christ's miracles in relation to this broad pattern. The miracles characterize the new commonwealth and prove its truth. Hilary's attention is focused upon the two churches, and he treats Christ's miracles as types of the creation of the church from Jews and Gentiles. Jerome is more concerned with the apostolic faith and, so to speak, looks more to the apostles themselves than to the allegorical figures that stand above them. Theodore and Cyril turn their attention to Christ himself and seek to place his wonderworking in the context of their accounts of his identity. The homilists to be examined in the next chapter are more concerned with the new Jerusalem and its life. For Ambrose the new Jerusalem and the new creation are a central preoccupation, while for Cyril Christ remains the focus even though his homilies shift our attention to the way Christians participate in his victory. Chrysostom draws attention to the life of virtue required by the new commonwealth, while Augustine thinks of the City of God and the two Resurrections that supply admission to it. What I am suggesting is that the different writers have significantly different things to say about the meaning of Christ's miracles, but that they are simply calling attention to different aspects of the same picture. Finally, we shall begin to see that in certain respects the miracles appear to resist an easy placement in this broader pattern. I shall wish to reserve direct discussion of the problematic character of miracles for later chapters, but the problem will begin to appear even in the course of a positive description of how they are interpreted.

HILARY OF POITIERS: THE MIRACLE OF THE CHURCH

Hilary's *Commentary on Matthew* was probably written very shortly before his exile in 356 and before he had become fully instructed in the Nicene response to Arianism.[2] It is not impossible that he was indebted to

Origen and to the two Latin commentators mentioned by Jerome, Victorinus of Poetovio and Fortunatus of Aquileia. Doignon's careful work, however, demonstrates that his major debt was to the Latin tradition found in Tertullian and Cyprian. As we shall see, his preoccupation with the church in itself argues for a Western orientation. The other preliminary point that needs to be made is that he appears to be writing for the *fratres*. We can probably imagine a quasi-monastic group of Christians that may well have consisted of Hilary's *presbyterium*, the priests over whom he presided as bishop.[3] The commentary is obviously erudite in character and is concerned with interpreting Matthew for an elite. It is with this in mind that we can turn to the way in which Hilary describes the wonderworker in the Gospel.

It is the creator of the universe that works miracles. Hilary makes this explicit in his interpretation of the feeding of the five thousand (Mt 14:13ff.). No wonder attaches to the way in which the earth brings forth grapes and produce in an annual cycle, but here the "author of this universe" acts beyond the ordinary course of nature. Christ's power as "the Lord of heavenly mysteries" is no different from the power that ordinarily produces wine and bread, but its exercise in the miraculous feeding defies explanation and arouses wonder (HM 14,12; SC 258, p. 26). Because of this and because of Christ's passion it sometimes happens that people fail to perceive that his miracles are the consequence of his divinity. For example, when Christ stills the storm on the Lake of Galilee (Mt 8:23ff.), "the men" marvel and say "What sort of man is this, that even winds and sea obey him?" Hilary identifies "the men" with "the pagans," who are misled by the passion and fail to grasp Christ's identity as God (HM 8,2; SC 254, p. 194).

It is not surprising that some would fail to understand that in Christ God works miracles, for the simple reason that Christ is human as well as divine. When Christ heals the man with the withered hand on the Sabbath (Mt 12:9ff.), the Pharisees see him only as a "man in the body" and do not understand "God in his works." This is why they "took counsel against him, how to destroy him" (Mt 12:14). Christ withdraws from these unbelievers and then commands the believers who follow him to keep silence about his miraculous healings. According to Hilary Christ's command of silence serves a double purpose. It indicates Christ's refusal of vainglorious boasting about his power and at the same time proclaims the mystery of silence by silence. The paradox is one that involves the tension between known and unknown and also seems to touch upon the double character of Christ. As human Christ seeks to avoid the adulation of the crowd; as divine his very insistence on silence proclaims him God beyond human words (HM 12, 8–9; SC 254, p. 274f.).

Hilary gives the same sort of interpretation to Christ's temptation by the devil to turn stones to bread (Mt 3:3). The devil understands that Christ is God incarnate, and his temptation is aimed at both his divinity and his humanity. The miracle of changing stones to bread would have made a show of Christ's divinity, and it would have made mockery of Christ's human endurance of the long fast. What seems to me most interesting about Hilary's interpretation is that he manages to treat the temptation narrative not merely as the triumph of the human Christ but also as the victory of God. And the paradox is that God's power is demonstrated not by performing miracles but by refraining from them.[4]

Let me turn now from the identity of the wonderworker to the wonders themselves. If Hilary can argue that only faith can rightly understand Christ's identity, he can also argue that faith is necessary in order to see the miracles. Without true faith the wonders that are accomplished through magic and by the power of the devil can be accounted miracles, as we find in the case of Simon Magus (HM 25,2; SC 258, p. 182). Moreover, Christ will reject those who claim they have prophesied, cast out demons, and done many mighty works in his name (Mt 7:22) because they sought glory for themselves and have failed to attribute the wonders to Christ (HM 6,5; SC 254, p. 176). When the Pharisees and Sadducees ask Christ to give them a sign from heaven (Mt 16:1), they betray their lack of faith and their failure to perceive his miracles. The miracles ought to have produced a proper knowledge of Christ, but did not (HM 16,1–2; SC 258, p. 48).[5] Only twice have I discovered Hilary arguing that the miracles actually do produce faith or repentance. His interpretation of John the Baptist's question "Are you he who is to come, or shall we look for another?" (Mt 11:3) shifts the apparent lack of faith to John's disciples, who are persuaded by Christ's miracles (HM 11,2–3; SC 254, p. 254). And he argues that the elder son in the parable of the two sons (Mt 21:28ff.) stands for the people from the Pharisees, who at first reject Christ but after the Resurrection repent when they see the miracles wrought through the apostles (HM 21,13; SC 258, p. 138).

The priority Hilary gives to faith is most clearly indicated by his interpretation of Christ's healing of the two blind men (Mt 9:27ff.). Of course, the text of Matthew does explicitly treat faith as the prerequisite of healing in this particular story. Christ asks the blind men whether they believe he is able to heal them, and only when they answer affirmatively does he work the miracle. But Hilary turns the pattern into a general rule (HM 9,9; SC 254, p. 212):

> The Lord shows them that faith does not come from healing, but rather that healing must be expected from faith. (For the blind

men saw because they believed; they did not believe because they saw. This obliges us to understand that what is asked must be deserved by faith and that faith cannot depend upon what we gain from our requests.) He promises sight if they have believed.

Hilary's interpretation can be regarded as the resolution of a problem posed by the text of the Gospels. The miracles are sometimes supposed to create faith and demonstrate the truth of Christ and his message, but sometimes they are made to depend upon faith. Hilary treats the first idea as usually true only in principle and the second as the key to the miracles. Proof becomes proof only to the eyes of faith.

Let me turn now to the significance the miracles take on once they are perceived in faith, since this is where Hilary's real interest lies. His interpretation of the healing of the paralytic (Mt 9:2ff.) suggests the broad outline of what all the miracles point towards. The narrative unfolds the "order of truth," while Christ's words explain the "image of the future." Hilary is suggesting that the narrative focuses upon the fact that, since only God can forgive sins, Christ in claiming to have that power is claiming to be God. At the same time, the double miracle he performs by forgiving the paralytic and by giving him bodily healing affords an image of redemption in both its moral and its physical redemptions. The Incarnation has the effect of forgiving souls their sins and promising bodies the resurrection. Miracles become paradigms of redemption (HM 8,6–7; SC 254, p. 200). Similarly, the apostles are sent upon their mission (Mt 10:1ff.) vested with Christ's power. Those who in Adam had been fashioned in the image and likeness of God now obtain the perfect image and likeness of Christ, their powers differing in no way from Christ's. Those who had been earthly now become heavenly (HM 10,4; SC 254, p. 218). Hilary goes on to describe their saving work as both physical and moral. Later he interprets the earthquake at the time of Christ's Resurrection (Mt 28:2) as indicating the power of the general resurrection (HM 33,9; SC 258, p. 258). And the faith that moves mountains (Mt 17:20) is related to the moral dimension of redemption that can overthrow the devil (HM 17,7; SC 258, p. 66f.).

The church, of course, is where the believer finds redemption; and for Hilary the real miracle is that of the church, towards which the wonders of Christ point in their "interior sense." The interior sense is really the spiritual meaning found in the order of the narrative, and the two meanings are never to be opposed to one another.[6] Hilary makes this point when he begins his discussion of the two miracles that follow the Sermon on the Mount: the healing of the leper and the healing of the centurion's servant (Mt 8:1–13). The narrative meaning, however, can be seen to conceal an interior sense that is already suggested by the preoccupation of the Sermon

on the Mount with the Jewish law. The miracle stories "contain in themselves the figure (*profectus*) of things to come" (HM 7,1; SC 254, p. 180).
They supply a "similitude of the future" (HM 7,5; SC 254, p. 184). What
Hilary means is that the spiritual meaning of the miracles may be found in
the constitution of the church from Jews and Gentiles. The leper stands for
the "healing" of the crowd that hears Christ's sermon, the believing Jews.
The command to be silent about the cure means that healing is offered
rather than sought. And the command that the healed leper show himself
to the priests indicates that the redemption brought by Christ, already
announced by the law, brings the law to perfection. The healing of the
centurion's servant, of course, stands for the redemption of the Gentiles.
The fact that the healing takes place by word alone means that the Gentiles are saved by faith alone. In a sense, the interior meaning is allegorical;
but, more accurately, we must describe it as a sort of typology whereby the
deeds of Christ in their spiritual meaning foreshadow the preaching of
Redemption to the Jew first and then to the Gentiles.

Hilary rings changes on the theme at a number of points in his commentary. Sometimes this involves supplying a catalogue describing the order of
the narrative so that the various stories may be seen in their relation to one
another. For example, he lists the details of the stories of the Gadarene
demoniacs and the healing of the paralytic (Mt 8:28–9:8) and goes on to
explain their meaning. The two demoniacs represent Ham and Japheth,
the two Gentile sons of Noah. They dwell outside the city, that is, outside
the synagogue of the law and the prophets, and are in death since they
dwell in the tombs. Their healing is the conversion of the Gentiles, and the
rejection of Christ by the townspeople is his rejection by the Jews. Thus
rejected, Christ returns to his own city in the little ship of the church. The
healing of the paralytic, then, represents the plenitude of the Gentiles. "In
one Adam sins are forgiven to all nations"(HM 8,5; SC 254, p. 198). If we
were to harmonize this section of Hilary's commentary with his interpretation of Matthew 8, we should have the following pattern: some Jews
believe, then redemption is taken to the Gentiles; this provokes Jewish
rejection of Christ and the ingathering of all the Gentiles. I am not sure,
however, that we should seek to force Hilary's description of the "image of
the future" into so tidy a pattern.

One reason for this conclusion is that there are several other places in
the commentary where the constitution of the church from Jews and
Gentiles is described with still more variation. Hilary treats another set of
episodes together when he interprets Matthew 9:18–34 (HM 9,5–10; SC
254, p. 208ff.). The ruler is the law and asks that his daughter, the people,
be brought to life from death. But before Christ can fulfill his promise, the
Gentiles, symbolized by the woman with the flow of blood, are healed.

Then Christ enters the synagogue (the ruler's house), where he raises the remnant of Israel (the daughter) but expels most of the Jews (the crowd). The two blind men whom Christ next encounters (Mt 9:27) are sons of David and represent the Pharisees and the disciples of John the Baptist.[7] Finally, the dumb demoniac of Matthew 9:32 stands for the Gentiles; and the reference to "all the cities and villages" in verse 35 suggests the universal scope of the Gentile mission. Still another variation begins with the healing of the man with the withered hand (Mt 12:9ff.). The withered hand represents the impotence of Judaism and is healed by Christ's word alone. Christ then turns to the Gentiles (the blind and dumb demoniac of Matthew 12:22), and defends himself against Jewish rejection in the Beelzebub controversy (Mt 12:24ff.). The undivided kingdom and city show that Christ does not divide Israel and Jerusalem. Finally, the unclean spirit that returns to its swept house (Mt 12:43ff.) symbolizes the expulsion of the devil by the law from the Jews and his turning to the Gentiles. Then, when the Gentiles are baptized, the devil returns to the Jews (HM 12,21–23; SC 254, p. 290ff.).

Hilary's most extensive commentary on the constitution of the church from Jews and Gentiles is found in his interpretation of Matthew 14. We are told that in the order of the narrative may be found an "interior meaning." Hilary first summarizes the narrative itself and then turns to its meaning. The law (John the Baptist) rebukes the Jews (Herod) for allying themselves with pagan disbelief and so selling the gifts of eternal life for sin and pleasure (Herod's birthday feast). The times of the law were buried with John the Baptist; and the Word of God then enters the little ship of the church, withdrawing to a desert place away from the synagogue (Mt 14:13). But the crowd leaves the synagogue for the church, receives Christ's healing in body and spirit, and so is enabled to receive the miraculous food of his new teaching of the law. Christ's walking on the water is his return at the end of the age to the little ship of the church, where he finds the remnant of Israel (HM 14,7–14; SC 258, p. 16ff.). Peter's walking on the water and his failure foreshadows his denial and repentance (HM 14,15–17; SC 258, p. 28ff.). The pattern is completed by the story of the Canaanite woman and her daughter (Mt 15:21ff.). The woman represents Gentile proselytes who become Christians, while her daughter symbolizes the people of the Gentiles (HM 15,1–5; SC 258, p. 34ff.). The feeding of the four thousand (Mt 15:34ff.) refers to the ingathering of the Gentiles.

The pattern that lies behind Hilary's interpretation is, of course, one that can be found in the New Testament. In Acts the remnant of Israel is first constituted in the Jerusalem church and only then does the Gentile mission begin. Moreover, the Paul of Acts consistently begins his mission by going to the Jews; only when he is rejected, as he always is, does he turn to the Gentiles. We may also think of Paul's argument in Romans 9–11, where he describes the mystery of God's purpose as the constitution of the church out of the remnant of Israel, which is the root of the olive tree into which the Gentiles are grafted. The final stage of Paul's vision is absent both for Acts and for Hilary. In Paul's view the conversion of the Gentiles will provoke the Jews to jealousy, and they will repent and return to the true Israel of the church. Hilary's understanding of the miracle of the church owes a debt not only to the New Testament but to the persistent themes of the remnant of Israel, the rejection of Christ by the Jews, and the Gentile mission as those themes are preserved in all of patristic literature.

Although Hilary must clearly be located in the mainstream of Christian thought, his emphasis is a particular one. Doignon has demonstrated his dependence upon the Latin tradition as found in Tertullian and Cyprian. Moreover, his emphasis upon the church seems to me specifically Western. We do not find any true ecclesiology outside the West, nor are the Eastern fathers very much concerned with who is in the church and who is outside it.[8] Hilary's attention is focused upon the allegorical figures representing the churches from the synagogue and from the Gentiles, to return to the analogy of the apse mosaic in Santa Pudenziana. He in no way denies the miracles of Christ, nor does he even seem to find them problematic in any way. His concern is with their meaning, their saving import. And that meaning finally resolves itself in the miracle of the church, the little ship that carries Christians towards their ultimate destiny.

Jerome: the Miracle of Faith

Jerome's *Commentary on Matthew* was written in Lent in 398 to satisfy an importunate request by Eusebius of Cremona, who wanted some profitable reading to while away the time during his return trip from the Holy Land to Rome. In his preface Jerome complains about the difficulty of the task, compounded by the fact that he is recovering from a serious illness; but he grudgingly complies with the request. As a result the commentary is a hasty work, and Jerome's comments are often sketchy. Moreover, they do not as clearly reflect a unified point of view about Matthew as do Hilary's comments.[9] A number of comments reflect Jerome's acquaintance with the Holy Land. He occasionally digresses into a discussion of textual matters.[10] Nevertheless, if there is one theme that dominates the commentary, it is that of faith.

We do, of course, discover that Christ's miracles bear witness to his person and work, even though Jerome tends to avoid language that would speak of proof. For example, when Christ stills the storm (Mt 8:26), we "understand that all creatures perceive the creator," even though we must not adopt the heretical understanding that they all have souls (JM 8:26; SC 242, p. 162). Moreover, after Christ's walking on the water Jerome supposes that the sea became calm and points out that the disciples acclaim Christ as Son of God (Mt 14:33), thus supplying a refutation of Arius (JM 14:33; SC 242, p. 316). Christ's healing of the blind men (Mt 20:34) is the creator's (*artifex*) gift of what nature had denied or in any case of mercy bestowing what infirmity had taken away (JM 20:34; SC 259, p. 100). And the miracles at the passion give strong testimony (*probabant*) to Christ's divinity (JM 28:2–3; SC 259, p. 310). In the temptation narrative the devil recognizes Christ's divinity, but Christ's refusal to turn stones to bread reveals his intention to defeat Satan by humility rather than power (JM 4:3–4; SC 242, p. 96).

In several places Jerome emphasizes the extraordinary character of Christ's miracles, and we may suppose that what underlies this emphasis is his conviction that it is as divine that Christ works wonders. For example, when Christ heals Peter's mother-in-law of her fever, she rises and serves him (Mt 8:15). Ordinarily, "human nature" is such that a fever leaves behind it a weakness scarcely compatible with the mother-in-law's recovery of immediate full health. The miracle shows the "intensity of might" (*epitasis fortitudinis*) that characterizes Christ's wonders (JM 8,14–15; SC 242, p. 158). The phrase "healing every disease and every infirmity" (Mt 9:35) prompts Jerome to remark that "nothing is impossible" for the Lord (JM 9,35; SC 242, p. 184). The darkness at the Passion cannot be regarded as an eclipse, since no eclipse can take place during a full moon (JM 27,45; SC 259, p. 296).

Christ's miracles not only reflect and proclaim his identity as the Son of God, they also function in relation to his words and his fate. The healing of the leper, which takes place immediately after the Sermon on the Mount (Mt 8:1ff.), confirms Christ's words for those who have just heard them (JM 8,1–2; SC 242, p. 152). The same pattern may be discerned in the mission of the disciples (Mt 10:5ff.). The twelve are told to preach, but Christ also gives them power to work miracles: "Heal the sick, raise the dead, cleanse lepers, cast out demons." The "uneducated" people to whom the disciples go will not believe the message unless it is confirmed by wonders (JM 10,7–8; SC 242, p. 190). Finally, the miracles that attend Christ's Passion are the testimony of "heaven and earth and all things" that it is their Lord who has been crucified (JM 27,51–52; SC 259, p. 300). In these passages Jerome comes close to arguing that the miracles provide persuasion and even proof of Christ's identity and saving work. This judgment stands in tension with Jerome's usual emphasis upon the miracles in their relation to Christ's education of believers and to the faith he wishes to teach. The tension is, of course, present in the biblical text at numerous points; but it is also reflected in Jerome's comments.

Christ as wonderworker is also a teacher. When he tells the disciples to give the crowd something to eat in the wilderness (Mt 14:16), he knows they have nothing. His command is simply designed to prepare the disciples for the greatness of the miraculous feeding (JM 14,16; SC 242, p. 306). At the Transfiguration Christ gives his three disciples the sign from heaven he had refused the scribes and Pharisees (Mt 16:1; 17:1ff.). His purpose is to "increase their faith" (JM 17,3; SC 259, p. 30). The miracles of Christ are in this way drawn into the motif of Christ's instruction of his disciples. Jerome's attitude betrays itself most clearly, however, in his remarks on Christ's cleansing of the temple (JM 21,15–16; SC 259, p. 116):

> Many people think that the greatest of the miracles (*signorum*) is that Lazarus was raised, that the man blind from birth received sight, that the voice of the Father was heard at the Jordan, or that transfigured on the mountain he displayed his triumphant glory. But in my opinion of all the miracles he did this seems the most marvelous, because a single man—at that time despised and so lowly that he was afterwards crucified, and with the scribes and Pharisees enraged against him and seeing their profits ruined— was able with the blows of a single whip to throw out so great a multitude, to overthrow their tables and break their chairs, and to do what an army without number could not have done.

The miracle is, of course, a prophetic act; and Jerome's remarks show that he not only refuses to attach value to the miracles as ends in themselves but also gives priority to the way in which they proclaim Christ's message. Jerome does not seem to betray any discomfort with the miraculous; it is simply a question of where his interest lies.

The same point can be made by noting that Jerome often argues that, however much miracles ought to produce faith, they fail to do so. His interpretation of Christ's rejection at Nazareth not only illustrates what I am suggesting but also shows how the tension is one to be found in the texts themselves. Christ worked no wonders at Nazareth. According to Mark he "*could* do no mighty work" because of the people's "unbelief" (Mk 6:5f.). But Matthew says "he *did not do* many mighty works there, because of their unbelief" (Mt 13:58; italics added). For Mark faith is the prerequisite for wonderworking. For Matthew it is a question only of Christ's unwillingness. Jerome explains this further by saying that, since Christ knew his fellow countrymen would not believe, he refused to perform miracles which would only have made them more culpable and would not have convinced them (JM 13,58; SC 242, p. 294). Indeed, the miracles performed in Chorazin, Bethsaida, and Capernaum (Mt 11:20–24) produced no repentance. Jerome's interpretation simply reproduces the obvious meaning of the text (JM 11,21–23; SC 242, p. 228f.). When the guards at Christ's tomb tell the chief priests the miracle of the Resurrection (Mt 28:11), the priests persist in their wickedness even though they ought to have been driven to repentance. They bribe the guards with money, just as they had given Judas the thirty pieces of silver (JM 28,12–14; SC 259, p. 314).

At one point in the commentary Jerome treats the theme as a general rule. He alludes to pagans who fault the Christians because they are unable to move mountains with their faith (Mt 21:21). He may be thinking of Porphyry or of Julian the Apostate. But he goes on to allude to John 21:25. The "world itself could not contain" the miracles performed by Christ, meaning that the world cannot *accept* his miracles because of its unbelief. Similarly (JM 21:21; SC 259, p. 122):

> We believe that the apostles also performed such deeds, but that they have not been written down lest greater opportunity be given for contradiction to unbelievers. Besides, if we should ask them whether or not they believe the miracles which have been narrated in Scripture, we shall see that they are incredulous and shall, consequently, show that they would not believe greater miracles if they did not believe lesser ones.

It becomes clear that in Jerome's view miracles seldom fulfill their function to produce repentance and faith.

One reason for this somewhat peculiar fact is that true miracles can be misunderstood as magic, while false miracles that are really magical impostures can be misunderstood as marvels. It all depends, of course, on how one defines the terms; one person's miracle is another's magic and vice versa. Jerome, quite gratuitously, comments that the same faithlessness that led Judas to betray Christ also led him to believe that Christ's miracles were accomplished "not by the majesty of God but by magical arts." He had heard of Christ's Transfiguration and feared that a similar transformation would enable him to escape those sent to arrest him (JM 26,48; SC 259, p. 258f.). The implication may be that Judas was attracted to Christ by the hope that he would be able himself to work wonders. In any case, Jerome explicitly says that Judas did work miracles (cf. Mt 10:8). But he is ranked with the false disciples of Matthew 7:22–23 and with other false prophets and exorcists like Saul, Balaam, Caiaphas, Pharaoh, Nebuchadnezzar, and the sons of Sceva (JM 7,22–23; SC 242, p. 148). The disciple whom Christ implicitly rejects by saying that "the Son of man has nowhere to lay his head" (Mt 8:20) comes to Christ the same way Simon Magus comes to Peter (Acts 8:19), namely, to gain profit by learning to work miracles (JM 8,19–20; SC 242, p. 160). Jerome speaks of true and false miracles rather than of miracles and magic, but we cannot escape the fact that what seem to be wonders are not necessarily true miracles. Faith is required to discern the true from the false, and in the final analysis is presupposed for an ability to see the true miracles.

At several places in the commentary Jerome follows what is either explicit or implicit in the Gospel to argue that faith must precede Christ's miracles. Christ's immediate response to the centurion's request that he heal his servant (Mt 8:7) finds its explanation in Christ's perception of the centurion's faith, humility, and wisdom. Christ's judgment (verse 10) that "not even in Israel have I found such faith" merely makes explicit what is implied by the narrative (JM 8,5–7; SC 242, p. 154f.). Similary, the woman with the hemorrhage (Mt 9:20ff.) and the Canaanite woman (Mt 15:21ff.) both display their faith before Christ makes it explicit by his commendation (JM 9,22 and 15,25; SC 242, p. 178 and p. 332). Finally, Jerome explains Christ's healing of the sick among the five thousand about to be fed miraculously in the wilderness as a response to their faith. Presumably, their following Christ into the wilderness implies their faith (JM 14,14; SC 242, p. 304). Moreover, the same pattern occurs at the feeding of the four thousand (Mt 15:30–31). The healing of the multitude prepares them for the nourishment they are to receive (JM 15,32; SC 242, p. 336).

Jerome's interpretation of the healing of the paralytic (Mt 9:1ff.) not only illustrates the importance of faith, but also introduces his conviction that healing can be spiritual as well as physical. Of course, the narrative itself suggests these themes. It is because Christ sees the faith of those carrying the paralytic that he first forgives him his sins and then cures his paralysis. Jerome notes that "a fleshly miracle takes place to testify to (probetur) a spiritual one, even though it is the same power that drives out the evils of both body and soul." We are, thus, able to see that most physical infirmities are the consequence of sin (JM 9,5; SC 242, p. 168). The healing of the soul sometimes appears in the commentary as an allegorical meaning of the physical miracles.[11] The sick who seek only to touch the fringe of Christ's garment (Mt 14:36) are those who obey the least of his commandments. Whoever transgresses one of these least commandments "shall be called least in the kingdom of heaven" (Mt 5:19). Jerome implies that the obedience of faith brings spiritual healing (JM 14,35–36; SC 242, p. 318).

A second example of moral allegory occurs in the comments on the epileptic boy Christ heals after descending from the mount of Transfiguration. The word translated in the RSV as "is an epileptic" literally means "is a lunatic" (Mt 17:15; Greek, *seleniazetai;* Latin, *lunaticus esse*); and Jerome's interpretation depends upon the association with the changes of the moon. The "tropological" (*iuxta tropologiam*) meaning identifies the "lunatic" as someone who "changes hour by hour in vices, does not persevere in what he begins but waxes and wanes, and now is swept into the fire by which the hearts of adulterers are inflamed, now into waters which are not strong enough to quench love" (JM 17,15–16; SC 259, p. 38). Later in the same narrative the "mountain" that faith can remove (Mt 17:20) refers to the "mountain" Christ removed from the lunatic boy, that is, the devil (JM 17,20; SC 259, p. 40).[12] Christ's healing enables the believer to win a moral triumph over Satan.

Jerome takes a rather different approach to the story of how Peter, instructed by Christ, catches the fish with the shekel in its mouth in order to pay the half-shekel tax for himself and his Lord (Mt 17:24ff.). The "mystical" (*secundum mysticos*) meaning of the story has to do with the deliverance of the first Adam by Christ, the second Adam. The coin symbolizes the confession made both by Peter and by Christ. Peter's is offered as "a price for a sinner"; Christ's because of "the likeness of flesh." What Jerome means is that, even though Christ "committed no sin" and "no guile was found on his lips" (1 Peter 2:22), he identified himself with the old Adam in the incarnation. In this way the same "price" ransoms both Lord and servant (JM 17,27; SC 259, p. 44f.). Let me suggest that here the moral meaning of Christ's miracles finds a spiritual dimension and expands into a summary statement of the meaning of Redemption. As the new Adam Christ delivers us from our bondage.

Jerome's allegorical treatment of the text sometimes approximates the sort of interpretation given by Hilary in that it can relate the miracle stories to the constitution of the church from Jews and Gentiles. Unlike Hilary, however, Jerome does not insist as carefully upon the typological or temporal dimension of the interpretation. Moreover, even in this context his emphasis seems as much upon faith and conversion as upon the miracle of the church. Let me begin by summarizing Jerome's interpretation of the narrative of the raising of the ruler's daughter and the healing of the woman with the hemorrhage, the two blind men, and the dumb demoniac (Mt 9:18–34). The ruler and his daughter stand for the Jews; the woman, for the Gentiles. The coincidence of the woman's twelve year illness and the twelve-year-old daughter (Luke 8:42) means that the "illness" of Gentiles became evident when faith first began to appear among the Jews. The fact that the woman is healed first refers to the fact that "Ethiopia will first bring her hand to God" (Ps 68:31) and that when "the full number of the Gentiles come in . . . all Israel will be saved" (Rom

11:25f.). The two blind men show that after Christ's return to his "home" at the Resurrection and Ascension Jews and Gentiles alike receive "the light of true faith." The dumb demoniac's healing signifies that those converted gain not only the sight of faith but are also enabled to voice their confession of Christ (JM 9,18ff.; SC 242, p. 176ff.).

Like Hilary's, Jerome's interpretation revolves around the constitution of the church from the synagogue and from the Gentiles. Moreover, he appeals to the pattern found in Romans 9–11. At the same time, throughout his discussion Jerome seems equally preoccupied with the issue of faith. It is the dawning of faith on the part of the Jews that reveals the wickedness of the Gentiles, since it is only by comparison with virtues that vice becomes evident. Faith is what brings the woman healing. Christ tests the blind men's faith before giving them "the light of true faith." Of course, all these comments directly reflect the text of the Gospel; and I should not wish to argue that we must oppose the theme of faith to that of the miracle of the church. Nevertheless, I find in Jerome's comments an emphasis upon the first and, consequently, a shift from what I take to be Hilary's major interest.

I should want to draw a similar conclusion from Jerome's interpretation of the cursing of the fig tree (Mt 21:18ff.). The fig tree is "the synagogue and assembly of the Jews," which possesses the law but is "by the wayside" because it does not believe in the Way (John 14:6). Christ "was hungry" either to show the reality of his humanity or because "he hungered for the salvation of believers and was thirsty because of the unbelief of Israel." Christ finds only "leaves" on the fig tree because the Jews bring forth fine words but "no fruits of truth." Mark's comment that "it was not the season for figs" (Mk 11:13) means "either that the time for the salvation of Israel had not yet come because the people of the Gentiles had not yet converted or that the time of faith had gone by because he had come first to Israel and when rejected had passed over to the Gentiles." The first of these possibilities reflects the pattern of Romans 9–11, as does also Jerome's comment that the withering of the fig tree leaves the root alive to symbolize the remnant of Israel and the root of the olive tree into which the wild olive is grafted (Rom 11:16ff.).[13] The second possibility betrays Jerome's concern with faith and shifts attention away from the church (JM 21,18–20; SC 259, p. 118ff.).

Faith becomes the dominant theme in Jerome's interpretation of the centurion (Mt 8:5ff.) and of the Canaanite woman (Mt 15:21ff.). The centurion's faith reminds us that the Gentiles will come from East and West to believe in Christ (JM 8,11; SC 242, p. 156f.). The Canaanite woman asks us to marvel at "the faith, the patience, and the humility of the church." Her belief that her daughter can be healed stands for faith. Her persistence signifies patience. And her willingness to be called a dog reveals her humility (JM 15,25; SC 242, p. 332). In these passages Jerome does not do away with the theme of the conversion of the Gentiles, but he is more interested in the faith that makes that conversion possible. What I take to be his emphasis finds clear expression in what he says about Christ's healing of the blind and dumb demoniac (Mt 11:22). He says that three miracles were accomplished (JM 12,22; SC 242, p. 244):

> Blind he sees; dumb he speaks; possessed by a demon he is freed. To be sure, this happened then in a carnal fashion. But it is also fulfilled today in the conversion of believers. As soon as the demon is expelled they see the light of faith and then, though previously silent, they open their mouths in the praises of God.

The miracle that chiefly concerns Jerome is the miracle of faith by which people turn to Christ. He by no means denies the reality of Christ's miracles, nor does he limit their meaning to faith. But what acts as a *basso continuo* in the commentary is, I think, the miracle of faith.

THEODORE OF MOPSUESTIA: THE WONDERWORKER INDWELT BY GOD THE WORD

Theodore's *Commentary on John*, discovered in 1868 in a Syriac translation, was not translated into any other language until Vosté published his Latin translation in 1940.[14] Theodore was bishop of Mopsuestia from 392 until his death in 428. While the *Commentary* cannot be dated, it was most likely written about 400 and so is contemporaneous with Jerome's *Commentary on Matthew*.[15] In his preface Theodore makes a distinction between the task of the interpreter and that of the preacher (V, p. 2). While the preacher must pay equal attention to the clear and to the problematic texts, the interpreter is obliged to focus on the difficult passages, particularly those the heretics use to support their errors. This distinction differs from our modern one between historical exegesis and theological interpretation. For Theodore both the interpreter and the preacher are engaged in a theological task. The difference is, rather, one that attaches to the audience envisaged. The interpreter seeks to resolve difficulties that appear in controversial theology; the preacher gives a positive theological interpretation for a popular audience. For this reason Theodore's preoccupation is with giving a proper account of Christ, and the most obvious feature of the commentary is that it interprets John in accordance with the divisive Christology of Antioch.

In two other respects the commentary reflects the peculiarities of Theodore's point of view. First, implicit in his comments is the anti-allegorical

stance of the Antiochenes. For example, when John tells us in the feeding
of the five thousand that there was "much grass in the place" (John 6:10),
Theodore remarks that this was because it was spring, the month of
Nisan, "when the earth usually is adorned with fresh grass" (V, p. 94).
Second, John's citation of Psalm 69:9 ("Zeal for thy house will consume
me" (John 2:17) should not be regarded as a prophecy fulfilled by Christ's
cleansing of the temple. Rather, the verse simply describes what is charac-
teristic of the righteous and is applied to Christ in this sense. Theodore
denies much of the Old Testament a prophetic character. For example,
only Psalms 2, 8, 45, and 110 prophesy Christ; and the only one of the
writing prophets to predict him is the last, Malachi.

One last preliminary remark. Theodore makes several assumptions
about John's Gospel. The faithful in Asia brought John the other three
Gospels, which had already been published, and asked for his opinion.
John praised the Gospels, but noted that there were many omissions and
that doctrine was almost completely absent. He agreed to the universal
request that he write his own Gospel, and by doing so he remedied the
deficiencies of Matthew, Mark, and Luke (V, pp. 3–4). Moreover, John was
more concerned with an accurate chronology than were the other evangelists. Theodore bases this view on the repeated time references in the first
two chapters of John (V, pp. 4, 39, 42). Thus, Theodore harmonizes the
Gospels by assimilating the synoptics to John.[16] Finally, Theodore notes
that, while John often adds what the other Gospels omitted, he also omits
some of their narratives and other events that he knew of. In part this
helps explain how we can fit the synoptic Gospels into John (V, p. 43). We
also need to remember, says Theodore, that people differ from one another in how they tell a story. Some tell everything, while others seize only
upon the crucial points (V, p. 233). But the idea that John has omitted
stories is sometimes implied or stated in the text of John. John does in fact
omit any narrative of the "signs" referred to in John 2:23 (V, p. 45). And
John 20:30–31 explicitly mentions "many other signs . . . not written in
this book" (V, p. 257).

With all this in mind let me turn to Theodore's interpretation of Christ's
miracles and begin by describing how he understands their function.
Christ's signs do produce faith in him, but Theodore follows John 2:23–25
and makes explicit the implication of the text that a faith based upon
miracles is not "true and steadfast" (V, p. 45). The same judgment must
be made about Nicodemus, who seeks Christ out because of his miracles
(John 3:2; V, p. 46). Theodore finds the same pattern in the story of the
official whose son was ill (John 4:46ff.). Christ's judgment that "Unless
you see signs and wonders you will not believe" (verse 48) is borne out by
the fact that only when the official learns that Christ's words, "your son

will live," were spoken at the hour when his son began to mend, does he believe (verse 53). The official's belief in Christ's words (verse 50) means only that he accepted the words, not that he believed (V, pp. 68–69).

Despite the fact that the miracles produce only a limited kind of faith, Christ uses them to their fullest power. His healing of the man blind from birth (John 9) confirms his words and the reaction of the Jews to them. Christ leaves the temple hidden from the sight of his enemies in a miraculous way (John 8:59). And he makes himself visible to the blind man by healing him. Theodore appears to use Christ's words in John 9:39, "For judgment I came into this world, that those who do not see may see, and that those who see may become blind," as the key to explaining Christ's words and his deed in the whole of John 7–9. Several other examples of Christ's careful use of miracles occur, according to Theodore. When Christ asks the paralytic whether he wants to be healed (John 5:6), he appears to ask a "useless" question. After all, the man had been ill thirty-eight years and had waited by the pool "a long time." Examined more carefully, however, the narrative shows that Christ works his miracles in a carefully ordered fashion, preparing the man for his healing (V, p. 70). Moreover, both in the healing of the paralytic and in that of the man blind from birth Christ acts providentially in order that the miracles may have the widest possible effect. By telling the paralytic to take up his pallet and walk and by commanding the blind man to go and wash in the pool of Siloam, Christ makes it possible for a crowd to be attracted and to see the signs (V, p. 134). Christ's refusal to go to Lazarus until he has died has the purpose of preparing a greater miracle than healing the sick and of confirming the disciples' faith by showing them he can raise even corpses that stink (V, p. 158).

Theodore can also interpret details from the narrative to argue that Christ works wonders so as to give us an example we can follow. For example, when he gives thanks before distributing the loaves to the five thousand (John 6:11), he does so in order to show us that we ought always give thanks before partaking of food (V, p. 94). Christ weeps at Lazarus's tomb (John 11:35), and he does this to teach us what proper and moderate grief for the Christian ought to be. Moreover, Christ works his miracles in such a way as to avoid the accusation of pride or of seeking vainglory. His miracles are greater than those of the prophets because they go beyond what is necessary. Moses, for example, supplies manna in the wilderness in such a way that only what is necessary is given day by day. Christ, on the other hand, gives the multitude in the wilderness "as much as they wanted" (John 6:11). Elijah gives the widow unlimited meal and oil, but only "until the day that the Lord sends rain upon the earth" (1 Kings 17:14). Similarly, when Elisha makes the widow's jar of oil overflow, the oil stops when all the available vessels have been filled (2 Kings 4:1–7). Because Christ's miracles go beyond what is necessary and so transcend those of the prophets, there is the risk he may be accused of pride. Consequently, he acts in such a way as to avoid the charge. He commands that the fragments left from the miraculous feeding be gathered; he obliges the woman healed of her hemorrhage to declare the miracle by asking who touched him (John 6:12; Lk 8:45). Christ avoids the accusation of pride by having others testify to the miracles (V, p. 95). Similarly, he avoids going everywhere and healing everyone so he may not appear to seek vainglory. Rather, "he heals one man and through him reveals himself to many" (John 5:1ff.; V, p. 69).

Theodore follows the text of the Gospel by arguing that, though the miracles are supposed to instruct and to produce faith, they do not always have that effect. The multitude that had been miraculously fed, "with the remnants of the food still between their teeth," ask Christ for a sign (John 6:30, V, p. 99). Although they have seen miracles, they do not believe (V, p. 102). Christ heals both the paralytic (John 5) and the man blind from birth (John 9) on the sabbath. The Jews pay no attention to the miracles, but accuse Christ of breaking the sabbath or of blasphemy (John 5:10, 18; 9:16; 10:33; V, pp. 99, 102, 112, 132, 153). Theodore's comments scarcely go beyond the obvious meaning of the text. Indeed, John 12:37 summarizes the theme by saying: "Though he had done so many signs before them, yet they did not believe in him." Christ's rejection by "his own" (John 1:11) is at one level a rejection of his miracles. Theodore employs the theme to explain why Christ is "deeply moved in spirit and troubled" immediately before the raising of Lazarus (John 11:33). His emotion is one of anger because he knows the Jews will not believe despite the miracle he is about to work (V, pp. 162, 164). The further irony is that the Jews will accept the miracles of Antichrist, the other who "comes in his own name" (John 5:43; V., p. 91).

The whole of my discussion thus far suggests that Theodore's comments seldom stray very far from the obvious narrative meaning of the text. He carefully describes the function of the miracles and shows how they are meant to produce faith but often fail to do so. What is largely missing in Theodore's commentary is any discussion of the meaning of the miracles.[17] In this respect he differs considerably from the other interpreters I am describing. In only one way does Theodore enter upon larger theological issues, and even here we cannot speak of a spiritual interpretation. He is concerned with the identity of the wonderworker, and he finds in the text of John warrants for his Christology. For Theodore "Christ" is a term that refers to the "*prosopon* of union." That is, Christ refers to the union of the Man and God the Word, two subjects that remain distinct in nature but are united in honor and grace. God the Word "indwells" the Man "by good pleasure as in a Son."[18]

The peculiarity of Theodore's view is that the Man is the wonderworker; but this peculiarity, which distinguishes Theodore even from his fellow Antiochene John Chrysostom, is qualified by recognizing that the Man's wonderworking power is really God the Word's and is simply bestowed graciously upon the Man. For this reason Theodore can maintain his Christology and equally recognize that John's chief theological concern is to emphasize Christ's divinity (V, pp. 3–4). When Christ tells the Jews "My Father is working still, and I am working" (John 5:17), he is arguing that he and the Father "have the power of working in the same fashion" because he is "of the same nature" as the Father, since he is "begotten of him" (V, p. 76). Moreoever, when Christ a little later says "the Son can do nothing of his own accord, but only what he sees the Father doing" (John 5:19), he does not mean to suggest he has no power but to show that his power is the same as the Father's "because of his undivided equality with the Father" and the unity of will effected by their "natural union" with one another (V, p. 78; cf. 98, 148). These discussions make it appear that Theodore is identifying the wonderworker with God the Word, but a closer reading of what Theodore says makes it clear that he distinguishes the wonderworking power from the wonderworker. The consubstantiality of Father and Word means that there is an identity of operation in the Trinity (V, p. 79). The miracles of Christ are accomplished by the divine power working through the Man.

Because of Theodore's emphasis on the divine character of the power to work miracles, he can sometimes treat Christ's miracles as acts of God. For example, when Christ makes clay of his spittle and anoints the blind man's eyes with the clay (John 9:6), the action alludes to God's formation of humanity from the dust of the ground (cf. Gen 2:7). "By this he revealed himself to be the creator of human beings" (V, p. 133f.). Moreover, John 5:25 refers to the resurrection accomplished now and in the future by "the voice of the Son of God." Theodore immediately appeals to Christ's raising of the widow's son, of the ruler's daughter, and of Lazarus (V, p. 84; cf. 81). Again it begins to look as though God the Word is the wonderworker. While this is not what Theodore means, it does seem to me important to insist that, despite his emphasis on the Man's agency, he wishes to make it clear that the miracles are wrought by God's power. Theodore's view is an odd one, but he does not part company in an absolute fashion from the other church fathers.

At a number of points in the commentary Theodore defines the agency

of the Man. In explaining the Father's gift of "all judgment" to the Son
(John 5:22) he says (V, p. 82):

> Scripture, when it refers to what pertains to the human nature of
> the Lord, customarily goes on at once to mention the majesty of the
> divinity, if there is a question of something transcending that na-
> ture. In this fashion it makes its message one that cannot be
> doubted by those who hear it. For example, when the blessed Paul
> says: "God has spoken to us by a Son, whom he appointed the heir
> of all things" (Heb 1:2), he means the assumed Man . . . and that
> he received universal dominion through his union with God the
> Word. . . . But since Paul understands that this statement tran-
> scends the nature of the one he is speaking of, he adds the words
> "through whom also he created the world." . . . Similarly, John is
> arguing here from what belongs to the divine nature . . . and turns
> his discourse to the human nature in order to teach that it received
> supernatural gifts from the divine.

The gift and power of working miracles must be understood in the same
way. The power is God the Word's, but the one who exercises the power is
the assumed Man (cf. John 5:30; V, pp. 86, 91). The same interpretation
explains Christ's statement in his prayer immediately before the raising of
Lazarus that "thou hearest me always" (John 11:43; V, p. 163). Theodore
succinctly states his view by saying that "the miracles, though worked by
the Man, obviously transcended the nature of the one who did them" (V, p.
193).

What seems to me remarkable about Theodore's interpretation of the
miracles in the Fourth Gospel is that he single-mindedly focuses upon the
Man as the wonderworker. The emphasis found upon explaining the obvious narrative meaning makes sense from this point of view. It is the
human Christ that occupies the forefront of the stage. And yet what is true
of the narrative cannot be allowed to obscure the theological point John, in
Theodore's view, wishes to make. That is, beyond the human activity of
Christ we find God the Word. It is his power that represents the gracious
gift enabling the Man to work wonders. Moreover, the grace in question
differs from that given the prophets. Moses, for example, was able to work
wonders; but for him the gift was not one of a constant power (V, pp. 39–
40, 74; cf. pp. 49, 94, 96). Christ's powers may be compared to those of the
prophets, but they are finally different in kind. However much the Man is
the wonderworker, Theodore does not wish us to forget that he is so only
in virtue of his union with God the Word.

CYRIL OF ALEXANDRIA: THE MIRACLE OF THE WONDERWORKER MADE FLESH

Although we cannot date Cyril's commentary with any certainty, it most probably is an early work written before the outbreak of the Nestorian controversy in 428.[19] Cyril adopts the same sort of view of John's purpose in writing the Gospel as Theodore does. John wrote at the request of "wiser" believers in order to halt a theological scandal that "was consuming like a plague the souls of the simpler" (P 1, p. 14). This explains why the Fourth Gospel emphasizes the divinity of Christ, and it also supplies Cyril with his own point of departure. If anything, his commentary is even more theological than Theodore's. He explicitly says that he is writing "a more dogmatic interpretation" (P 1, p. 7); and much of the commentary represents a theological treatise written polemically against heretics, particularly the Arians.

Cyril firmly ties the miracles of Christ to the incarnation of God's eternal Word and relates them to the condescension of the Word and his accommodation of the revelation to the world (P 1, p. 114):

> For "She [Wisdom] appeared upon earth and lived among men" (Bar 3:37). He made his presence in the world more manifest in this way. He who of old had been comprehended by the mind was seen now by the very eyes of the body. So he entrusted us with a grosser perception of divine knowledge, if I may put it this way, since he made himself known by wonders and mighty deeds.

Positively, the miracles do reveal God the Word; but Cyril's emphasis is upon their limitation. They give only a "grosser" knowledge of God because the mind is not "firmly founded upon new miracles" (P 1, p. 214). Cyril bases this opinion upon Christ's refusal to "trust himself" to the people who are drawn to him because of his miracles (John 2:24). He also draws the conclusion that novices in the faith must have full instruction before they can be admitted to the mysteries of the church. Nicodemus, who is one of those attracted to Christ by his miracles, is not even able to understand from the miracles that the wonderworker is God (P 1, p. 216f.).

To a greater degree than Theodore, Cyril underlines the fact that Christ's miracles more often than not fail to function in practice as they are meant to in principle. Perhaps this is because he tends to find their true meaning in a spiritual interpretation rather than at the narrative level. In any case, the failure of the miracles to function adequately finds expression for him in the disbelief of the Jews and in their quest for a sign.[20] For example, John "brings the wonderworker back to Jerusalem" to heal the paralytic at the pool (John 5:1). Although his miracles in Samaria and Galilee produced belief, the reaction in Jerusalem is hostile. The Jews immediately accuse Christ of breaking the sabbath (John 5:10), and "they do not even accept with their mind the obligation of marvelling at the power of the one who healed" (P 1, pp. 304, 309; cf. p. 611f.). In the same way the multitude miraculously fed in the wilderness "saw, they saw that the Lord was God by nature, when he fed a multitude exceeding number. . . . But they 'have seen and not believed' (John 6:36) because of the blindness which from God's wrath like a mist overshadowed their understandings" (P 1, p. 477). The Jews have no further excuse. "It is obvious, then, that they altogether misunderstand the signs; and pretending a willingness to marvel at them, they are led to serve the unclean pleasure of the belly" (P 1, p. 455).[21] Cyril can also associate the quest for a sign (P 1, p. 210) and the accusation that the wonders are demonic and magical (P 1, p. 270; P 2, pp. 195, 287) with the disbelief of the Jews.

Perhaps because of this negative assessment of the function of the miracles Cyril can say that at the end of the world Christ will make his kingdom "more manifest." Then he "shall descend in the glory of the Father, no longer known to be truly and by nature Lord through miracles as before, but confessed without hesitation to be King because of a glory suitable to God" (P 1, p. 425). On the other hand, Cyril can speak of what Christ will do at the end of the world as miraculous. The judgment of the world and the raising of the dead are greater miracles before which the "lesser miracles" of the Incarnation pale in significance (P 1, pp. 330, 348).

In contrast to Theodore, Cyril is more interested in the meaning of the miracles than in their function. To be sure, he sometimes makes the same sort of remarks Theodore does about the narrative and the way Christ uses the miracles to instruct.[22] And he can treat the miracles as giving us examples we should follow. We should give thanks before meals (P 1, p. 416). We should practice hospitality (P 1, p. 419). We should despise vainglory (P 1, pp. 422, 583). But his preoccupation is with the significance of the miracles. We should not put Cyril in the same camp as Origen, since he admits that not every passage in Scripture admits an allegorical interpretation.[23] But he is faithful to John by seeing that the miracles are "signs" that point beyond themselves to a deeper meaning. This meaning need not be allegorical. For example, Cyril describes the narrative meaning of the miracle at the wedding in Cana as follows (P 1, p. 203):

> Many most excellent things were accomplished at once through the one first miracle. For honorable marriage was sanctified, the curse

on women put away (for no more shall they "bring forth children in pain" [Gen 3:16], since Christ has blessed the very beginning of our birth), and the glory of our Saviour shone forth like the sun's rays; and more than this, the disciples are confirmed in faith by their marvelling.

The allegorical meaning of the miracle has to do with the transformation of the water of Judaism into the wine of Christianity.

Cyril's allegorical interpretations sometimes depend upon the details of the text. The five barley loaves at the miraculous feeding (John 6) signify the five books of Moses, while the small fishes stand for the apostolic teaching of the fishermen found in the New Testament (P 1, p. 417f.). Thus, the miracle may be understood to refer to the nourishment believers receive from Scripture. And, of course, Cyril also follows the implication of John's narrative and interprets the miracle in terms of the Eucharist. Similarly, Cyril reflects upon the fact that the paralytic at the pool has been ill for thirty-eight years (John 5:5). The number signifies imperfection, and Cyril thinks of the paralysis of Israel under the law (P 1, p. 306f.). This interpretation begins to show that Cyril tries to weave the meaning of the miracles into a larger pattern not unlike the one I have suggested can be found in Hilary's interpretation of Matthew. Negatively, the miracles are drawn into the pattern of the Jews' rejection of Christ and the consequent Gentile mission. This represents the burden of Cyril's interpretation of the healing of the man born blind. Positively, however, the miracles point towards the faith of the church and the consummation of the age to come. When the disciples cross the Sea of Galilee after the miraculous feeding (John 6:17ff.), we must think of the little ship of the church, buffeted by the storms of this world. When the church reaches its goal, the age to come, Christ also appears "having the whole world under his feet" (P 1, p. 430f.). The negative side of the broader picture reflects Cyril's attitude toward the Jews; the positive, his understanding of the message of salvation.[24]

All Cyril's observations about the function and the meaning of the miracles tend to point towards his interest in a correct assessment of Christ's identity. This is what he means by saying that he has given "a more dogmatic interpretation." Practically the whole of the first book of his commentary is devoted to the elaboration of an orthodox Christology that will not only expound the meaning of John but also refute the heretics. Christ's miracles demonstrate "a might and power suitable to God" (P 1, p. 310). They show that he is of one essence with the Father, and that Father and Word have an identical will and power (P 1, p. 328). Christ can heal "by a word as God" (P 1, p. 398). The miracles proclaim him the creator (P 1, pp. 202, 314f.), and that explains why he is "unrestrained by the nature of things" (P 1, p. 427). The contrast between John the Baptist, who "did no sign" (John 10:41), and Christ is that between a prophet and "he who is God the wonderworker" (P 2, p. 263).

Cyril's attribution of Christ's miracles to his divine nature requires no further discussion, but I do need to point out that he does not forget that it is the Word incarnate who accomplishes the miracles of the Gospel. At one point Cyril says that Christ's miracles on earth in no way "surpass the power essentially in him." What he means is that the miracles fade in significance when compared with God's creative power exercised apart from the Incarnation. That is why Christ's miracles can be misunderstood (P 2, p. 41):

> For it was likely that some would say he made a suitable statement by the words "Of myself I do nothing" (John 8:28), interpreting his words to mean that he borrowed power from God the Father. He drove out the demon. He freed the paralytic from his infirmities. He delivered the leper from his disease. He gave blind people sight. He satisfied a numberless multitude with five loaves. He stilled the raging sea with a word. He raised Lazarus from the dead. Shall we, then, say that these deeds demonstrate a might stronger than the one essentially his?

Cyril goes on to speak of Christ's creative power as the Word of God and the agent of creation. The miracles of the Incarnation are "small matters" by comparison.

One other example of the way Cyril keeps the Incarnation in view needs to be cited. He relates Christ's words about "the Son of man ascending where he was before" (John 6:62) to Christ's claim in the same context that his flesh gives life. Flesh is not capable by nature either to give life or to ascend to heaven. Nevertheless, the "flesh" or humanity of Christ receives both these powers. "For the one who made what is from earth heavenly will also render it lifegiving, even though its nature, considered alone, is to decay" (P 1, p. 550). From one point of view, Cyril and Theodore sharply disagree. Cyril's wonderworker is the Word incarnate; Theodore's, the Man indwelt by God the Word. But viewed somewhat differently, the two interpreters are not so much in disagreement as might first appear. If Theodore can recognize that the Man's power is really God's, Cyril can argue that God exercises his power through the humanity he has appropriated in the Incarnation.

Conclusion

It seems reasonably clear to me that Christ's miracles play a central role in the way the Gospels find interpretation. All four commentators examined take the miracles seriously, and none of them so much as hints at any doubt with respect to the historical truth of the narratives. At the same time, the miracles receive a function and a meaning that places them in a larger framework of thought. They become constitutive of the new commonwealth of the church. They testify to Christ, who has established the church, and to the meaning of his saving work both in this world and in the age to come. And they take on their proper significance only when they are seen through the eyes of faith. All these themes find iconographical expression in the apse mosaic of Santa Pudenziana. Believers have access to the church and to Christ through the apostles, and this places them in the new commonwealth symbolized by the walls and buildings of Jerusalem. Finally, it is the four Gospels enshrining the victory of the cross that confirms believers in their faith.

At one level the miracles reveal the identity of the wonderworker himself. They proclaim him as divine or, for Theodore, as the vehicle through which God acts. And we perceive in him the same power found in creation. The one who made the sea commands it; the one who gives growth to the vine and the wheat supplies their fruit in a marvelous fashion. At the same time, as the Gospels themselves recognize, the miracles often fail in their proper function. They do not always produce faith in Christ, and in part this is because miracles are by no means limited to Christ. Pharaoh's magicians could rival Moses in wonderworking. Evil people can work wonders by Satan's power and by magic. For this reason the miracles tend to function as proof only provided one sees them with the eyes of faith.

Perhaps more important than their function is the meaning of the miracles. They are useful examples of how we should behave; we must give thanks, practice hospitality, and avoid the pursuit of vainglory. Still more they point toward the fullest miracle of all, Redemption. They help define the moral and spiritual transformation effected by incorporation into the church. And they are signs that point toward the age to come when the moral and spiritual transformation will be perfected and when the resurrection of the body will complete the bodily healing foreshadowed by Christ's acts of healing.

In one sense all these conclusions suggest a certain downplaying of miracles. Only in part does this seem to me correct. It is true that Christ's miracles are located within a broader theological context. They are the tail of the dog, and not the dog itself. But, I should argue, this way of regarding the miracles accurately reflects the way the Gospels treat them. It cannot be denied that the interpreters we have examined have a developed ecclesiastical theology in mind and read the text in its light. On the other hand, they *are* reading the text and are doing so with great care and attention to detail. We cannot speak of an imposition of theology on the text, nor can we say that the text is read apart from theology. Instead, we are dealing with a hermeneutical circle that may well be inevitable regardless of the assumptions and methods employed by the exegete. Finally, if I am correct in concluding that the miracles of Christ, while taken with utter seriousness, are the tail of the dog, then there exists the possibility that the tail will wag the dog. This possibility becomes actual for the homilists to be examined in chapter 2.

2

The Wonderworker Proclaimed from the Pulpit

 In this chapter I wish to continue my examination of the way Christ's miracles in the Gospels were interpreted in the church during the fourth and fifth centuries. From one point of view there is no difference from what we saw in the last chapter. Ambrose on Luke, Augustine on John, Chrysostom on Matthew and John, and Cyril on Luke all say pretty much the same things about miracles as the commentators already examined. In other words, I can find no shift of theological interpretation nor any significant difference in the theological context in which miracles find their proper setting. Once again we shall find a set of variations on the same themes. Nevertheless, we shall be dealing with preachers concerned in some degree to explain their theological convictions to a popular audience. And we shall begin to find, particularly in Chrysostom's sermons, a concern that some Christians are misunderstanding or misusing the notion of miracles. The tail, in other words, shows signs of beginning to wag the dog.

One other preliminary remark is in order. I shall begin my discussion in the West with Ambrose and Augustine and then turn to the East with Chrysostom and Cyril. The treatment, therefore, will not be chronological, since Ambrose and Chrysostom are writing within a few years of 390, Augustine and Cyril about thirty and forty years later. I do not mean to suggest any rigid or absolute distinction between West and East or Latin and Greek. Ambrose, for example, often reads like a Latin Origen. And we should remember that in late antiquity the line between East and West was not so firmly drawn as it was once the collapse of the Empire in the West began to isolate it from the Byzantine Empire. At the same time, differences do begin to appear by the late fourth century. The language barrier becomes increasingly important even for highly educated people like Augustine. Moreover, upon the death of Theodosius the Great in 395 two imperial courts were established. My real reason, however, for choosing this particular order of treatment is simply that Ambrose and Augustine seem to belong together, while Chrysostom and Cyril will supply the Eastern dialogue between Antioch and Alexandria.

AMBROSE: THE MIRACLE OF THE NEW CREATION

Aristocratic and well educated, Ambrose was born into a Christian family, though, like Augustine, he remained unbaptized till past his youth. His father had been the prefect of Gaul, and he had begun his own ascent of the *cursus honorum* of the Roman imperial civil service when he became bishop of Milan in 373.[1] As the *consularis* in Milan he intervened in the dispute between Arians and orthodox over the selection of a bishop. He found the honor and the duty thrust upon himself, and was baptized and consecrated. His episcopate lasted just short of a quarter century. Sometime about 389 he edited and published his homilies on Luke's Gospel. What is clear is that with the exception of Book 3 Ambrose simply reworked and pasted together homilies he had already preached, possibly over a period of ten years. What is less clear is how to recover the earlier materials he is using.[2] The only point of concern to us is that Ambrose's editing may in some degree have obscured the way in which the homilies originally functioned. At the same time, other considerations create the same problem. A sermon read is not the same as a sermon heard, which, in fact, handicaps our reading of all patristic homiletical material. Moreover, it is clear from Augustine's account in *The Confessions* that Ambrose's preaching aimed high and was persuasive to the intelligentsia.[3] What this means will become clearer when we turn to Chrysostom, whose writings help us imagine the situations to which they are addressed. With these caveats in mind let me turn to Ambrose's sermons.

The prologue to the collection of homilies sets the stage for Ambrose's interpretation. Luke is writing an historical narrative (AL, prol. 1; SC 45, p. 40; *stilum ... historicus*). From one point of view this aim stands in contrast to wisdom, whether natural, moral, or rational. John fits the category of natural wisdom; Matthew, of moral; and Mark, of rational. Nevertheless (AL, prol. 4; SC 45, p. 42):

> Saint Luke maintains the order of an historical narrative and re-
> veals to us a great many miraculous deeds accomplished by our
> Lord in such a way that the narrative of this Gospel embraces the
> powers of every form of wisdom.

Ambrose by no means rejects or minimizes the significance of the narrative meaning. "Each book has its own mysteries, deeds, and miracles that
distinguish it" (AL 1, 11; SC 45, p. 52). And yet Ambrose is obviously more
interested in the allegorical meaning of the text and always moves quickly
to what engages his delight.

Ambrose does, however, pay some attention to the identity of the wonderworker; and it need come as no surprise that he attributes Christ's
power to his divinity. "Jesus appears in his works, and in the works of the
Son the Father is also discerned." Jesus works the miraculous transformation of water to wine at Cana (John 2:9), but only the "Lord of the world"
could have such power. Jesus anoints the blind man's eyes with clay (John
9:6), and we recognize the one who made humanity from clay. Forgiving
the paralytic (Mk 2:5,7) and raising Lazarus (John 11) require the same
double interpretation. And Ambrose appeals to Romans 1:20 to argue that
these visible works proclaim Christ's "invisible" nature (AL 1, 7; SC 45, p.
50).[4] When Christ heals the leper (Lk 5:13), he says "I will; be clean." And
the fact that the leprosy leaves "immediately" shows Ambrose that Christ
is God, since there is no interval between his word and his deed (AL 5, 4;
SC 45, p. 184). At the healing of the paralytic the same word "immediately" (Lk 5:25) suggests the same interpretation (AL 5, 15; SC 45, p. 188).

Ambrose does not forget, however, that Christ's divine miracles are
accomplished in the Incarnation. When Christ "comes down" to heal before his sermon (Lk 6:17), we are to understand that he "came down" so
that we might be "made participants in his nature" by our union with
him. In other words, the text suggests to Ambrose the doctrine of
divinization. Christ became human that we might be made divine (cf. also
2 Pt 1:4). When Ambrose interprets Christ's stilling of the storm (Lk
8:22ff.), he understands Christ's sleeping in the middle of the storm as a
sign of his divinity. Christ does not share the terror of the disciples, and
this is because he is not in every respect of their nature. Even if "his body"
sleeps, his divinity is at work. Ambrose has not thought through his Christology quite so carefully as one might have expected, and he seems in some
degree to follow the Western tendency to seize upon the paradox of
Christ's double character rather than to explain it. But the important point
is that it is the divine Christ who works wonders.

Because Christ is God incarnate his birth and infancy are attended by
miracles. The greatest of these, of course, is the virgin birth. Elizabeth

gave birth to John the Baptist and Sarah to Isaac in a marvelous fashion because "age is often an impediment to nature." In these cases, however, "it is not unreasonable that the lesser cause yield to the greater and that the more powerful prerogative of nature exclude the functioning of the lesser cause, age." In contrast, Christ's birth from the virgin Mary is truly miraculous (AL 2, 17; SC 45, p. 80). Ambrose's comments on Luke's infancy narrative includes treatment of Matthew's stories. Both evangelists make it clear that Christ's infancy "was by no means deprived of divine acts." Although his fleshly age prevented him from working miracles, God was there to do wonders (AL 2, 50; SC 45, p. 95). Perhaps the greatest of these is the story of the Magi.[5] They saw the star as "a new creation," and worshipped the infant because they knew who he really was and because, as magicians, they knew their art was at an end (AL 2, 48; SC 45, p. 94).

Most of Ambrose's interpretations press beyond the identity of the wonderworker to the meaning of his miracles. Let me begin by describing how he relates this meaning to the two peoples that constitute the church. The theme is the same as what I suggested is the focus of Hilary's commentary on Matthew, and Ambrose is quite clearly drawing upon Hilary's interpretation. I shall argue that he incorporates the theme into a somewhat larger framework by thinking of the church in terms of the new creation it adumbrates and the Christian life it requires. In other words, I am suggesting that the ecclesiastical interpretation leads Ambrose toward the mystical and moral allegory that dominates his homilies.

In several places Ambrose explains the text of Luke as a reference to the Gentile mission. When Christ in his sermon at Nazareth mentions the widow of Zarephath and Naaman (Lk 4:25ff.), he prefigures the church, which is "a people assembled from strangers, a people once leprous, a people once stained, before its baptism in the mystical river; yet after the mysteries of baptism, now washed of bodily and spiritual stains, it begins to be no longer leprous, but an immaculate virgin without spot" (AL 4, 50; SC 45, p. 171). The text keeps its reference to the Gentile mission, but Ambrose's attention wanders from this theme to that of the moral transformation effected by baptism. I should make the same observation about Ambrose's discussion of the healing of the centurion's servant and the raising of the widow of Nain's son (Lk 7:1–17). His opening comment implies the point I wish to make (AL 5, 83; SC 45, p. 213):

> [Christ] teaches us how to conform to his teachings. For immediately the servant of a Gentile centurion is presented to the Lord to be healed. In him is expressed the people of the nations who are bound by chains of slavery to the world, are sick with deadly passions, and must be healed by the kindly act of the Lord.

Again the theme of moral transformation appears to take precedence over the ecclesiological theme. Similarly, the widow of Nain is the church receiving "a younger people" raised from the dead; but Ambrose immediately drifts into an allegorical interpretation that identifies the four "bearers" with the four elements and the (wooden) bier with the cross, which once touched by Christ brings life.

Only occasionally does Ambrose allow the ecclesiological interpretation to dominate. His discussion of the healing of the woman with the hemorrhage and the raising of Jairus's daughter (Lk 8:40–56) is in its main lines like Hilary's treatment of Matthew's version of the stories.[6] Christ's leaving the Gerasenes (Lk 8:39) is his departure from the synagogue. Jairus, then, stands for the Law, interceding for its dying daughter, the synagogue. But before its request can be granted, the Gentiles find healing in the person of the woman with the hemorrhage. Ambrose appeals to Romans 9:11 and 25 to show that the apostasy of Israel leads to the conversion of the Gentiles. Finally, the raising of Jairus's daughter stands for the believing Jews, who are few in number compared with the "crowd" whom Christ expels (a detail Ambrose imports from Matthew 9:23ff.).

Two other themes employed by Ambrose reflect Hilary's interpretation. First, the "unclean spirit" (Lk 11:24ff.) is that driven out of the Jewish people and into the Gentiles by the Law, and then expelled by baptism from the Gentiles in order to return to the Jews (AL 7, 91f.; SC 52, p. 39f.).[7] Second, Ambrose notes that Luke tells of a single Gerasene (or Gadarene) demoniac and a single blind man on the road to Jericho, while Matthew has two demoniacs and two blind men (Lk 8:27, 18:35; Mt 8:28, 20:30). Despite the evangelists' disagreement the "mystical" interpretation is identical, since it has to do with the conversion of the Gentiles, who can be symbolized by a single person or by two, who stand for Ham and Japheth (AL 6, 44; SC 45, p. 243f. and AL 8, 80; SC 52, p. 135f.).[8]

One last ecclesiological interpretation Ambrose offers seems to me different both from Hilary's usual view and from Ambrose's tendency to think in terms of the moral dimension of conversion. The woman "bent over" for eighteen years (Lk 13:10ff.) is a "figure of the church." The eighth day of the resurrection added to the ten commandments makes up the number eighteen. "When the church shall have completed the measure of the Law and of the resurrection, lifted on high in that perpetual rest, she will no longer be able to sense the wearying bending over of our infirmity" (AL 7, 173; SC 52, p. 72). We are no longer to think of the church of those converted on earth or of its constitution out of Jews and Gentiles. Instead, Ambrose directs our attention to the church triumphant, its destiny accomplished in the age to come.

In this sense the church for Ambrose becomes the sign of the new creation effected by Christ's death and Resurrection. When John the Baptist sends two of his disciples to ask Christ whether he is "he who is to come," Christ replies by appealing to his miracles (Lk 7:18ff.). He appeals, says Ambrose, to "marks not of a human but of divine power." Moreover, Christ's miracles can be seen in relation to the cleansing of Naaman (2 Kings 5:14) and the feeding of the widow of Zarephath (1 Kings 17:16), and we are in the presence of "the figure of a mystery" and "the image of a sacrament." What Ambrose seems to mean is that the miracles can be related to baptism and the Eucharist, the life of the Christian in the church. But he goes on to say that "the fulness of faith is the Lord's cross, his death, his burial." The meaning of the miracles drives towards the pattern that characterizes Christian perfection (AL 5, 99ff.; SC 45, p. 220f.). The "grain of mustard seed" (Lk 13:18f.) is faith in Christ's Incarnation, death, and Resurrection. It is the seed which, dying, bears much fruit (John 12:24) and the bread which comes down from heaven (John 6:33). Ambrose continues with a meditation on the kingdom of God in its present and its future dimensions (AL 7, 181ff.; SC 52, p. 75ff.). In this way the moral and the mystical elements of Ambrose's allegorism hold together.[9]

Ambrose can locate the saving work of Christ's death and resurrection in the wider context of the Incarnation and can also refer to it as a new creation. The first point appears in a lyrical meditation on Christ's birth (Lk 2:1ff.). Luke does not disagree with John, but tells the story of Christ's birth, omitted by John, to show that Christ came to abolish sin and death. Ambrose continues by saying (AL 2, 41; SC 45, p. 91):

So, therefore, he was a tiny little child so that you might be a grown man. He was wrapped in swaddling cloths that you might be freed from the bonds of death. He was in the manger that you might be on the altar. He was on earth that you might be among the stars. He had no place in the inn that you might have many rooms in heaven. "Though he was rich," it says (2 Cor 8:9), "yet for your sake he became poor, so that by his poverty you might become rich."

The riches given believers are ultimately the life of the resurrection, and Ambrose can speak of this as the new creation. One of the "mysteries" found in the miraculous feedings of the five and the four thousand with five and seven loaves is the new creation. Five refers to the five bodily senses; and four, to the four elements from which the world was created. The five loaves show that those fed are equal to the world, because though in it they are not of it. And the seven loaves stand for the sabbath, the new creation which follows the six days of the old one (AL 6, 79f.; SC 45, p. 257f.).[10]

The new creation, while it finds its consummation in the age to come, can also refer to the moral transformation of believers in the present. For example, the allegorical meaning of the healing of the man with the withered arm (Lk 6:6ff.) is that Adam's hand, which he stretched out to take the forbidden fruit, finds healing by good works. And the moral for us is that we should stretch out our hands only toward the poor and those who need our help (AL 5, 39ff.; SC 45, p. 197f.). Moreover, Ambrose describes Christ's victory over Satan (Lk 4:1ff.) as a triumph of the new Adam where the old Adam failed. Gluttony, vanity, and ambition fail to conquer Christ, who wages the battle on human grounds (AL 4, 4ff.; SC 45, p. 152ff.). The new creation is, then, a transformation of the old. We see this in the miracle of Cana (John 2:6ff.). Midas was able to turn all he touched to gold, but this brought death. Christ transforms water to wine, and this brings the life of the new creation (AL 6, 88; SC 45, p. 261).

If anything, Ambrose's emphasis is upon the present and moral meaning of the new creation; and his allegory tends to be moral more often than mystical. He gives such a meaning to the story of the first creation by equating Adam with the soul and the image of God, and Eve with the body. The body rebels against the soul and causes it to rebel against God. The new creation restores and heals these broken relationships, subordinating the soul to God and the body to the soul (AL 4, 66f.; SC 45, p. 178). First the soul is delivered from the devil, and then it gives life to the body by governing it (AL 4, 62; SC 45, p. 176). It is the soul that can choose whether to obey God or not. Just as the demons expelled from the Gerasene demoniac themselves request to be sent into the pigs, so we bring punishment upon ourselves (AL 6, 46ff.; SC 45, p. 244f.). The sick mind cannot embrace the Word of God (AL 6, 51; SC 45, p. 246). Contrariwise, someone who seeks healing in a dutiful and religious way finds it. This is why, though there were many lepers in Israel in the time of Elisha, only Naaman the Syrian was healed (Lk 4:27; AL 4, 49; SC 45, p. 170).[11] Because the mind or soul is more important than the body, spiritual healing transcends physical; and spiritual fevers and leprosy are more in need of healing than their corporeal counterparts. Peter's mother-in-law's fever and Naaman's leprosy provoke these comments from Ambrose (AL 4, 51, 63; SC 45, p. 171, 176). The same conclusion enables the paralytic (Lk 5:17ff.) to be allegorized as spiritual paralysis (AL 5, 10; SC 45, p. 186).

If I am correct in arguing that Ambrose's interpretation of Christ's miracles ends by referring them to the new creation in its mystical and moral dimensions, the question that remains is whether he means the allegorical meaning to discount the narrative meaning. The answer would seem to be an immediate no. He does not so much dispose of the literal miracles as press beyond them to their deeper meaning. And we must certainly remember that it is Ambrose who insists upon the miracles that attended the discovery of the bodies of Gervasius and Protasius in Milan. His letter to his sister telling the story betrays no hesitation in affirming the importance and value of the wonderworking relics of the two martyrs.[12] At the same time, at least three passages in his homilies on Luke seem to betray some uneasiness with miracles. In speaking of the stilling of the storm he argues that we can think of the stilling of the storms caused by the "unclean spirit." And so "you have a miracle in the elements; you have a teaching in the mysteries." Both are important and should not be thought contradictory (AL 4, 69; SC 45, p. 179). It is Ambrose's insistence upon both that interests me. More clearly, his interpretation of what Luke means by "the things which have been accomplished among us" (Lk 1:1) argues that what is true and false about Christ may be ascertained not by "miracles and prodigies" but by understanding (verbo). "And so our faith is founded on understanding and reasoning and not on miracles" (AL 1, 4; SC 45, p. 48). Finally, Christ's command to the leper he heals to "tell no one" (Lk 5:14) suggests to Ambrose that Christ thinks the faith of those who believe "spontaneously" is better than that of those who "hope for benefits" (AL 5, 5; SC 45, p. 185).

At first sight we seem to have encountered a puzzle. Ambrose encourages belief in miracles as a bishop, but he can attack or at least voice suspicion about belief in miracles in his sermons. Yet I do not believe there is finally any real contradiction. Ambrose never attacks miracles. He does not doubt them, nor does he seek to deny their importance. Rather, his concern is partly to be sure that the miracles are harnessed to the church and made to serve its purposes. And it is partly to insist that the miracles retain their place in a broader theological structure. They are, indeed, signs of the new creation which can be seen at work in the new life of Christians and which point further toward the consummation of the new creation in heaven. Moreover, the theological framework in which the miracles belong is that of Christian Platonism. When Ambrose says that the mind brings punishment upon itself, he implies the usual fourth-century understanding of providence and freedom as simultaneously active in human life. Large issues begin to appear, but I shall reserve further discussion until chapter 6. Let me conclude by saying that however difficult it is to penetrate the text of Ambrose's reworked sermons to the situation in which they were preached, we find at least hints of a worry not about miracles in and of themselves, but about the dog's tail getting out of hand.

AUGUSTINE: THE MIRACLE OF THE TWO RESURRECTIONS

It was as he was approaching his thirtieth birthday, in the autumn of 384, Augustine went to Milan and encountered Ambrose. Almost two years later he heard the child's voice chanting "take it and read" and, by reading Saint Paul's words in the thirteenth chapter of Romans, experienced his conversion (*Conf.* 8.12). Baptism and his return to Africa shortly followed, and by 396 he was bishop of Hippo. His *Tractatus in evangelium Ioannis* consists of 124 sermons preached or dictated at some time during his episcopate.[13] Reading these sermons gives us a stronger sense of Augustine's actual preaching than is true of a reading of Ambrose's homilies. He wages war on the Arians and the Donatists, and at one point he alludes to the feasts of St. Lawrence and St. Xystus, martyrs who abided in Christ (AJ 27.12; *NPNF* 1.7, p. 178).

As we should expect, Augustine treats Christ's miracles as deeds accomplished by God. When the blind man whom Christ heals says "If this man were not from God, he could do nothing" (John 9:33), Augustine commends him. "With frankness, constancy, and truthfulness [he spoke]. For these things that were done by the Lord, by whom were they done but by God?" (AJ 44.13; *NPNF* 1.7, p. 248). Moreover, because the miracles are God's they are in a sense "not marvelous" once this is understood. Augustine means that the changing of water to wine at Cana differs in no absolute fashion from the way in which the creator ordinarily changes "what the clouds pour forth . . . into wine." We can see that giving existence to someone from nothing is more marvelous than restoring to life someone who has already existed. But the very regularity of the miracle of nature dulls our perceptions. Therefore (AJ 8.1; *NPNF* 1.7, p. 57):

> God has, as it were, reserved to Himself the doing of certain extraordinary actions, that by striking them with wonder, He might rouse men as from sleep to worship Him.

The works of creation are really more marvelous than Christ's miracles.[14] Indeed, Augustine takes a further step and argues that still more marvelous than the miracles is the very fact of the incarnation. "It is of greater importance to our salvation what He was made for men, than what He did among men: it is more important that He healed the faults of souls, than that He healed the weaknesses of mortal bodies" (AJ 17.1; *NPNF* 1.7, p. 111).

Although Augustine attributes Christ's miracles to his divinity, he by no means forgets that the wonderworker is God incarnate. He gives a curious interpretation of Christ's words to his mother at the wedding in Cana: "O woman, what have you to do with me? My hour has not yet come" (John 2:4). The question is a repudiation of Mary by Christ's divinity and means: "That in me which works a miracle was not born of thee." The statement supplies a balance by promising from the point of view of Christ's humanity that "because my weakness was born of thee, I will recognize thee at the time when that same weakness shall hang upon the cross" (AJ 8.9; *NPNF* 1.7, p. 61). Going a step further Augustine suggests that even the miracles themselves bear witness to the double character of Christ. That the hour had not yet come means that much remained to do (AJ 8.12; *NPNF* 1.7, p. 62):

> Disciples had to be called, the kingdom of heaven to be proclaimed, the Lord's divinity to be shown forth in miracles, and His humanity in His very sympathy with mortal men. For He who hungered because He was man, fed so many thousands with five loaves because He was God; He who slept because He was man, commanded the winds and the waves because He was God.

Christ's divine miracles must be balanced by his human weaknesses and suffering.[15]

Augustine repeats the theme, already familiar to us, that even though Christ's miracles ought to produce faith in the incarnate Lord, they as often as not fail to do so. Indeed, people can believe in Christ without seeing any miracles at all. The Samaritans, for Augustine, are the paradigm example. In Galilee only Christ's few disciples believe in him because of the miracle at Cana (John 2:11), and the ruler in Cana believed only after he had confirmed the miracle by comparing the hour of his son's healing with the hour of Christ's promise to him. In contrast (AJ 16.3; *NPNF* 1.7, p. 109):

> The Samaritans had waited for no sign, they believed simply His word; but His own fellow-citizens deserved to hear this said to them, "Except ye see signs and wonders, ye believe not" (John 4:48); and even there, notwithstanding so great a miracle was wrought, there did not believe but "himself and his house."

Augustine does relate his interpretation to Christ's rejection by the Jews and acceptance by the Gentiles, but his emphasis is upon the superiority of a faith that does not require miracles. "We" are like the Samaritans because we "have believed on Christ through the gospel; we have seen no signs, none do we demand" (AJ 16.3; *NPNF* 1.7, p. 109).

Augustine certainly does not wish to deny the reality or the importance of miracles, but he is concerned that they be related to a deeper spiritual meaning. The "greater works" mentioned by Christ (John 5:20) are to raise the dead, something greater than healing the sick (AJ 19.4f.; *NPNF* 1.7, p. 123). This might lead us to suppose that Christ's miracles of healing in the present point toward the future general resurrection. But a deeper truth finds expression in Christ's words "the hour is coming, and now is, when the dead will hear the voice of the Son of God, and those who hear will live" (John 5:25). The two resurrections implied by these words are not to be understood as Christ's raising of Lazarus, the widow of Nain's son, and Jairus's daughter in contrast to the resurrection on the last day. Instead, we must think of a resurrection of the soul that precedes the resurrection of the body. In other words, the first resurrection is spiritual and moral; the second, physical. And those who are given the first resurrection find deliverance from the second death, otherwise the fate of all Adam's children.[16] Of greatest importance is the resurrection of the soul, quickened by finding its life in God (AJ 19.9ff.; *NPNF* 1.7 p. 125ff.).[17]

For this reason the true significance of Christ's raising the dead is not found in the physical miracle. After all, Lazarus, though brought back to life, is doomed to die like everyone else. The message for Augustine's congregation is both moral and spiritual (AJ 22.7; *NPNF* 1.7, p. 147):

> Rise in thy heart; go forth from thy tomb. For thou wast lying dead in thy heart as in a tomb, and pressed down by the weight of evil habit as by a stone. Rise, and go forth. What is Rise and go forth? Believe and confess. For he that has believed has risen: he that confesses is gone forth.[18]

Moreover, the three people Christ raised from the dead "have some figurative significance of that resurrection of the soul which is effected by faith" (AJ 49.3; *NPNF* 1.7, p. 271). Jairus's daughter, who was not yet carried out of the house for burial, stands for those dead by latent sin. The widow of Nain's son, carried out for burial, represents those who have actually committed sin. Finally, Lazarus, buried for four days and stinking, symbolizes those dead by evil custom. By a similar allegorical interpretation the "deaf, blind, lame, impotent" are those who refuse the spiritual healing of the divine physician (AJ 17.15; *NPNF* 1.7, p. 116). And contrariwise, those whose eyes and ears are healed are those who are enabled to see and hear God (AJ 2.16, 112.5; *NPNF* 1.7, pp. 18, 417).

One of Augustine's most extended allegories is in some sense related to the notion of the first resurrection. Homily 9 expounds the mystery of the miracle at Cana (John 2:1–11). Until Christ's Resurrection "prophecy was water." But when the risen Lord explains the scriptures to the disciples who were on the road to Emmaus (Lk 24:13ff.), they discern Christ in those books where they had not previously found him. This is the sense in which Christ transformed the water to wine. When the believer has "passed over to the Lord," he finds the veil removed from the Law so that he can read its true meaning (2 Cor 3:14ff.; AJ 9.3; NPNF 1.7, p. 64). The allegory is extended to the six stone jars that contain the water, which symbolize the six ages into which Augustine, following Matthew's genealogy of Christ, divides human history. He embarks upon a long discussion of the prophecies associated with Adam, Noah, Abraham, David, Daniel, and John the Baptist; and he shows in detail how the water of their prophecies is changed to wine by the risen Lord.

The first resurrection enables the believer to understand the truth of Christ, but from another point of view it merely makes him a convalescent or a pilgrim. Augustine emphasizes the discontinuity between the two resurrections. Our present life is a long Lenten fast in which we abstain from wickedness and unlawful pleasures; but it is also a life of hope, because we are "awaiting our blessed hope, the appearing of the glory of our great God and Saviour Jesus Christ" (Ti 2:13: AJ 17.4; NPNF 1.7, p. 162). Another metaphor makes the same point. Life is a broad and stormy sea that separates us from our homeland. But God has supplied us with a plank to get us across. "For no one is able to cross the sea of this world, unless borne by the cross of Christ" (AJ 2.2; NPNF 1.7, p. 14). Similarly, even though we can board the little ship of the church, the storms through which it must sail are terrifying. Christ treads the waves (John 6:16ff.; AJ 25.6f.; NPNF 1.7, p. 162):

> Thus it goes on, so long as time endures, so long as the ages roll. Tribulations increase, calamities increase, sorrows increase, all these swell and mount up: Jesus passeth on treading upon the waves. And yet so great are the tribulations, that even they who have trusted in Jesus, and who strive to persevere unto the end, greatly fear lest they fail; while Christ is treading the waves, and trampling down the world's ambitions and heights, the Christian is sorely afraid.

The first resurrection, so to speak, represents a decisive moment; we are on board ship. But the voyage that takes us to our homeland in the City of God and to the second resurrection is a hard and dangerous one.

Let me now raise the difficult question of Augustine's attitude toward miracles. One impression conveyed by the passages in his homilies just examined is that the important dimension of miracles is their spiritual or even allegorical meaning. This impression is strengthened by several passages in the homilies attacking magic and superstition. Christ was no magician; this is what the pagans think, supposing to praise him (AJ 100.3; *NPNF* 1.7, p. 386):

> For they reproach Christians as being destitute of skill; but Christ they laud as a magician, and so betray what it is that they love: Christ indeed they do not love, since what they love is that which Christ never was. And thus, then, in both respects they are in error, for it is wicked to be a magician; and as Christ was good, He was not a magician.

Not only does Christ supply no warrant whatsoever for magic, he also cannot be understood to support astrology by speaking of his "hour" (John 2:4; AJ 8.10; *NPNF* 1.7, p. 61f.). Christ's miracles, then, are not to be confused with magic; and this point might prove sufficient had not the Christians sometimes brought magic with them into the church.

Augustine attributes this to the work of evil spirits, who seek to deceive Christ's followers by seducing them with "amulets and incantations." He exhorts his congregation by saying "When our head aches, let us not have recourse to the superstitious intercessor, to the diviners and remedies of vanity" (AJ 7.6f.; *NPNF* 1.7, p. 50). I am obliged to admit that a certain amount of reading between the lines is necessary, but Augustine seems here to betray a worry that Christian miracles will be given a magical interpretation. This would help explain his insistence on the theological framework for Christ's miracles. At the same time, the problem seems somewhat more complex, which I can indicate by citing what Augustine goes on to say after he attacks the use of amulets for headaches. He recommends placing the Gospel at one's head (AJ 7.12; *NPNF* 1.7, p. 52):

> For so far has human weakness proceeded, and so lamentable is the estate of those who have recourse to amulets, that we rejoice when we see a man who is upon his bed, and tossed about with fevers and pains, placing his hope on nothing else than that the gospel lies at his head; not because it is done for this purpose, but because the gospel is preferred to amulets. If, then, it is placed at the head to allay the pain of the head, is it not placed at the heart to heal it from sin?

Is it simply a question of one person's magic being another person's religion? Is Augustine grudgingly allowing a sort of Christianized magic in the church? Or does he really "rejoice" that such a thing is possible and merely expresses concern that the health of the soul not be forgotten in pursuing the health of the body? I must defer these questions for later and fuller treatment, but one final passage in Augustine's homilies requires attention.

Miracles, says Augustine, cannot prove the church to be true. He refers to the Donatist claim that one of their bishops, Pontius, worked a miracle and that Donatus himself had his prayer answered by God from heaven (AJ 13.17; NPNF 1.7, p. 93). Even if true, the claim would not prove the Donatist church the true one. Charity is more important than moving mountains (1 Cor 13:2). There can be false prophets working "signs and wonders" (Mk 13:22). Simon Magus and Pharaoh's magicians did wonders. And even those in the church who worked true miracles, like Peter, rejoiced not in what they did but because their names were written in heaven (Lk 10:20). The important thing is not the miracles but the church in which alone they have significance. The church proves the miracles; the miracles do not prove the church.[19] In a sense, we can draw the conclusion I suggested earlier about Ambrose's attitude. Augustine's concern is not to deny or minimize the importance of miracles, but only to insist that miracles be placed firmly in their proper theological context and that they be controlled by the church. I should wish to adopt this conclusion, but also to argue that it does not go far enough. Again further discussion must be reserved for chapter 6, when I shall attempt to examine more directly the theological problem posed by miracles.

JOHN CHRYSOSTOM: THE MIRACLE OF THE NEW VIRTUE

John Chrysostom, born in Antioch of a prosperous Christian family, educated under the famous pagan rhetorician Libanius and the Christian teacher Diodore, was ordained priest by Bishop Flavian of Antioch in 386, the year of Augustine's conversion. From that time until his consecration as patriarch of Constantinople in 398 his principal duty was preaching. The epithet by which he is known (Chrysostom means "golden-mouthed") testifies to his great success in his work. There survive his homilies on Matthew, probably delivered in 390, and his homilies on John, to be dated a year or so later. Chrysostom's sermons, therefore, are roughly contemporaneous with Ambrose's homilies on Luke. They represent a verse-by-verse exposition of the Gospels, although the homilies on John are much shorter and less discursive than those on Matthew. All the homilies are preoccupied with persuading the Christians in Antioch to take the demands of the Gospel seriously in their daily lives. Consequently, Chrysostom's writings are a mine of information about what it was like to be a Christian in a large city toward the end of the fourth century.

Chrysostom seeks to engage his congregation in the study of the Gospels

and urges them to meditate beforehand upon the passages that will be
read at the liturgy (ChJ 11.1; *NPNF* 1.14, p. 38). In this way he will be able
to preach to people who have already considered the text and its problems.
One problem, of course, involves the relationship of the Gospels to one
another and their apparent disagreements. These can always be resolved,
and Chrysostom shares with his time the conviction that harmonization is
always possible. The evangelists deliberately aim at completing one another. Matthew, for example, omits what Christ did after his Baptism and
before John the Baptist's imprisonment; John turns particular attention to
this part of Christ's ministry (ChJ 17; *NPNF* 1.14, p. 58). In any case,
whatever difficulties remain, the evangelists never disagree regarding the
chief points of Christian teaching (ChM 1.6; *NPNF* 1.10, p. 3):

> That God became man, that He wrought miracles, that He was
> crucified, that He was buried, that He rose again, that He as-
> cended, that He will judge, that He hath given commandments
> tending to salvation, that He hath brought in a law not contrary to
> the Old Testament, that He is a Son, that He is only-begotten, that
> He is a true Son, that He is of the same substance with the Father.

Two of Chrysostom's additions to this succinct statement of the creed
deserve notice. First, his reference to "commandments" fits his preoccupation with teaching Christians to live virtuously. We must glorify Christ
both by faith and by works, since "sound doctrines avail us nothing to
salvation, if our life is corrupt" (ChJ 4; *NPNF* 1.14, p. 19). Second, he adds
the working of miracles to the credal narrative of Christ's story. They are
integral to the message of salvation, which includes the victory over Satan
(ChM 1.4; *NPNF* 1.10, p. 2).

Yet even here there is a tension in Chrysostom's point of view. Several
times in the homilies on John he notices that John includes fewer miracles
than do the other evangelists. John himself explains this by referring to
"many other signs . . . not written in this book" (John 20:30; cf. 21:25).
John is more concerned to preserve Christ's teaching. It is the "grosser
sort" of people who are attracted to Christ by miracles, for "miracles are
not for believers, but for unbelievers" (cf. 1 Cor 14:22; ChJ 42.1; *NPNF*
1.14, p. 151).[20] Chrysostom does not hesitate to give miracles their proper
place. As we shall see, they function along with prophecy to demonstrate
the truth of Christ and the church. At the same time he wants to make
sure that miracles remain subservient to the Gospel they help to vindicate;
and he relegates them to a safe place in the past, arguing that they no
longer happen.

Let me turn directly to the way Chrysostom treats miracles as proof of

Christ and begin by discussing the wonders that attend Christ in contrast to the wonders he does. Miracles surround Christ's birth; and the greatest of all is, of course, his virgin birth.[21] The star the Magi follow bears miraculous witness to this greatest wonder. Indeed, it is not even a star but "some invisible power transformed into this appearance" (ChM 6.3; NPNF 1.10, p. 37). We can tell this because it does not move like an ordinary star. It disappears from view while the Magi consult Herod; it moves from north to south rather than from east to west; it shines in broad daylight; it descends and comes to rest "over the place where the child was" (Mt 2:9). The entire story witnesses to the power of Christ in two ways. The Gentiles turn to him; and far from indicating that we should trust the stars and astrology, it shows that Christ has put down astrology, taken away fate, stopped the mouths of demons, cast out error, and overthrown sorcery (ChM 6.1; NPNF 1.10, p. 36).

The miracles attesting Christ cease after his birth, and Christ remains hidden until "another more glorious beginning" (ChM 7.2; NPNF 1.10, p. 44). Chrysostom refers to the baptism by John, when the miraculous dove descends "not bearing an olive branch, but pointing out to us our Deliverer from all evils, and suggesting the gracious hopes" (ChM 12.3; NPNF 1.10, p. 77). The contrast between the type of Noah's ark and its fulfillment in Christ is between the deliverance of one man and his family and the leading up to heaven of the whole world. Christ's work of redemption is completed on the cross, and once more miracles attest to its truth. The darkness from the sixth to the ninth hour (Mt 27:45) fulfills the type of the darkness in Egypt preceding the Exodus (ChM 88.1; NPNF 1.10, p. 520). Even though three were crucified, the miracles pointed to Christ alone and so thwarted the devil's attempt "to cast a veil over what was done" by including the two thieves with Christ. Moreover, the devil was defeated in another way, since "it was not a less matter than shaking the rocks, to change a thief upon the cross, and to bring him unto Paradise" (ChJ 85; NPNF 1.14, p. 317).[22]

The miracles that Christ performs primarily demonstrate his identity as God and creator. Chrysostom observes that Christ did no miracles before his baptism, repudiating the infancy miracles as "inventions of certain who bring them into notice" (ChJ 17.3; NPNF 1.14, p. 60). John the Baptist's ignorance of Christ and the need of the multitude for his teaching make it clear that there had been no miracles earlier. The implication of Chrysostom's view is that Christ's miracles are firmly associated with his public ministry and so tied to his message and its authority in his person. Once the wonderworker begins his mission, however, there are "showers of miracles" (ChM 14.4; NPNF 1.10, p. 89). When Christ brings forward the woman healed of her hemorrhage (Mt 9:22), he does so "to glorify her, and to amend others, and not to show Himself glorious." There was no need to call attention to himself, "for the miracles were pouring around Him faster than the snow-flakes" (ChM 31.2; *NPNF* 1.10, p. 207).

Chrysostom summarizes the purpose of these showers and snow storms of miracles by saying that "where His name was great, He did not greatly display Himself: but where no one knew Him . . . He made His miracles to shine out, so as to bring them over to the knowledge of His Godhead" (ChM 28.4; *NPNF* 1.10, p. 192). Christ proclaims himself Lord of the sea by commanding Peter to walk on it and by bringing up the gift of the sea in the form of the fish with the shekel in its mouth (Mt 14:29, 17:27; ChM 58.2; NPNF 1.10, p. 359). The children's hosannas in the temple (Mt 21:15ff.) are miraculous. The proof text from Psalm 8 proves that Christ as the creator of nature caused the children to utter praises beyond their years (ChM 67.1; *NPNF* 1.10, p. 409). "Again, that He created the world and all things therein, He demonstrated by the fishes, by the wine, by the loaves, by the calm in the sea, by the sunbeam which He averted on the Cross; and by very many things besides" (ChM 16.2; *NPNF* 1.10, p. 104). That Christ "used the creation itself as a groundwork for His marvels" refutes Marcion and proves Christ to be the creator (ChJ 42.2; *NPNF* 1.14, p. 152). Indeed, the miracles can be understood as the completion of an unfinished creation (ChJ 56.2; *NPNF* 1.14, p. 201).

Chrysostom sometimes associates the proof from miracle with that from Scripture or prophecy. More often than not, however, the context in which the idea occurs is one in which the two proofs fail to convince. "His own" reject Christ (John 1:11); they see but "do not believe" (John 6:36).[23] He also can treat the proof from Scripture as greater than that from miracles. When Christ appeals to Scripture to explain what believers receive (John 7:38), he implicitly reproves those who have believed because of the miracles (John 7:31) and shows that true conviction must come "not so much from the miracles as from the Scriptures" (ChJ 51.1; *NPNF* 1.14, p. 183). Miracles are somewhat less convincing because they can lead to boasting, because they can be slandered, and because they can be imitated by the devil (ChJ 19.2; *NPNF* 1.14, p. 68).

Despite Chrysostom's qualifications, the miracles not only establish Christ's identity as God and creator, they also demonstrate the truth of the new commonwealth he establishes. We can appeal to a general principle, namely that "whensoever anything is done strange and surprising, and any polity is introduced, God is wont to work miracles, as pledges of His power, which He affords to them that are to receive His laws." This is why we find miracles associated not only with the Incarnation but also with Adam, Noah, Abraham, and Moses (ChM 14.4; *NPNF* 1.10, p. 88). Moreover, this means that the miracles were done "for the aliens' sake, to increase the number of the proselytes." From this point of view the miracles of the apostles must be considered together with Christ's miracles as designed to establish the new commonwealth. Nevertheless, "afterwards they stayed, when in all countries true religion had taken root." In other words, miracles no longer take place, though Chrysostom is obliged to admit some exceptions to this rule. For example, when the Emperor Julian encouraged the Jews to rebuild the temple in Jerusalem, miraculous divine punishments stopped the work (ChM 4.2; NPNF 1.10, p. 20f.).

Chrysostom's interpretations often downplay the question of the function of the miracles to prove the identity and the truth of Christ and the church and simply attempt to explain the narrative meaning of the stories in the Gospels. In this respect what he says resembles the way Theodore interprets the miracles in John. Let me mention several themes in a summary fashion and ask the reader who is interested to consult Chrysostom's sermons. We may distinguish between miracles Christ works with power and those he works by prayer and humility. The difference is one between greater and lesser deeds, but the lesser deeds also accommodate Christ's works to the weak condition of those receiving it.[24] A second theme is that the miracles function together with Christ's teaching. His words and deeds reinforce one another, whether it is the multitude or the disciples that are the object of his teaching.[25] Chrysostom qualifies this judgment the same way he qualifies the proofs from miracle and prophecy by arguing, particularly in the homilies on John, that it is the "grosser sort" of people who are persuaded more by the miracles than by the teaching.[26]

Three other themes reflect Chrysostom's understanding that the miracles must be considered as an aspect of Christ's careful teaching and his concern for his pupils. Occasionally he does not require faith before the miracle; more often he makes that requirement of the person to be healed or of his friends. And he often displays the faith of those who have been healed.[27] The emphasis is clearly upon the importance of faith, and Chrysostom's interpretations do little more than repeat the obvious meaning of the Gospel text. The second theme is that Chrysostom notes that Christ sometimes seeks out people to heal and sometimes waits to be called.[28] He does the first out of divine compassion and the second from modesty or in order to prepare people for the miracle. Finally, the careful way Christ works miracles is reflected by his occasionally heightening miracles and by his refraining from them. He does the first in order to make the miracles more persuasive.[29] But the second equally suits his excellence as a teacher.

Three points are involved. First, Christ knows the Jews will not be persuaded by miracles because they consistently reject him even when they witness his wonders.[30] That is why he refuses their demand for a sign.[31]

Nothing can change the fate of the Jews, and their doom came inevitably with the destruction of Jerusalem under Titus.[32] Even that doom did not put an end to their wickedness, and Chrysostom attacks the Jews of his own day as evil magicians (ChM 43.4; *NPNF* 1.10, p. 276). Christ's refusal to work wonders for the disbelieving Jews, however, can find in Chrysostom's view a more positive explanation. He does not wish to increase their envy and worsen their punishment.[33] A second pedagogical reason for refraining from miracles is Christ's wish to avoid vainglory and to set an example of humility.[34] Finally, refraining from miracles enables Christ to demonstrate the truth and reality of his humanity.[35] His power to work wonders must always be balanced by an insistence upon the reality of his passion.[36]

Chrysostom takes seriously the way the miracles demonstrate Christ's identity and the truth of the new commonwealth. And he pays considerable attention to the way Christ uses the miracles as an important part of his pedagogy. But his central concern is to show how the miracle stories may be used as a warrant for the virtue he supposes were required by the new commonwealth. Several assumptions lie behind this concern. Miracles as such do not necessarily produce faith and virtue. Indeed, they usually presuppose faith on the part of those who benefit from them. Moreover, miracles apart from virtue are meaningless.[37] Even the wicked can perform miracles.[38] What counts, therefore, is the miracle of the soul's healing. Christ in the Gospels is a healer not merely of bodies but, more importantly, of souls. The rich young man who comes to Christ asking about eternal life (Mt 19:16ff.) understands this, as do those who ascend the mount to hear Christ's sermon.[39] The soul is most precious of all and is superior to the body that it governs.[40]

Chrysostom, then, appeals to his congregation to use their freedom for the choice of virtue. He by no means wishes to deny the importance of grace. The apostles' disclaimer that they have not made the lame man walk by their own power (Acts 3:12) teaches us "a great doctrine, that a man's willingness is not sufficient, unless any one receive the succor from above; and that again we shall gain nothing by the succor from above, if there be not a willingness" (ChM 82.4; *NPNF* 1.10, p. 494). Human life is like a sea voyage. The wind makes the ship sail, but the sailors must hoist the sails correctly. So God's providence guides our life, but it is up to us to respond to him aright (ChJ 1.5; *NPNF* 1.14, p. 3). Within this framework of thought, however, Chrysostom's emphasis is upon our own efforts and our choice of virtue.[41] Most of his homilies end with a section of moral exhortation only loosely associated with the text he has been expounding, and it is in these passages that we chiefly see Chrysostom the moralist.

We also find, however, a good many passages where Chrysostom gives a

moral interpretation to miracles. The exegesis seems to me more meta-
phorical than strictly allegorical, since Chrysostom tends to say that the
miracle is like a corresponding moral miracle than that it directly bears
that significance. However one assesses his method, what he says is clear
enough. For example, the burning fiery furnace of Daniel 3 reminds him of
the furnace of poverty which cannot harm the poor Christian and into
which the rich Christian must descend in order to give alms (ChM 4.19–
20; NPNF 1.10, p. 29ff.). Or it is the furnace of our warfare with the devil
and the passions, a furnace that cannot harm us because God descends to
give us his help (ChM 16.14; NPNF 1.10, p. 115). The Eucharist is a potion
that kills the worms and serpents of the passions (ChM 4.17; NPNF 1.10, p.
28). The following passage sums up the way Chrysostom treats the miracles of Christ as a way of exhorting his listeners to virtue (ChM 32.11;
NPNF 1.10, p. 219):

> For, as to miracles, they oftentimes, while they profited another,
> have injured him who had the power, by lifting him up to pride
> and vain-glory . . . but in our works there is no place for any such
> suspicion, but they profit both such as follow them, and many
> others.
>
> These then let us perform with much diligence. For if thou
> change from inhumanity to almsgiving, thou hast stretched forth
> the hand that was withered. If thou withdraw from theatres and go
> to the church, thou hast cured the lame foot. If thou draw back
> thine eyes from an harlot, and from beauty not thine own, thou
> hast opened them when they were blind. If instead of satanical
> songs, thou hast learnt spiritual psalms, being dumb, thou hast
> spoken.
>
> These are the greatest miracles, these the wonderful signs.[42]

The miracle that engages Chrysostom's interest is that of the new virtue.
    To seek that new virtue is to enlist in Christ's army for warfare against
the devil and his hosts. Chrysostom supposes this to be a central meaning
of the Christian life, and it explains why we are taught to say in the Lord's
prayer "deliver us from the evil one" (ChM 19.10; NPNF 1.10, p. 136). The
battles of Themistocles and Pericles against Xerxes the Persian are "children's toys" compared with the Christians' war with Satan. The armies of
the monks who attack the devil in his desert stronghold supply a noble
example of how all Christians ought to fight (ChM 33.5, 8.6; NPNF 1.10,
pp. 223, 53). Sometimes the warfare seems trivialized to our modern
sensibilities. Chrysostom repeatedly attacks the theater and the baths.

Dancing also betokens the presence of Satan. God gave us feet not for dancing "but that we may walk orderly: not that we may behave ourselves unseemly, not that we may jump like camels, (for even they too are disagreeable when dancing, much more women,) but that we may join the choirs of angels" (ChM 48.5; *NPNF* 1.10, p. 299).

More important, however, for success in this warfare are the weapons of the virtues, particularly charity and humility. When Christ cites the verse "You shall not tempt the Lord your God" (Deut 6:16) to reject Satan's temptation, he teaches us "that we must overcome the devil, not by miracles, but by forbearance and long-suffering, and that we should do nothing at all for display and vainglory" (ChM 13.4; *NPNF* 1.10, p. 82). The true marvel concerns those who have renounced wickedness and "from thence have gone up to Heaven, and from the stage and orchestra have passed over unto the discipline of angels, and have displayed so great virtue, as to drive away devils, and to work many other such miracles" (ChM 26.7; *NPNF* 1.10, p. 181). It is this kind of miracle that persuades unbelievers. "For not even a dead man raised so powerfully attracts the Greek, as a person practising self-denial" (ChM 43.7; *NPNF* 1.10, p. 278. Cf. ChJ 72.5; *NPNF* 1.14, p. 266).

We cannot escape the conclusion that Chrysostom is not merely insisting that the life of virtue and warfare against Satan is more important than concentrating on miracles but is actually engaging in a kind of polemic against miracles. He is responding to a question and a demand from his congregation that seem to be more than merely rhetorical fictions. The question is: How can we be expected to imitate Christ and the apostles when we have no miracles. The demand is: Give us miracles in our time. The question evokes from Chrysostom the answer that it is not their miracles that make the apostles worthy of emulation but their willingness to endure persecution and to practice self-denial. It is by denying oneself and by defeating the passions that we can imitate the apostles (ChM 33.6; *NPNF* 1.10, p. 224). Scriptural examples abound. John the Baptist is an example for us, even though he "did no sign" (John 10:41). Elijah is admirable because of his boldness to Ahaz, his zeal for God, and his voluntary poverty, not for the miracles he performed. Chrysostom goes on to speak of Job, David, and the patriarchs (ChM 46.3; *NPNF* 1.10, p. 290).

Chrysostom concludes this last discussion by arguing that what "commends" our life is not "a display of miracles" but "the perfection of an excellent conversation." Christ himself worked wonders "that having made Himself thereby credible, and drawn men unto Him, He might bring virtue into our life." Turning to his congregation, Chrysostom demands (ChM 46.3; *NPNF* 1.10, p. 291):

Why, even thou, should one give thee thy choice, to raise dead men by His Name, or to die for His name; which I pray thee, of the two wouldest thou rather accept? Is it not quite plain, the latter? and yet the one is a miracle, the other but a work. And what, if one offered thee to make grass gold, or to be able to despise all wealth as grass, wouldest thou not rather accept this latter? and very reasonably. For mankind would be attracted by this more than any way.

We should not lament our inability to perform miracles. We are not required "to raise the dead, or to cure the lame." We can be like Peter by following him in renouncing wealth (ChM 90.4; NPNF 1.10, p. 533). Nor should we be sorry and vainly wish we had "lived in those times, and had seen Christ working miracles." Christ himself tells us "Blessed are those who have not seen and yet believe" (John 20:29; ChJ 87.1; NPNF 1.14, p. 327).

Sometimes the question becomes a demand, and Chrysostom's congregation says, "we seek miracles." What this demand fails to perceive is that miracles have fulfilled their function and have ceased.[43] Their function was to demonstrate the truth of Christ and of the commonwealth he introduced. Only when that commonwealth is in danger, as in the time of Julian the Apostate, should we expect miracles (ChM 4.2; NPNF 1.10, p. 21). Moreover, miracles, as the apostle Paul says, are signs "not for believers but for unbelievers" (1 Cor 14:22). Chrysostom generalizes from what Paul says about speaking with tongues. Whether or not his interpretation is justified, he clearly argues that miracles serve to convert people to Christ and have no place in the lives of believers.[44] And he can cite Paul's words about love (1 Cor 13) and Christ's words, "do not rejoice . . . that the spirits are subject to you; but rejoice that your names are written in heaven" (Lk 10:20), to prove the superiority of virtue over miracles and to repudiate the demand for signs (ChM 32.11; NPNF 1.10, p. 218).

The final question to ask is what is Chrysostom worrying about. I am strongly tempted to associate the demand for miracles he perceives on the part of his congregation with the practices Chrysostom directly attacks. He warns his people against astrology, sorcery, and necromancy (ChM 6.1, 37.8; NPNF 1.10, pp. 36, 249). And he associates sorceries and magical arts with the Jews (ChM 43.4; NPNF 1.10, p. 276). It seems likely that Chrysostom identifies the quest for miracles with the magical practices he naturally supposes Christians must avoid. Still more, the Jews tend to become scapegoats in Chrysostom's polemic.[45] For the moment let me leave the question, since it demands more extensive treatment. I shall turn to miracles as a practical and a theological problem in chapters 5 and 6.

CYRIL OF ALEXANDRIA: THE MIRACLE OF THE INCARNATE WORD'S VICTORY

We have already met Cyril as an interpreter of the Fourth Gospel. Here we shall encounter him as a preacher. Only three of Cyril's homilies on Luke exist in the original Greek, but almost 156 survive in a sixth- or seventh-century Syriac translation. Frequent allusions by Cyril to the Nestorian controversy require a date somewhat later than that of the *Commentary on John*, and a possible allusion to Cyril's Anathemas in homily 63 means that we can probably date the homilies to the end of 430, the year of Augustine's death and some forty years after Chrysostom preached in Antioch.[46] Cyril's point of view is not obviously different from that found in the *Commentary on John*, even though his Christology is expounded against Nestorius. But the character of the work is quite different, since he employs his theology for the purpose of exhorting his flock and encouraging them in the Christian life as participants in Christ's victory over Satan.

There is no need to discuss the way in which themes in his commentary find expression in the homilies. Suffice it to say that he rings changes upon his interpretation of the function and meaning of Christ's miracles in much the same way as in his comments on John. The miracles ought to have the effect of proving the truth of Christ and his work, but seldom do largely because the Jews consistently reject Christ despite his miracles.[47] Their significance is found partly in the way they help constitute the church out of the remnant of the Jews and the Gentiles and partly in the way they point to the meaning of Redemption, including the resurrection of the dead.[48] Moreover, Cyril retains his preoccupation with providing a proper account of Christ's person. He is the eternal Word of God, consubstantial with the Father, who has emptied Himself by becoming human in the Incarnation. The miracles, then, prove Christ to be God and the agent of creation; but they also reflect the importance of the humanity God the Word has appropriated as his instrument.[49] In all his interpretations Cyril clearly employs his theology, but he also pays close attention to the text. For example, he underlines the irony that it is those who reject Christ (the "elders of the Jews") who implore him to heal the centurion's slave (Lk 7:3ff.; T 35, p. 41). Cyril reads Luke carefully and notes the details, which differ from those in the Matthaean and Johannine parallels.

What is new, however, and what reflects Cyril's purpose is that he is concerned to employ his interpretation for the edification of the people. Central, I believe, is his desire to explain to them Christ's victory over Satan and their share in that victory. Christ was born to destroy the power of the devil, and this is what the story of the Magi told by Matthew proclaims (T 2, p. 4f.). But the victory is not one that Christ wins merely for himself.

The mission of the twelve indicates that Christ commissions all his disciples to embark upon this victorious warfare. His specific instructions (Lk 9:1–5) show how we must arm ourselves with fasting and poverty, with a zealous purpose and an enlightened mind, with the confidence of pilgrims sure of our goal (T 47, p. 101ff.). The victorious return of the seventy after similar instructions provokes Christ to say "I saw Satan fall like lightning from heaven" (Lk 10:18). And the truth of his judgment is evidenced by the triumph of Christianity over paganism (T 64, p. 169).

The conquest of Satan may be equated with the constitution of the church. This is the plundering of the strong man's goods that Christ speaks of (Lk 11:21f.; R 1.143, p. 127). This is the gathering "into one the children of God who are scattered abroad" (John 11:52; R 1.144, p. 127f.). The healing of the Gerasene demoniac (Lk 8:26ff.) moves Cyril to exclaim (T 44, p. 82f.):

> Let us then see the tyranny of the devil struck down by Christ and the earth freed from the wickedness of demons. Let us see the very heads of the dragon broken by Christ and the crowd of poisonous snakes driven out by force and fear. Formerly they wantonly and audaciously held all beneath heaven under their hands and received glory in many ways in the temples of this world.

The victory is one any Christian in Alexandria may see by looking around. And we may also think of Cyril's own war upon paganism.

The defeat of Satan is, however, a challenge as well as a promise. Thinking of Christ struggling with Satan in the wilderness reminds Cyril of the monks who follow his example. And the monks, of course, are an encouraging example to Christians in Alexandria. To defeat Satan is to win the war against our passions (T 12, p. 19f.). We are helped in the struggle by Christ's touch, just as he touched the bier on which the widow of Nain's son was carried out for burial (Lk 7:14; T 36, p. 46). But like Chrysostom Cyril underlines the Christian's responsibility in the effort to achieve virtue. For this reason the miracles of Christ sometimes afford us an example of virtue to imitate. The collection of the fragments after the miraculous feeding (Lk 9:17) shows us that we must practice hospitality no matter how little we have to give (T 48, p. 107).The character of Cyril's moral exhortation finds expression in his discussion of Christ's promise that the Father will "give the good Spirit to those who ask him" (Lk 11:13, in a variant reading). The goodness belongs to the grace that makes the person receiving it "most blessed and marvelous." But when someone fails to receive his request, he is to blame for having asked wrongly (T 79, p. 223f.):

If you seek riches, you will not receive them from God. Why? Because they drive the human heart away from him. . . . If you seek worldly power, God turns away his face. . . . If you seek the ruin of others or that they be hurled into inescapable torments because they have afflicted you or have caused you grief, God will not grant it. . . . Seek for yourself an abundant supply of spiritual gifts. Seek strength to be able to conquer all carnal lust; seek from God what is guileless, by no means eager for money, longsuffering, the mother and nurse of all good things—seek, I mean, patience. Seek endurance, temperance, a pure heart, and most of all seek wisdom from him.

The war against Satan is really a moral one, and Cyril's homilies drive toward urging his people to the new life of virtue.

It comes as no surprise that Cyril can contrast this central aspect of the Christian life to seeking miracles. Like the disciples we should rejoice because our names are written in heaven (Lk 10:20). We should not rejoice in working wonders and terrifying throngs of demons, because these marvels lead to vainglory (T 64, p. 171). At least one passage in Cyril's homilies shows that the theme is more than exegetical or abstractly homiletical. He explains the story of the strange exorcist (Lk 9:49f.) by focusing upon the error of the disciples, who are unprepared to accept the man using Christ's name to cast out demons because "he does not follow with us." Cyril imagines two examples. There are Christians in the church who "use incantations and certain abominable murmurings, who sometimes fumigate certain things, and who order amulets to be used." They are not to be commended, because even though they are Christians they do not behave so. The second example is a simple man, who has spent time in the desert with the monks and who seems to be an outsider in the church. This man, like the strange exorcist, must be welcomed (T 55, p. 138).

Even though the evidence is not as clear as it might be, I should conclude that Cyril sees the same problem Chrysostom had noted some forty years earlier. There is a real danger that, by bringing magic into the church, Christians will corrupt the true meaning of the faith. And it looks as though this has some connection with the miracles of Christ. Cyril has not left us as large a body of homiletical material as has Chrysostom, and he does not seem as preoccupied with the problem of miracles as does Chrysostom. Nevertheless, his point of view does not seem so very different. Moreover, both the Eastern fathers examined in this chapter appear to differ considerably in their attitude from Ambrose and Augustine, who appear to handle the problem of miracles not by rejecting them but by making sure they are Christian and ordered by the church. These conclusions probably ought to be put in the form of questions and will be reexamined later in the argument.

CONCLUSION

From one point of view, examining homilies on the Gospels has taught us nothing new. The same set of assumptions is at work, and we find an insistence that the miracles of Christ be placed in a broad theological context. The miracles proclaim the identity of Christ as God incarnate. That he heals the man born blind with clay reminds us that he made humanity from clay; and his sovereignty over water and his ability to produce wine and bread reflect the fact that he is the agent of creation. At the same time details of the stories proclaim him also human, and we are told not to forget his human experience and his Passion. The function of the miracles, both those that attend Christ at his birth, baptism, and Passion and those that he works, is to proclaim his identity and the truth of his saving work. The "signs" are primarily for unbelievers and are designed to persuade those who witness them to embrace the new commonwealth of the church. But they seldom fulfill that function. At least the Jews remain unpersuaded to this day.

The meaning of Christ's miracles embraces the entire meaning of the Christian faith. They reflect the promise of salvation in two ways. First, they help create the church out of the remnant of Israel and the Gentiles. Second, they help give Christians the hope of salvation both by pointing toward the resurrection of the age to come and by promising a new vision of life and a new virtue in the present. The new creation has future and present, mystical and moral dimensions. Moreover, the miracles can be used as a basis for the challenge of faith as well as its promise. They supply warrants for the demands made upon Christians by the Gospel, and they can be interpreted to refer to the healing of the soul in which human freedom plays a large role. In all these respects, despite my attempt to distinguish the different writers from one another and the interpreters from the homilists, there is broad agreement. Christ's miracles are part of a larger picture.

One difference to be found in the homiletical writings, I think, is that emphasis has shifted to the last point I have just described. The preachers we have examined are all concerned with applying their understanding of the miracle stories to the exhortations they deem appropriate for their people. And here what begins to take pride of place is the battle with Satan. Christ, of course, has already won the victory; and so the Christian can be assured of the outcome of his own struggle. It is also true that divine help is always available for the faithful warrior. But neither of these observations takes away the importance of the individual's obligation to join the Christian army and enter the fray. It may not be going too far to suggest that the central meaning of Christianity in late antiquity has to do with Christ's victory over Satan. I shall seek to explore this somewhat more fully in chapter 3 by discussing the liturgical and catechetical context in which Christ's miracles were placed.

Another difference to be found in the preachers' writings is an uneasiness with and, in the case of Chrysostom, a polemic against miracles. Partly this involves an insistence upon the theological framework in which the miracles belong; partly it has to do with a determination to keep the miracles in the church where they can be controlled by the bishops. But a problem has begun to develop. We learn from at least three of our preachers that Christians are resorting to amulets, incantations, and magical arts. This resorting to wonders appears to lead to a misunderstanding of Christ's miracles or even a use of them to justify magic. The tail, as I have suggested, runs the risk of wagging the dog. Ambrose and Augustine wish only to moderate the wagging, but Chrysostom wants to cut the tail off. At least these are my tentative conclusions. The practical problem of miracles needs further attention, and I shall return to it in chapter 5.

Finally, we discover at least hints that miracles pose a theological problem. All the writers examined reflect the problem of the relationship between human freedom and divine providence. And, with the exception of Augustine, all of them resolve the problem by insisting that we are dealing with two activities or forces that work simultaneously but on different levels. The miracles Christ works are acts of providence, but they are properly understood and received only by a right use of freedom. A related theological problem has to do with what we mean by nature. The providence exercised by Christ in creation is in one sense the same that he exercises in working wonders. And yet there is an obvious difference. Nature is speeded up or made more remarkable. Or it can even be that nature is transcended. It would be premature to say more, and I must defer discussion of these difficult theological issues until chapter 6. As the reader will understand, chapters 3, 5, and 6 will explore further dimensions of what we have learned in the first two chapters. Chapter 4 will be concerned with wonderworking Christians during the time of the Christian Roman Empire and will also prepare the way for chapters 5 and 6.

3

Christ the Wonderworker in Context

 To think of miracles in Roman imperial Christianity is, of course, to think in the first instance of Christ's miracles in the Gospels and the way they were understood by Christians. Yet it has already become evident that their interpretation does not take place in a vacuum. The very fact that the Gospel stories were preached to congregations of Christians means that we must immediately think of the public worship of the church. Indeed, while from one point of view Scripture clearly supplies the basis for Christian teaching, from another point of view Scripture can scarcely be considered apart from its liturgical context. By that context I mean a number of different things. Obviously, I am thinking of the liturgy, primarily that of baptism and that of the Eucharist. And I include the preaching that regularly took place as an integral part of the liturgy. But I am also thinking of the sort of architectural and iconographical setting in which the liturgy took place, of the lectionary system that required the regular public reading of Scripture, and of the conventions that surrounded catechetical instruction and the rites associated with baptism. All this supplies the larger context in which we must consider the wonderworker in the Gospels.

S. APOLLINARE NUOVO AND THE MIRACLES OF CHRIST

There is no better point of departure for the discussion of this chapter than a cycle of remarkable mosaic pictures in the church of S. Apollinare Nuovo at Ravenna. The basilica was built during the first quarter of the sixth century by Theodoric the Ostrogoth, who ruled an Italo-Gothic empire in Italy from 493 until his death in 526. Theodoric, of course, was an Arian; and the basilica, originally dedicated to Christ himself, was an Arian church. At the same time, we can also use what remains of the original iconographic program as evidence for what orthodox Christians might have experienced in the early sixth century. By 540 Justinian had reconquered Ravenna, and within a quarter of a century the basilica had been appropriated for use by orthodox Christians and rededicated to St. Martin of Tours. The primary change made at that time in what survives of the iconography was that the figures of Theodoric and his family were obliterated from the arches of the mosaic depicting his palace. This explains the ghostly fingers left from the portraits that were destroyed that can still be seen on the columns of the palace. Moreover, we learn from the experts that the mosaics of Ravenna supply excellent evidence for Christian ecclesiastical art in the late antique and early Byzantine period.[1] Changes since the seventh century have altered the basilica and its iconographic program only by destroying the mosaics in the apse and on the west wall. The dedication was changed to S. Apollinare in the ninth century, when his relics were moved from S. Apollinare in Classe.

The nave of the basilica is lined north and south by two rows of classical columns that support the walls on which the lateral mosaic program has been placed. This program consists of three zones. The lowest, immediately above the columns, depicts on the north wall the port and city of Classe, a procession of virgins, the three Magi presenting their gifts (a nineteenth-century reconstruction), and closest to the altar a large and magnificent mosaic of the Virgin, holding the Christ child and surrounded by four angels. At the same level on the south wall we move from Theodoric's palace to a procession of saints, and finally, nearest the altar, to an enthroned Christ clothed in purple and flanked by angels that marks a counterpoint to the portrait of the Virgin. The middle zone of the program is interrupted by windows and consists of thirty-two figures of saints and prophets. The upper zone is the one of most interest to us. On the north wall there are thirteen scenes from Christ's ministry, while on the south wall the events of his Passion and Resurrection are depicted.

Let me list the scenes in this upper zone, in sequence from the apse end of the nave to the entrance wall:

north wall

1. The miracle at Cana
2. The miraculous feeding
3. Calling of Peter, Andrew
4. Blind men near Jericho

south wall

1. The Last Supper
2. Gethsemane
3. Judas's betrayal
4. Christ arrested

5. The woman with hemorrhage	5. Christ and Sanhedrin
6. The woman of Samaria	6. Peter's denial predicted
7. Raising of Lazarus	7. Peter's denial
8. Pharisee and publican	8. Judas repentant
9. The widow's mite	9. Christ and Pilate
10. The sheep and the goats	10. Christ to Calvary
11. The paralytic	11. The Marys at the tomb
12. The Gerasene demoniac	12. The road to Emmaus
13. The paralytic at Bethesda	13. The risen Lord

I need to add that one of the remarkable features of the two sets of scenes is that the figure of Christ on the north wall differs strikingly from that on the south. The north wall Christ is beardless, serene, clothed in purple, and haloed. In all but scenes 2, 8, and 10 he is accompanied by a single apostle who stands beside him. In some degree this seems peculiar, particularly in scenes 3 and 6. We should not expect Christ to be accompanied by an apostle when he is calling his first disciples (Mt 4:18ff.). And the disciples are not present for Christ's conversation with the woman of Samaria (John 4). The south wall Christ, though still clothed in purple and haloed, is bearded and somehow seems more human. Moreover, the scenes on the south wall convey a more dramatic effect, are more crowded with figures, and tell a consecutive story in a way the first set of scenes does not.

It is difficult to know exactly how to interpret the program in the upper zone. The contrast between the two sets of scenes must in part be explained by a difference in technique and artistic temperament. We probably must reckon with two different workshops. At the same time, both series seem to have been produced together and to have been meant to reinforce one another. The wedding at Cana, the miraculous feeding, and the Last Supper are all located toward the east end of the basilica; it is hard to escape the conclusion that a eucharistic connotation is envisaged. Certainly, the three stories repeatedly receive this interpretation in the ancient literary sources. Moreover, we can also assume that the second set of scenes proclaims the central message of the church, the death and Resurrection of Christ. The major problems revolve around the meaning of the first series, which does not tell any obvious story, and around the relation of the two series to one another. To take the second problem first, we can see some correlations between the two sets. For example, the Last Supper corresponds to the wedding at Cana; the betrayal of Judas contrasts with the call of Peter and Andrew. But it is difficult to force the correspondence of the two series much further than this. Turning to the problem of the first set of scenes, what of the apostle who usually stands beside Christ. Is he a witness or an assistant? Does he stand for the Christian's presence in the story? There is simply no way to tell.[2]

There is only one interpretation I feel confident enough to suggest: The iconography draws our attention to the paradox of the majesty and the humility of Christ. The majestic Christ works miracles, calls his disciples and the Samaritan woman, persuades people to a new piety symbolized by the publican's true prayer and the widow's offering, and expressing itself in the power of judging between sheep and goats. The humble Christ goes to the cross, which is transformed to victory by the Resurrection. We have already seen in the first two chapters that an appeal to this sort of paradox is common in the literature that interprets the Gospels and that it often correlates with the double judgment about Christ that appears in Scripture and is articulated in the church's dogma of the two natures of Christ. The mosaic scenes I have been discussing would impress upon the ordinary Christian in Ravenna this double judgment. Christ's victory manifests itself not only in the miracles and deeds of his life but also in his Passion. Once again we find that the miracles are placed in the total theological context of the church's teaching.

THE LECTIONARY CONTEXT

We can take a further step by noting that the first set of mosaic scenes at S. Apollinare Nuovo has been explained as corresponding to the lectionary readings that were used in the basilica.[3] Although it probably is impossible to recover with any certainty the lectionary used at Ravenna, the suggestion is reasonable and even likely. If it is true, then Christians at S. Apollinare Nuovo would have encountered the stories of Christ's miracles in what they heard read, in what they saw, and in the sermons they heard. Exactly how this happened is surely impossible to know, but that it happened seems to me beyond doubt. From the fourth century on it was usual to have three lessons at the liturgy. The last of these, of course, was the Gospel. Much ceremony became associated with the reading of the Gospel, and it became one focus of the liturgy.[4] Not all Gospel lessons are, of course, miracle stories. Nevertheless, such narratives cannot be escaped and must have seemed typical of the Gospel reading. Of the thirteen scenes on the north wall at S. Apollinare Nuovo eight are miracles. It is surely not extravagant to claim that some such proportion inevitably characterizes any lectionary system.

One way of making my point is to show that, although the Byzantine lectionary that later developed was clearly not in use in Ravenna, the stories in the mosaic series do appear at prominent points in it. The miracle at Cana by which Christ turns water to wine (John 2:1–11) is the

Gospel for both the Wednesday after Easter Day and the Monday of the second week of Easter. The miraculous feeding is probably that of the five thousand, since Christ is blessing four (closer to five than to seven) loaves and two fishes. Matthew's narrative (14:14–22) is the Gospel for the eighth Sunday of Pentecost, while John's version (6:5–14) is listed for the fifth Wednesday of Easter. The healing of the blind men on the road to Jericho, which must be from Matthew (20:29–34) because there are two blind men, is listed as the Gospel for the twelfth Saturday of Pentecost. The story of the woman with the hemorrhage cannot be from Matthew because there she does not fall down at Christ's feet. The Lukan version (8:41–56) is used on the twenty-third Sunday of Pentecost. The paralytic, who is let down by the roof in Luke and Mark but not in Matthew, appears as the Gospel on the eighteenth Saturday of Pentecost (Lk 5:17–26) and the second Sunday of Lent (Mk 2:1–12). The Gerasene demoniac (Matthew has two demoniacs) in the Lukan version (8:27–35, 38–39) is used the twenty-second Sunday of Pentecost. Finally, the healing of the paralytic at the pool of Bethesda (John 5:1–15) is the Gospel for the fourth Sunday of Easter.[5]

My point is not to explain the series of mosaic scenes at S. Apollinare Nuovo but simply to argue that the miracle stories depicted there would have been read at one time or another in churches using the Constantinopolitan lectionary. The same point can be made more generally by leaving the Ravenna mosaics behind and turning to the lectionary itself. For example, during Lent the Gospels for Saturday and Sunday are from Mark except for the Sunday of the first week and both Saturday and Sunday of the sixth week, when they are from John. Of a total of twelve Gospels, six are miracle stories, including the raising of Lazarus on the Saturday of the sixth week of Lent.[6] One final example may be taken from the fifth-century Syriac lectionary published by F. C. Burkitt in 1923.[7] On the Sunday of the middle week of Lent seven lessons precede the Gospel, which is the story of the raising of Lazarus (John 11:1–44) "or read in Lk about the widow's son (vii 11–17), or read in Mk about Jairus' daughter (v 21–43)."[8] The name Jairus, of course, occurs only in Luke; but the motive of the lectionary appears to be to give equal time to the Gospels and to read one of the three stories in which Christ raises someone from the dead.

My argument up to this point is that ordinary Christians encountered Christ's miracles not only in the sermons they heard but also in what they saw in their churches and in the reading of the Gospel. The obvious question to ask is how all these impressions would have been ordered and made sense of for Christians. The answer revolves around the catechetical practices of ancient Christianity. Although infants were probably baptized from earliest times and certainly were baptized during the period we are studying, it is important to emphasize that the statistical norm almost certainly remained adult baptism. Many people were converted to Christianity as adults, and even people who were brought up in Christian families usually deferred baptism until they had reached maturity. For example, one major purpose of Gregory Nazianzen's *Oration on Holy Baptism* (*NPNF* 2.7, p. 360ff.) is to exhort his people to abandon their habit of refusing baptism until adulthood. The reason for emphasizing the likelihood that adult baptism was the statistical norm is that it gave the church the opportunity of indoctrinating and socializing its members while they were preparing for baptism. Let me turn, then, to the church's catechetical practices in order to examine how miracles functioned in the instruction given catechumens and in the rites in which they participated.

THE CONTEXT IN THE BAPTISMAL RITES

Four writers from the second half of the fourth century have left us homiletical materials associated with baptism. The earliest of these is Cyril of Jerusalem, whose episcopacy lasted from 348 until his death in 386. Even though he became embroiled in the Arian controversy and was expelled from his see three times, he was ultimately vindicated as orthodox and his point of view is probably to be regarded as typical of conservative Eastern bishops in the middle of the fourth century. Nineteen homilies (a procatechesis and eighteen catechetical lectures) are certainly his, and he probably delivered them in the church of the Holy Sepulchre in Jerusalem in 350. Five mystagogical lectures, delivered to the newly baptized, cannot confidently be attributed to him largely because they are assigned to his successor John in one of the manuscripts; but their content certainly differs in no way from that of the catechetical lectures.[9]

We have already met the three other writers. A. Mingana in 1932 discovered a Syriac translation of Theodore of Mopsuestia's catechetical homilies. The first ten are on the Nicene Creed and were almost certainly delivered to the candidates before their baptism. The eleventh on the Lord's Prayer, and five others on baptism (12–14) and the Eucharist (15–16) are in all likelihood to be understood as mystagogical lectures for the newly baptized. Theodore probably gave these homilies in Antioch sometime after 388 and before 392, when he became bishop of Mopsuestia, though perhaps they are to be dated during his time as bishop (392–428).[10] John Chrysostom has left us twelve baptismal homilies, most of which have been discovered in this century.[11] Since there are references in the text to people not speaking Greek and since this fits the situation in Antioch better than that in Constantinople, we should date the homilies during the time Chrysostom was active as a preacher in Antioch (386–

398). Finally, Ambrose of Milan published a small treatise in the form of a homily called *De mysteriis* about 390. This work seems to have been based upon earlier homilies, and the collection of sermons called *De sacramentis* may supply a case in point and represent what was preserved for Ambrose by shorthand stenographers. A third work, *Explanatio symboli ad initiandos*, should also be included.[12] Consequently, Theodore, Chrysostom, and Ambrose are all preaching at about the same time, the very end of the fourth century.

Let me begin by discussing the rites of baptism to which these sources bear witness. At the beginning of Lent the catechumens who wished to present themselves for baptism at Easter enrolled themselves as *photizomenoi* or *competentes*. They then received instruction followed by exorcism, probably daily. When the time for baptism came the candidates were anointed, required to renounce Satan, were baptized with a triple immersion, clothed in a white robe, and anointed again. They then participated in the Paschal Eucharist. Within this broad framework certain differences may be found. In Antioch, for example, two anointings preceded the baptism itself; the first was simply a signing of the forehead with oil, while the second was an anointing of the entire body. In Milan, on the other hand, only one anointing took place before baptism, though it was a total one. Then after baptism proper the head was anointed with *muron*; and a *spiritale signaculum*, probably the sign of the cross with oil, completed the rite. Moreover, in Milan immediately before the first anointing and the renunciation of Satan, the bishop touched the ears and nostrils of the candidates in the ceremony of the "opening" (*apertio*). Also in Milan the ceremony of the footwashing and the reading of John 13 took place between the second and third anointing.

With this broad framework of the rite in mind let me turn to the literary sources in order to illustrate how some of its different aspects found explanation. Both Theodore and Chrysostom strongly emphasize the enrollment that began the preparation of the candidates. For Theodore the enrollment makes the candidate "the citizen of a new and great city" (WS 6, p. 24). Chrysostom makes the same point and urges the candidates to "resolve to do the things which can show that you deserve your citizenship in heaven" (ACW 31, p. 108). Theodore elaborates his interpretation and associates it with the rite of exorcism. The enrollment is not possible unless a judgment can be rendered against Satan, who claims legal title to the candidate. The exorcist is the lawyer who pleads the case against Satan (WS 6, p. 26f.). The candidate stands on sackcloth, silent, with head down and arms outstretched in supplication. This posture symbolizes the candidate as a captive of Satan, and it is described in Isaiah 30:3–4 (WS 6, p. 31f.; ACW 31, p. 154f., 48).

The renunciation of Satan, then, completes what has already begun in the preliminary rites of exorcism. According to Cyril[13] the candidate turns to the West, "the region of sensible darkness," and says: "I renounce thee, Satan, and all thy works, and all thy pomp, and all thy service." He then turns to the East and says: "I believe in the Father, and in the Son, and in the Holy Ghost, and in one Baptism of repentance" (*NPNF* 2.7, p. 144ff.). What Chrysostom and Theodore say implies a similar ritual, though they do not refer to the orientation of the candidate. The renunciation may have been followed by spitting at Satan. Certainly, the renunciation of Satan (*apotasso*) was followed by enlisting in Christ's army (*syntasso*). What is remarkable about Chrysostom's evidence is that he treats the renunciation of Satan as a ceremony taking place on Good Friday at the ninth hour.[14] Though still part of the baptismal rite it takes place more than a day before the baptism itself. Chrysostom draws from the time the "mystical lesson" that it was then that Christ commended his spirit to the Father and then that the penitent thief entered paradise.

Although Ambrose gives no elaborate interpretation of the renunciation of Satan, he does consider with some care the meaning of the anointings. He finds the *muron*, the chrismation following the baptism itself, spoken of in Scripture. It is "the precious oil upon the head running down upon the beard, upon the beard of Aaron" (Ps 133:2) and the "oil poured out" which gives the fragrance that attracts the "maidens" (Song 1:2f.). The good smell is that of the Resurrection; the head stands for the wise man's "eyes in his head" (Eccles 2:14); the beard, for the "grace of youth;" Aaron, for the fact that "you have become an elect race, priestly, precious" (1 Peter 2:9; SC 25*bis*, p. 172). The anointing of the total body that precedes the baptism finds a different interpretation. The candidate is anointed as "an athlete of Christ" and made ready for the contest that will enable him to be crowned by Christ (SC 25*bis*, p. 62). For Cyril the anointing reflects Christ, the "anointed," and conveys the gift of the Spirit. The oil is applied to the forehead to wipe away Adam's mark of shame, to the ears to open them to divine mysteries, to the nostrils to make the baptized the sweet savor of Christ, to the breast to guard him against Satan in the warfare he now enters (*NPNF* 2.7, p. 149f.).

Theodore treats the first anointing as a signing, made immediately after the renunciation of Satan and stamping the candidate "as a lamb of Christ and as a soldier of the heavenly King" (WS 6, p. 46). Peculiar to Theodore's account is what immediately follows. The godfather "spreads an orarium of linen on the crown of your head, raises you and makes you stand erect." This shows that "you" have been freed from your ancient slavery and enlisted as a free soldier of Christ (WS 6, p. 47). The total anointing that follows is "a mark and a sign that you will be receiving the covering of immortality, which through baptism you are about to put on" (WS 6, p. 54). The signing with oil that follows baptism is like the dove that descended upon Christ at his baptism and signifies the descent of the Spirit (WS 6, p. 68). Chrysostom pays no attention to the anointing following baptism, but he treats the two earlier anointings as preparing the Christian athlete for his contest with Satan (ACW 31, pp. 51, 58, 169). In general, the meanings attributed to the anointings tend to revolve around the two themes of the grace and promise of baptism and the demand and challenge implied by thinking of it as a consecration for a contest.

The baptism itself, of course, has many different meanings. It is a conformity to Christ's death and Resurrection (Rom 6:1ff.; WS 6, p. 51ff.; ACW 31, p. 151; NPNF 2.7, p. 148; SC 25bis, pp. 86, 90, 140). It is a new birth from the waters of the church's womb (WS 6, p. 55; NPNF 2.7, p. 148). Less emphasis attaches to baptism as a washing away of sin, but both Theodore and Chrysostom use the metaphor of refashioning a damaged pot (WS 6, p. 57; ACW 31, p. 138f.). The Old Testament helps explain the meaning of baptism. It is a new creation, a new deliverance from the deluge in Noah's time, and a new Exodus by which the Christian is enabled to escape Egypt and cross the Red Sea. The cleansing of Naaman by bathing in the Jordan foreshadows baptism (SC 25bis, p. 160ff., 78; NPNF 2.7, p. 15; ACW 31, pp. 64, 71f., 170). Christ's own baptism by John supplies a warrant for baptism. The triple immersion symbolizes either the three days before Christ's Resurrection (NPNF 2.7, p. 148) or the three persons of the Trinity (WS 6, p. 63; SC 25bis, p. 166). In sum, the focus seems to be upon conformity to Christ's death and Resurrection understood according to the major types of creation and the Exodus.

I have not attempted to examine the evidence in detail. To do so would be beyond my purpose, which is simply to suggest that baptism receives a rich and complicated interpretation that in some degree focuses upon the details of the rite itself. Several conclusions are suggested. Antioch seems to emphasize what precedes the actual baptism. The enrollment, the renunciation of Satan, and the anointings almost overshadow the baptism itself. The concern has to do with treating baptism as a consecration for the Christian life more than with its initiatory meaning.[15] The Christian is freed from slavery to Satan in order to become Christ's athlete or soldier. A second conclusion is that Ambrose's point of view seems rather different from that of the three Easterners. His emphasis is more strictly on the baptism proper, and he passes over the renunciation of Satan rather quickly. Moreover, the "opening" ceremony in which the bishop touches the eyes and nostrils of the candidates is explained largely in terms of the grace given. Certainly, Ambrose by no means omits the consecration theme; and the footwashing rite, peculiar to Milan, implies an emphasis upon the new virtue required of the baptized, as well as upon the grace given. Nevertheless, the initiatory theme seems to prevail in Ambrose's understanding of baptism.

Let me suggest that the complicated and varied images we have encountered ultimately all focus upon a very simple underlying pattern. The rite itself basically enacts a transition from an old servitude to Satan to a new freedom in Christ. The same pattern holds together all the specific interpretations we have encountered. And I should go one step further and argue that the transition demands to be understood in the light of the story of the two Adams. Even Ambrose uses this fundamental pattern. "In the beginning the Lord our God made humanity so that if it had not tasted sin, it would not have died." But Adam sinned, died, and was driven from paradise. Christ's death and Resurrection puts an end to sin and death. "Death is the end of sins, and resurrection is the remaking of nature." Baptism enables us to enter the story and share in Christ's triumph over Satan (SC 25*bis*, p. 82f.). "You, therefore, have been crucified with him, you have been fastened to Christ, you have been fastened with the nails of our Lord Jesus Christ so that the devil cannot drag you away from there" (SC 25*bis*, p. 88). It is because the devil poisoned Adam's foot that the footwashing has the effect of washing away the serpent's venom (SC 25*bis*, p. 96).

Theodore tells the story in the clearest fashion. He explains the words in the creed "He was incarnate and became a man" as follows (WS 5, p. 59f.):

> They [the fathers of Nicea] rightly said that He [God the Word] assumed a man who resembles those from whom He was assumed, because the man whom He assumed resembles Adam who introduced sin into the world, so that He might abolish sin by one who was of the same nature. Indeed, He put on a man resembling Adam who after having sinned received the punishment of death, so that He might eradicate sin from us and abolish death by similar means. . . . And because when we were subjected to sin we had no hope of deliverance, the grace of God kept that man whom God put on for us free from sin, but Satan came with his deceitfulness and brought death upon Him as upon (any other) man. . . . and since He was not touched by sin which would subject Him to death, Christ our Lord received also upon Himself the death which with wickedness the tyrannical Satan brought upon Him. He showed to God that there was no sin in Him and that it was through injustice that He was enduring the trial of death. And He effected the abolition of condemnation with ease, and He rose from the dead by the

power of God and became worthy of a new and ineffable life which
He generalised to all the human kind.

It is obvious that Theodore's Christology is at work in this statement of the
meaning of the Christian faith, but equally clear that it focuses upon
Christ's death and Resurrection as what overcomes both sin and death. My
point, however, is that the propositions are firmly located within the
framework of the two Adams. Christ as the new Adam delivers the human
race from the servitude of the old Adam to Satan. This basic schema
governs Theodore's account of baptism in the first two of his three homilies on baptism.[16]

The same story appears in Cyril's and in Chrysostom's sermons. Cyril
attributes the fall of Adam and Eve to "the envy of the Devil" (*NPNF* 2.7, p.
73) and in doing so probably alludes to Wisdom of Solomon 2:23f.: "God
created man for incorruption, and made him in the image of his own
eternity, but through the devil's envy death entered the world, and those
who belong to his party experience it." This text, I suggest, is very much in
the minds of the church fathers; and it helps explain why Satan is, if
anything, more strongly associated with death than with sin. Cyril completes the story by saying that by "the very same weapons, therefore,
wherewith the Devil used to vanquish us, have we been saved" (*NPNF* 2.7,
p. 75). What he means is the Incarnation by which God the Word took
human nature and rendered it incorruptible. Chrysostom agrees. The devil
drove Adam from paradise and brought upon him the penalty of death.
"But God in His love did not fail to regard mankind. He showed the devil
how foolish were his attempts; He showed man the great care He manifested in his regard, for through death He gave man everlasting life. The
devil drove man from Paradise; God led him to heaven" (ACW 31, p. 45f.;
cf. p. 63).

The moral of this simple story by which the central meaning of Christianity and of baptism in particular is articulated is a double one. First of
all, those whom the story has grasped in baptism receive power against
Satan. Baptism, says Chrysostom, is a new Exodus from Egypt (ACW 31, p.
64):

The Jews saw miracles. Now you shall see greater and much more
brilliant ones than those seen when the Jews went forth from
Egypt. You did not see the Pharaoh and his armies drowned, but
you did see the drowning of the devil and his armies. The Jews
passed through the sea; you have passed through the sea of death.
They were delivered from the Egyptians; you are set free from the

demon. They put aside their servitude to barbarians; you have set aside the more hazardous servitude to sin.

The defeat of Satan is the victory over, first, death and, second, sin. The assurance of triumph is constantly renewed, and Chrysostom can point out that prayers at the martyrs' tombs encourage Christians to overthrow the tyranny of Satan (ACW 31, p. 107). This means, of course, that however much the victory has been won for the believer in baptism, the baptized life must be a translation of what is true in principle into what is true in fact.

The grace given in baptism remains active in this process. The white baptismal robe blinds the devil and drives him away afraid (ACW 31, p. 74). This may be why Chrysostom calls the newly baptized "spiritual stars" that shine in broad daylight and outshine the sun, blinding the devil and bringing confusion and flight upon him (ACW 31, p. 67f.). The Eucharist, which in a sense is the completion of baptism, has the same effect. When the devil sees a Christian returning from the Eucharist, it is as though he had seen a lion breathing flames. He sees the mouth "all crimsoned and ruddy" and runs away. He will no more enter the Christian than the destroying angel dared to cross the doors marked with blood at the passover in Egypt (ACW 31, p. 60f.). Finally, the sign of the cross made by the anointing prevents the devil from looking the baptized Christian in the face "when he sees the lightning flash which leaps forth from it and blinds his eyes" (ACW 31, p. 52).[17]

Chrysostom's comments, which could in some degree be duplicated by passages from the other writers we are considering (with the possible exception of Ambrose), imply that baptism supplies a grace meant to be used in freedom by entering the contest against Satan. Part of what this means for Chrysostom and the others is that the baptized Christian must renounce practices that are regarded as demonic. Cyril includes in one such list observation of the stars, auguries, omens, divinations, witchcraft, enchantment, and necromancy (*NPNF* 2.7, p. 28).[18] Theodore lumps together astrology and the superstitious practices of the Jews: "the purifications, the washings, the knots, the hanging of yeast, the observances of the body, the fluttering or the voice of birds and any similar thing" (WS 6, p. 41f.). Purely religious observances seem to be equated and confused with magical practices, but we must remember both the problem of the attraction of Judaism to Christians in Antioch and that the Jew in the ancient world was stereotyped as a magician.

Once again Chrysostom supplies the best evidence. The "pomps" of the devil the Christian must renounce include not only immorality, the theater, horse racing, and coarse banquets, but also "portents, oracles, omens, observances of times, tokens, amulets, and incantations." The cross and the name of Jesus are far better amulets. "Call upon that name and every disease will flee, every attack of Satan will yield" (ACW 31, p. 168; cf. p. 39). In another passage Chrysostom attacks as demonic omens, incantations, amulets, and "those who tie bronze coins of Alexander of Macedon around their heads and feet." "You bring into your house drunken and witless old hags." The remedy for all this is the constant renewal of the baptismal renunciation of Satan (ACW 31, p. 190f.):

> When you are going to cross the threshold of a doorway, first speak these words: "I renounce thee, Satan, thy pomps and service, and I enter into thy service, O Christ." And never go forth without saying these words. This will be your staff, this will be your armor, this will be your impregnable tower. And after you speak these words, make the sign of the cross on your forehead. In this way no man will be able to hurt you, nor will the devil himself be able to do so, when he sees you appear with these weapons to protect you on every side.

Christians must arm themselves with Christ's weapons and not with demonic and magical practices.

The choice of armor, however, merely prepares the Christian for the main event, the moral contest with Satan. Repeatedly in our sources Satan is virtually equated with vice. It is he that incites us to evil. But, as Cyril insists, he "indeed suggests, but does not get the mastery by force over those who do not consent" (NPNF 2.7, p. 8). The devil "has not the power to compel against the will" (NPNF 2.7, p. 24). Indeed, Satan's own transformation from a good nature "was of his own free choice." Similarly, he can only persuade "the willing" (NPNF 2.7, p. 28). The devil, then, becomes "the father of men (John 8:41) not by nature, but by fraud" (NPNF 2.7, p. 46). Satan's angels, according to Theodore, are evil people who seek to deceive us whether by idolatry, by vain philosophy, or by heresy (WS 6, p. 39f.). Chrysostom can even identify demons with vices. There is the "demon of drink" (ACW 31, p. 84), and swearing is the "arrow of Satan" (ACW 31, p. 156; cf. p. 141). To consent to vice is to acknowledge Satan, but Christians are free to avoid such consent.

Their freedom to do so must be exercised in the contest with Satan, which is really a struggle to renounce vice and to attain virtue. Chrysostom points out that in the games the herald first leads forth the contestant to be sure he is a free man. But in the contest with Satan slaves may participate, presumably because they are free in Christ. Moreover, "the combat does not consist in wrestling grips but in the philosophy of the soul and the virtue of the heart" (ACW 31, p. 183). Theodore uses the soldier metaphor to make the same kind of point. After the signing which marks the candidate as Christ's, the linen orarium "denotes the freedom to which you have been called." Once "you have been singled out and stamped as a soldier of Christ our Lord you receive the remaining part of the sacrament and are invested with the complete armour of the Spirit" (WS 6, p. 47).[19]

The argument has taken me rather far afield from Christ's miracles into the miracle of the renunciation of Satan and the enlistment in the new Adam's army. What we find, however, is that those miracles can be drawn into the baptismal framework. Ambrose supplies us with the most interesting evidence. He uses the story of Christ's healing of the deaf mute (Mk 7:31ff.) as a warrant for the ceremony of "opening." Christ touches the ears and the tongue of the man healed and says "Ephatha," that is "Be opened." Similarly, the bishop touches the ears and nostrils of the candidates; and Ambrose supplies some rather far-fetched explanations as to why nostrils have replaced the tongue (SC 25*bis*, p. 60f., p. 156). A second Gospel story given the same treatment is that of the paralytic at Bethesda (John 5:1ff.). The story is one of the lessons that has been read, and Ambrose interprets it in relation to baptism. Christ is the angel who descends to trouble the water and the "man" who is able to help the paralytic. Or the angel is the Holy Spirit. And there is a contrast. In the story only one man is healed; in baptism a whole people (SC 25*bis*, p. 74ff., 166f.). Finally, the healing of the man blind from birth by anointing his eyes with clay and by having him wash in Siloam refers to the dirt (*lutum*) placed on the candidates' eyes after their penitence at the beginning of Lent, while the pool of Siloam stands for the font of baptism (SC 25*bis*, p. 98ff.).

In a similar way Cyril of Jerusalem relates the Gospel miracle stories to different aspects of baptism. He provides a long list of examples to explain the kind of faith required of the candidates for baptism. When Peter walked on the water, he "found his faith safer upon the waters than any ground; and his heavy body was upheld by the buoyancy of his faith" (Mt 14:29). The paralytic at Capernaum was healed not by his own but by his bearers' faith (Mt 9:2). Lazarus's sisters had the proper kind of faith (John 11:14ff.)). And even if one thinks he lacks faith, he can say with the father of the epileptic lad (Mk 9:24) "I believe; help my unbelief" (*NPNF* 2.7, p. 30f.). In another passage Cyril draws together the miracle at Cana and the Eucharist. If Christ turned water to wine "akin to blood," "is it incredible that He should have turned wine into blood?" (*NPNF* 2.7, p. 151).

We must, I think, add to our consideration the evidence described in chapter 2 that interprets the miracle stories in relation to the promise and the demand of the Gospel. That is, if baptism is fundamentally the way a person joins in Christ's victory over sin and death, then passages that discuss the double victory apart from baptism are really making the same point. The miracle stories are very much drawn into what clearly represents for the fathers of the church the central meaning of Christianity. They are no longer understood for themselves but in their function as signs. Christ's victory over Satan supplies the hope that physical death will be overcome at the general resurrection and the promise that the Christian will be enabled to beat down Satan under his feet by making progress in virtue. Moreover, the victory over Satan in this second dimension carries with it the demand that the Christian win his own moral and spiritual battle with evil. In other words, the victory over Satan is at one level a ringing assertion that the human quest for virtue can be freely pursued, encouraged as it is by God's persuasive love expressed in Christ. The victory of Christ is both promise and challenge, and the cross symbolizes both these aspects. As a trophy of victory it stands for the triumph of God over death and sin. But as a banner it leads the Christian into his own struggle, conceived in large measure in terms of late antique notions of virtue.[20]

THE PATTERN IN EUSEBIUS OF CAESAREA'S DEMONSTRATION

It was probably in the years immediately after Constantine's victory at the Milvian Bridge (312) and certainly before the outbreak of the Arian controversy in 318 that Eusebius of Caesarea published his *Demonstration of the Gospel.*[21] Ten of the original twenty books survive, though a good many fragments of Book 15 are also extant. Eusebius treats the work as a sequel to his *Preparation for the Gospel* and, therefore, the completion of a large apologetic task involving the refutation of, first, pagan and, second, Jewish objections to Christianity. Certainly, the *Demonstration* is a massive assembling of Old Testament prophecies in order to show how they have been fulfilled in Christ. Nevertheless, it is more than an apology to the Jews. Eusebius himself says that "the importance of my writing does not lie in the fact that it is . . . a polemic against the Jews" (*D* 1.1.8; p. 5). It is also aimed at the Gentiles, and Eusebius has in mind chiefly Porphyry's *Against the Christians* even though his refutation of Porphyry is less direct than in his treatise *Against Porphyry*. Still more the *Demonstration* transcends its apologetic purpose by setting forth "the character of the religion set before Christians" (*D* 1.1.11; p. 7).

It is this last aspect of the work that concerns me. What I wish to argue is that the *Demonstration* yields a view of the central meaning of Christianity coherent with what I have taken to be the point of view in the catechetical writings just examined. Consequently, very much the same theological structure appears at the beginning as well as at the end of the fourth century. The *Demonstration* begins with two books that discuss Christian claims in their relation to the Old Testament and that function as an introduction to the entire work. Book 3 turns to the humanity of Christ, while Books 4 and 5 turn attention to his divinity. Books 6 through 10 treat the incarnate life of Christ from his birth to his Passion. The lost books presumably complete the story with the Resurrection and Ascension and with an account of the spread of the church. One of the fragments of Book 15, for example, treats the church in the light of the four kingdoms mentioned in Daniel 7. The argument, in fact, summarizes the Gospel by relating how the incarnate Lord defeats Satan and establishes the church as the community in which all people are invited to participate in Christ's victory. In examining it I shall attempt to focus upon the miracles of Christ and their incorporation into this simple structure of thought.

The miracle of Christ begins with his birth of the Virgin and the Incarnation (*D* 7.1.328b; p. 66):

> If, then, the prediction was wonderful, and the result of the prediction yet more wonderful, and beyond all reason, why should we disbelieve that the actual entrance of Him that was foretold was allotted a miraculous and superhuman kind of birth, especially as the clear evidence of the other miracles, as marvellous (as the Birth itself) in their sequence from that Birth compels us to accept the evidence of the other wonders connected with Him.[22]

The proof from prophecy and that from miracle are woven together, and the miracles are treated as all of a piece: those that attest Christ and those he does unite to prove his truth and power. The "final miracle" is the Resurrection itself (*D* 10.8.493c; p. 219). Even Christ's death is not an ordinary one, and Eusebius observes this in his list of Christ's "marvellous works," which includes detailed reference to the Gospel miracles. By implication Christ's death is miraculous because it is voluntary; he "commends" his spirit to the Father (Lk 23:46) to show that "uncompelled and of His own free will He departed from the body" (*D* 3.4.108d; p. 125).

The miracles that chiefly concern Eusebius, however, are those Christ performs during his ministry. He performs no marvels as a child, since this is "before the time" (*D* 9.4.426d; p. 159). The implication is that the miracles belong in the context of Christ's public ministry. Eusebius summarizes this context in an interpretation of the words "spoken by the Lord in the prophecy" of Zechariah (11:12f.) about the thirty pieces of silver (*D* 10.4.480ab; p. 207f.):

> I the Lord from the very first day ceased not to give to you Jews
> proofs of My kindness, and in countless ways I did you good, not
> only through the earliest prophets, but also by My presence in
> moral teaching and spiritual education, in signs and wonders, and
> other miracles, and in cures and attentions: now you that were
> privileged to receive such benefits, give My price or refuse it, de-
> manding of them, it would seem, the fruits of holiness, and the
> proof of their faith in Him. But they . . . instead of loving Me spoke
> evil of Me . . . weighing out thirty pieces of silver, as if they valued
> at that price Him that was sold.

Eusebius obviously takes the miracles seriously, but he treats them in a
moral context that binds them to Christ's teaching and to the moral and
spiritual effects they are meant to produce.

One important effect is a correct understanding of Christ. At first the
disciples saw Christ only as "a remarkable man because of His miracles"
or as a prophet. But the miracles gradually showed them that Christ had
"destroyed the enemy and the avenger, and death the prince of this world,
together with the other unseen hostile powers." By understanding that his
miracles were the final victory over Satan and death they came to the
realization that he was God "and worshipped Him" (D 8.1.377ab; p. 111).
Christ's miracles are, of course, the product of his divinity (D 9.13.448a; p.
178). But the instrument used by God the Word to heal was his humanity.
Like "a musician showing his skill by means of a lyre" Christ brought
healing to souls and bodies "through the human organism which He had
assumed" (D 4.13.168d; p. 189). We are to see in Christ the divine healer.

Two chapters (5–6) of Book 3 are Eusebius's defense of Christ's miracles. He first refutes those who refuse to believe the miracles. His argument revolves around insisting upon the reliability of the evangelists. They
bound themselves to Christ and to his precepts, which are "those of a
philosopher's life." They could not, therefore, have sworn falsely; indeed,
they were forbidden to swear at all. Even if they were untrustworthy, how
would it be possible for so many, the twelve and the seventy, to agree in a
lie? Would they have been willing to die for a lie? How could deceivers have
successfully proclaimed a false message to the whole world? Why would
they have included in their account "incidents of shame and gloom?" With
these as his major arguments Eusebius establishes that Christ did work the
miracles attributed to him by the evangelists (D 3.5; p. 126ff.). The second
polemic mounted by Eusebius is against those who accept the miracles
but say they are those of a sorcerer. His argument focuses upon Christ's
lofty moral character and his successful opposition to demons. And he
adds an appeal to the character of Christians, who repudiate magic,

charms, and amulets (*D* 3.6; p. 144ff.) What we begin to see is that the miracles are not ends in themselves, but rather function to establish a new commonwealth that will proclaim Christ's victory over Satan and enable its members to practice a new virtue.

For Eusebius the most remarkable effect of Christ's work is the triumph of the church, which he sees completed by the Constantinian revolution. The rise of Christianity coincides with "Rome's attainment of the acme of power" (*D* 3.7.139d; p. 161). And the church is the working out as well as the proof of Christ's divine power (*D* 9.13.448d; p. 179):

> And the strongest confirmation of the Divine Power of the Saviour . . . by which He really used to cure the lame, the blind, the lepers and the palsied with a word . . . is the power even now energizing through the whole world from His Godhead. . . . He attracts to Himself great multitudes from all the world, and releases them that come to Him from all kinds of evil and diseases and troubles of the spirit; He summons to His holy school all races, Greek and Barbarian; He leads countless hosts to the knowledge of the one true God, and to a healthy and pure life, as befits those who promise to worship Almighty God.

The miracles of Christ point to the miracle of the church, and Eusebius can follow the familiar path that interprets this as including the Gentile mission and the destruction of Jerusalem as a punishment meted out to the unbelieving Jews (*D* 7.pr.308; p. 48).

The miracle of the church, moreover, involves Christ's victory over Satan, first because the gods renounced by the Gentiles are demons. To renounce Satan is to repudiate the pagan gods. Just as Moses led Israel out of Egypt, so Christ summons "the whole human race from their impious Egyptian idolatry under evil daemons." He effects "the rout of the idolatry that embraced the whole world." And so he is "the first to introduce to all men the knowledge and religion of the one Almighty God. And He is proved to be the first Author and Lawgiver of a new life and of a system adapted to the holy" (*D* 3.2.91bcd; p. 105).[23] The evil demons explain the entire apparatus of paganism. They are not only identified with the gods and goddesses, but are also the spirits that give oracles. Their weakness betrays itself by false and ambiguous oracles, by the immorality associated with them, and by their extinction (*D* 5.pr.203d; p. 223). Eusebius also ventures an historical explanation that repeats what he says in Book 1 of the *Praeparatio*. The earliest humans did not worship demons, but were only later enslaved by them. And so paganism, demonstrated to be a novelty, finds its refutation (*D* 4.9159–60; p. 178ff.).[24]

The second aspect of the miracle of the church is that the defeat of Satan is the triumph of Christ and Christians over vice. In a complicated interpretation of Isaiah 7 Eusebius identifies the "two smoldering stumps of firebrands" (Isa 7:4) with Damascus and Samaria (Isa 8:4) and weaves the verses into the prophecy of Christ's birth. But the spiritual interpretation of the two firebrands identifies them with "two ranks of invisible enemies and hostile daemons, warring in different ways against humanity, one active always and everywhere in promoting idolatry and false beliefs among mankind, the other occasioning the corruption of morals" (D 7.1.330b; p. 68). The distinction is not one to which Eusebius strictly adheres, since he can argue that it is the demonic pagan gods who have legislated immorality. Using tried and true, conventional arguments he refers to laws of the nations that sanction cannibalism, incest, sexual license, and even the throwing of "their aged people to the dogs" (D 5.pr.205bc; p. 224). The demons are, of course, also responsible for the wicked persecution of the church (D 6.20.299b; p. 41). Christ has overcome them. "He converted and changed those who listened to Him from lust to purity, from impiety to piety, from injustice to justice, yea, verily from the power of the malicious demons to the divine acceptance of true holiness" (D 4.10.164; p. 183).

Let me attempt to come full circle and argue that the broader context of Christ's victory over Satan enacted in the church by the conversion of people from idolatry and immorality governs the interpretation of Christ's miracles. At one point Eusebius is discussing Christ's claim in his sermon at Nazareth (Lk 4:21) to have fulfilled the prophecy of Isaiah 61:1 by his preaching "good news to the poor" and by proclaiming "release to the captives and recovering of sight to the blind." The first accomplishment is equated by Eusebius with the first Beatitude: "Blessed are the poor in spirit" (Mt 5:3). The second refers to Christ's freeing those enslaved to evil demons by proclaiming "forgiveness, inviting all to be free and to escape the bonds of sin." This is why he said: "Come to me, all who labor and are heavy laden, and I will give you rest" (Mt 11:28). Finally, Christ restores bodily sight but also gives "the vision of the light of true religion" to "those who of old in their minds were blind to the truth" (D 3.1.88cd; p. 102). With the exception of restoring physical sight to the blind the miracles are spiritual and moral ones, and they are associated with Christ's victory over Satan.[25] Eusebius creates a hermeneutical circle; the miracles of Christ find their meaning in Christ's victory over Satan primarily as that is understood in spiritual and moral terms, while Christ's victory over Satan tends to define the meaning of the miracles.

Eusebius makes it apparent that miracles healing the soul are more important than those healing the body. Christ quite literally fulfills the prophecy of Isaiah 35:1–7 by opening the eyes of the blind, unstopping the ears of the deaf, and making the lame man leap like a hart and the tongue of the dumb sing for joy. Nevertheless (*D* 6.21.301c; p. 43):

> . . . figuratively, even today, they that were before so blinded in soul, as to bow down to wood and stone and other lifeless substances, earth-bound daemons, that were deaf in the ears of their mind, and lame, and palsied in all their life, are even now being released from all these and many other sufferings and weaknesses by the teaching of our Saviour Jesus Christ, receiving far better healing and benefit than that of the body, and shewing forth clearly the divine and superhuman power of the presence of the Word of God among men.

Christ's wonders revolve around his overcoming spiritual evil. Indeed, Eusebius employs Job 9:8 ("who alone stretched out the heavens, and trampled the waves of the sea") to interpret Christ's walking on the water (Mt 14:25ff.) as a symbol of the whole of his wonderworking mission. The sea is Satan, whom Christ trampled beneath his feet (Ps 74:13, Ps 69:2, Job 38:16f.). And so "when He walked on the sea in our human life, and rebuked the winds and the waves, He performed a natural symbolism of something unspeakable" (*D* 9.12.447b; p. 177). The ineffable mystery, of course, is Christ's victory. Eusebius's summary of the meaning of Christianity correlates with what we found by examining the baptismal homilies delivered later in the fourth century.

CONTEXTS IN THEOLOGY

My argument boils down to the claim that if one were to ask for a single, simple proposition that would summarize the meaning of Christianity in the patristic period, it would be: Christ has triumphed over Satan. We have already seen that the statement bears a twofold meaning. It refers both to the conquest of death, which will be consummated at the general resurrection, and to the moral triumph over vice which enables the Christian's life of virtue in the present. However, the fathers of the church sometimes seek to understand the basic proposition in a more sophisticated fashion. They are rather like the preacher who repeatedly assured his people that they were "washed in the blood of the lamb," and decided one day that he had better figure out for himself what he meant by repeating that cliché. In some such way Athanasius and Gregory of Nyssa, among others, sought to make sense of Christ's victory over Satan, not by denying that the claim was true but by explaining the claim by relating it to more complicated theological structures. Athanasius wrote *On the Incarnation* as the second volume of a larger apologetical work, probably after the Constantinian revolution (312) and before the outbreak of the Arian controversy (318). Gregory's *Address on Religious Instruction* was written about 385 as a manual for catechists. Gregory explicitly recognizes that the apologetical and the catechetical tasks do not fundamentally differ from one another, and so in a broad sense the two works in question, as well as Eusebius's *Demonstration*, are of a piece.

At the foundation of Athanasius's view is the story of the two Adams, the first seduced by Satan and the second victorious over him. The fall of Adam and its consequences bring to mind for Athanasius the succinct statement of the Wisdom of Solomon 2:23f.: "God made man for incorruption, and as an image of his own eternity; but by envy of the devil death came into the world" (*OI* 5; LCC 3, p. 60). Satan, therefore, primarily stands for death and for physical corruption. In addition, though, Athanasius speaks of a moral corruption. Satan obscured the truth and persuaded humans to worship devils, to practice magic, to consult oracles and the stars, and to fall into a veritable flood of immorality (*OI* 11; LCC 3, p. 96).[26] Christ's victory, then, is first of all the conquest of death. His miracles, which demonstrate his divinity (*OI* 18–19; LCC 3, p. 72f.), find their completion in his turning "the corruptible to incorruption" (*OI* 20; LCC 3, p. 73). The victory of the cross abolishes the power of death and is evidenced by the Christian martyrs, who despise death (*OI* 48; LCC 3, p. 102). It is also a victory of virtue over vice, demonstrated by the conversion of Greeks and barbarians and by the life of absolute chastity lived by many Christians.[27]

Athanasius goes one step further in his description of Christ's triumph over Satan by using the metaphor of a ransom paid by Christ to Satan. The idea is that the human race has been taken captive by Satan and that Christ's sacrifice on the cross pays the ransom necessary to deliver the captives. Even though Athanasius does not say so explicitly, it is obvious that the ransom is paid to Satan. The context of the discussion (*OI* 9–10; LCC 3, p. 63ff.) also enables us to understand where Athanasius finds the idea of the ransom, namely in Scripture. He cites 2 Corinthians 5:14f, and emphasizes the words "one died for all." Christ's death, then, is a sacrifice that is efficacious for all; and Athanasius may well have in mind Pauline passages that use the sacrificial metaphor.[28] A parallel discussion helps confirm this conclusion. Christ's death breaks down "the dividing wall of hostility" (Eph 2:14), and the explicit citation of this verse may well imply a reference to the previous verse and its words "you who were once far off have been brought near in the blood of Christ" (*OI* 25; LCC 3, p. 79). The ransom almost certainly derives from Hebrews 2:14f.: "that through death he might destroy him who has the power of death, that is, the devil, and deliver (*apallakse*) all those who through fear of death were subject to lifelong bondage" (*OI* 10, 20; LCC 3, p. 64, 74). Athanasius simply fuses the two biblical metaphors and makes of them a story about how Christ's death ransoms Satan's captives.

Thus far we can see that Athanasius is simply repeating the popular Christian understanding of Christ's work and elaborating it by using the biblical metaphors of sacrifice and ransom. What interests me, however, is that he seeks to explain the triumph of Christ over Satan by a far more sophisticated understanding of the meaning of Redemption. Two themes predominate in his discussion. First, if the defeat of Satan is the defeat of death, then we can understand this by explaining the Incarnation. The Word of God appropriated a human body, "and that of no different sort from ours." By making it his own and using it "as an instrument" he gradually divinized it, rendering it incorruptible by raising it from the dead (*OI* 8; LCC 3. p. 62f.). The logic of a Stoicizing view of human nature is pressed so that the mind's governance of the body actually results in its rendering the body physically incorruptible. The Word of God, of course, is a kind of supermind; and that is what explains the extraordinary way in which he governs the body he appropriates. But the pattern of the new incorruptible humanity thus established is capable of drawing the whole race to it.

If Athanasius interprets the conquest of death by appealing to the sort of view found earlier in Irenaeus and by employing philosophical common-places to understand it, he can also interpret the conquest of vice by using an Origenist account of the way humanity is created after the image of God. The Father is the archetype, while God the Word is his image. When Genesis says that humanity is made "after the image and likeness of God" (cf. Gen 1:26), it means that we are modeled after the Word of God by being made "rational." Thus, because of our mind or soul we are, in principle, capable of knowing God through his Word in whom we have a share. And since knowing the good is doing the good, the knowledge translates itself into virtue. The Fall, however, deprives us of our use of this capacity. Consequently, the Incarnation restores it to us by sending the image (the Word) accommodated to our condition (*OI* 11–16; LCC 3, p. 65ff.).

I do not wish to argue that Athanasius desires to substitute the theologi-cal structures he borrows from Irenaeus and Origen for the popular and biblical notion of Christ's victory over Satan. All I am suggesting is that the two structures give him a way of explaining the victory as a double one, over death (corruption) and over sin (ignorance). The sophisticated philo-sophical ideas, though they appear as commonplaces and as a kind of *lingua franca*, serve the simple purpose of trying to make sense in a Graeco-Roman world of the Resurrection and of Christian virtue. Moreover, Athanasius has clearly left more problems than he has solved. His account of the incarnate Word is, technically, Apollinarian, since he omits any reference to a human soul. And he fails to think through the relationship of the two themes to one another. It is true that in chapter 3 he tells the story of the Fall in such a way that we might suppose the knowledge of God subordinated to physical incorruption. That is, Adam and Eve in paradise had the grace of the contemplation of God and the "promise of incorruption in heaven." Before that promise could be redeemed they turned from the knowledge of God and so became corrupted, first morally, and finally physically. This account of the Fall implies that the restoration of knowledge would enable the promise to be fulfilled. That is, the knowledge of God is what empowers the mind so to control the body as to render it physically incorruptible. We might read Athanasius this way and suppose that he has subordinated the Origenist theme of knowledge to the Irenaean framework that is dominant for him. But the difficulty is that his discussion begins with the incorruption theme (4–10) and then turns to the knowledge theme (11–16), treating the two as different and unrelated aspects of Redemption.

The major point I wish to make has to do not with Athanasius's success or failure but with his aim to place the popular understanding of Christianity as Christ's victory over Satan in a more sophisticated theological account of Redemption. The same sort of point can be made with respect to Gregory of Nyssa's treatment of Satan in his *Address on Religious Instruction*. Like Athanasius, Gregory starts with the story of how Satan deceived Adam. He regards the story as "a traditional explanation" and not "a fanciful story" (*ARI* 6; LCC 3, p. 278). Satan was originally an angel entrusted with the governance of earth. But when he saw Adam created with such blessing and beauty as to be "the image of the archetypal beauty," he envied him. By envy he fell from goodness and by deceit persuaded humanity to disobey God (*ARI* 6; LCC 3, p. 279ff.). In the Incarnation Christ defeated Satan, as may be demonstrated by the destruction of paganism and of Judaism (*ARI* 18; LCC 3, p. 295). We are clearly on ground by now familiar.

Gregory also expounds a ransom theory to explain Christ's defeat of Satan. People, he says, can sell themselves into slavery. The only way of ransoming them is to offer the master of the slave a price in return for freeing the slave (*ARI* 22; LCC 3, p. 299). So it is with humanity. We are all Satan's slaves, and a persuasive price is necessary if we are to be ransomed from servitude. Christ supplies a dazzling price. His virgin birth and his astonishing miracles led Satan to regard him as "a bargain which offered him more than he held." Like a greedy fish Satan swallowed "the Godhead like a fishhook along with the flesh, which was the bait" (*ARI* 23–24; LCC 3, p. 300f.). The punishment of Satan may seem deceitful, but God dealt justly with him because the punishment fits the crime. Satan had deceived Adam with "the bait of pleasure," and God simply serves him the same sort of turn (*ARI* 26; LCC 3, p. 303).

Gregory takes the story seriously, but his major concern is to understand it in the light of his own theology and, in particular, his understanding of providence and freedom. In this way he goes somewhat further than Athanasius by considering the defeat of Satan not merely in terms of what Redemption means but in its relation to freedom and how God trains it for perfection. Satan's fall is the product of his own free choice and is defined as a movement toward evil and non-being. "But it [that angelic power] closed its eyes to the good and the generous; and just as one only sees darkness when one closes the eyelids in sunlight, so that power by its unwillingness to acknowledge the good contrived its opposite. That is how envy arose" (*ARI* 6; LCC 3, p. 280). Gregory is employing the usual patristic understanding of providence and freedom. Providence is a general and universal operation of God that has differing effects depending upon how it is received. Wrongly used, providence brings punishment; but in a sense by wrongly using providence we bring punishment upon ourselves. And the wrong use of providence involves a movement away from the good toward its deprivation, which has no ontological status.

A second theme follows this first. If the wrong use of freedom brings punishment, and a punishment that is just because it is retributive, God nonetheless uses the punishment to educate us. In other words, we are enabled to learn from our mistakes. Life is an education, and it requires both providential teaching and free learning. Moreover, we may also re-member that in Greek the same word (*paideusis*) means both punishment and education. Gregory applies the idea to Satan's defeat. To be sure, Christ's defeat of Satan must be understood as a justly retributive punish-ment. Nevertheless, Christ's victory benefited "not only the one who had perished [humanity], but also the very one who had brought us to ruin." Satan may well come to understand his punishment and "to recognize its benefit." Christ, then, "freed man from evil, and healed the very author of evil himself" (*ARI* 26; LCC 3, p. 303f.). What is unusual is Gregory's opinion that even Satan will find Redemption. But what I wish to call attention to is the way he draws the popular story of Satan's defeat into the framework of his teaching concerning providence and freedom, a teaching that owes much to Greek philosophy.

Conclusion

I have attempted to examine a number of different contexts in which Christ's miracles appear or from which they may be regarded. Those who preached his wonders did so in a liturgical setting. The iconographic programs found in Christian basilicas, the lectionary systems that were used, and the rites associated with baptism together with the way they found interpretation are simply different aspects of the liturgical setting. I should conclude that what emerges as a least common denominator in the evidence examined is the concise summary of Christianity as the victory of Christ over Satan. This, in turn, means the conquest of death, idolatry, and immorality. This conclusion seems to me confirmed by examining Eusebius's *Demonstration of the Gospel*, Athanasius's *On the Incarnation*, and Gregory of Nyssa's *Address on Religious Instruction*.

From one point of view the miracles of Christ seem almost to dissolve into the basic party platform; from another point of view they are dissolved by it. Obviously, no one denies that the miracles took place; nor is there any sign that they are not taken quite seriously. Nevertheless, the hermeneutical circle that is drawn between the miracles and the victory over Satan tends to redefine the miracles so that they become primarily signs that refer to the meaning of the Christian faith. That meaning has partly to do with the Christian hope. It is not just the raising of Lazarus that points toward the general resurrection. All the miracles are capable of pointing beyond this world order to the age to come. Only then will the marvelous power of God at work in Christ find its consummation.

I should, however, want to conclude that another dimension of the Christian message predominates. The defeat of death not only supplies the Christian hope for the age to come but also makes that hope a force in this world. More often than not the fathers of the church attribute our tendency to sin to our mortality. Once death is robbed of any final power over us, it becomes possible to live the virtuous life in a way that would otherwise be impossible. And so, in some such way, the miracles of Christ become signs for a healed life in the present. The moral meaning of the miracles is paramount and is articulated largely in terms of conventional philosophical ideas. What is involved is the knowledge and contemplation of truth and goodness together with the empowering effect that has upon the human mind or soul. The mind, then, is enabled to govern the body and its passions. In this way vice is overcome and transformed to virtue.

What I am suggesting is that our study of Christ's miracles has led us to a Christianized version of the late antique quest for virtue. Human freedom is at center stage, and affirming freedom means effecting the mind's hegemony over the passions and the body. Of course, the realization of this

human freedom is not a question of what we should think of as human-
ism. Few people in late antiquity would have thought this way. Indeed, the
Epicureans were despised precisely because they refused to allow the gods
a role in human life. The Christians see freedom as something that must
necessarily be exercised within the context of God's providence. And so
their definition of the quest for virtue is in some respects congruent with
that of the philosophers. At the same time their understanding of how God
informs and assists human freedom in its quest for virtue is unusual
simply because it is based upon convictions about Christ. In this sense just
as Christians sought to Christianize the Roman Empire, so Christians
sought to Christianize the quest for virtue that characterized the best in
their culture.

If this conclusion is warranted and it is possible to argue that a study of
Christ's miracles really leads us to Christian freedom turned toward virtue, then one important qualification must be made. We have already seen
signs that the basic fabric we have examined is unstable at points. The fact
that the fathers express an uneasiness or even a repugnance to miracles
suggests to me that they perceive miracles as a possible threat to the vision
that lies at the heart of their Christian convictions. Before turning to this
aspect of the matter we must turn our attention away from Christ's miracles to wonderworkers in the church. Chapter 4 will examine this phenomenon and seek to answer the question whether miracles contemporaneous with the fathers of the Nicene and post-Nicene church can be understood as congruent with the basic perspective I have sought to describe.
Not everyone agrees with Chrysostom that miracles no longer happen.

4

Wonderworkers in the Church

 At the beginning of the eighth book of his *Ecclesiastical History* Eusebius turns from the past to a narration of "a few of the most important occurrences of our own times" (*NPNF* 2.1, p. 323). His last three books tell the story of the Diocletian persecution, the victory of Constantine, and the peace of the church. Almost a century later Rufinus of Aquileia translated Eusebius's work into Latin and added two books, continuing the history to the death of Theodosius the Great in 395. Still half a century later two writers in Constantinople continued Eusebius's history by adding what they clearly regarded as second volumes. Socrates's *Ecclesiastical History* begins with the abdication of Diocletian and the first proclamation of Constantine as emperor (305) and ends during the principate of Theodosius II (439). Sozomen's *Ecclesiastical History* covers roughly the same period, ending somewhat earlier with the death of Honorius in 425. The same is true of Theodoret's *Ecclesiastical History*, which ends on the eve of the Nestorian controversy in 428.

If we add to the list Palladius's *Dialogue on the Life of St. John Chrysostom* (408) and his *Lausiac History* (420), we have mentioned the chief historical writings that give us access to the church during the fourth and fifth centuries. What strikes me most forcibly, however, is what Eusebius says about turning to the events of his own day. Not only do the histories become in large measure eyewitness accounts of the life of the church, but we also begin to see more clearly the personal involvement of the writers with the stories they are telling. In the first three chapters I was dealing largely with the way in which the miracle stories in Scripture shaped and were shaped by the Christian message. Here I am turning more directly to the experience of people like Eusebius with the miraculous. What begins to emerge is that, in addition to their commitment to the Gospel, the lives of these writers reveal a range of personal associations that bind them to specific Christian communities.

Eusebius himself explains what I mean by having adopted the name "son of Pamphilus" as his own. Pamphilus was a presbyter of the church in Caesarea who collected and guarded the works of Origen. He and Eusebius wrote an apology for the great Alexandrian, who had spent the last years of his life in Caesarea (*EH* 6.32f.; *NPNF* 2.1, p. 277f.). For Eusebius, Pamphilus "was the great glory of the parish of Caesarea, and among the men of our time most admirable" (*EH* 8.13; *NPNF* 2.1, p. 334). It was not merely as a spiritual father and a disciple of Origen but also as a martyr that Pamphilus was "a man thrice dear" to Eusebius (*Mart. Pal.* 11; *NPNF* 2.1, p. 351). The ties are intellectual and spiritual, but they are also personal. There are hints of the same sort of personal association in Socrates's *History*. He was a native of Constantinople and a lawyer there, but the peculiar feature of his work is its sympathetic interest in the Novatian church. There is no evidence that Socrates was himself a Novatian, but he obviously had happy associations with that schismatic group. He speaks with admiration of Paul, a teacher of Latin who became Novatian bishop of Constantinople in 419. Paul was remarkable for his asceticism, and Socrates says, "I myself found him just such a person as Evagrius says the monks dwelling in the deserts ought to be" (Soc. 7.17; *NPNF* 2.2, p. 161).

In many ways Sozomen is the most interesting case in point. He, too, was a lawyer in Constantinople; but he was originally from a small town near Gaza called Bethelia. He never forgot his home town, and his family associations were Christian. He tells the story of the monk Hilarion, who became Antony's disciple in Egypt and returned to his native village of Thabatha near Gaza.[1] Disposing of his patrimony Hilarion established himself as an anchorite not too far from his native village. Though buried in Cyprus, where he had gone before his death, a monk named Hesychas later "stole the body, conveyed it to Palestine, and interred it in his own monastery." Even now, says Sozomen, "many afflicted and possessed people are healed at his tomb" (Soz. 3.14; *NPNF* 2.2, p. 293). The story of Hilarion, moreover, is bound up with Sozomen's own. Hilarion expelled demons and even stopped a flood by prayer, but for Sozomen the important miracle was that he expelled a demon from his grandfather's friend Alaphion. "My grandfather was of pagan parentage; and with his own family and that of Alaphion, had been the first to embrace Christianity in

Bethelia, a populous town near Gaza." Sozomen speaks with veneration of his grandfather, who was skilled in the exposition of Scripture and was "much beloved by the Christians of Ascalon, of Gaza, and of the surrounding country." The family of Alaphion holds equal importance for Sozomen. Its members founded the first churches and monasteries in the area; "and in my youth I saw some of them, but they were then very aged" (Soz. 5.15; *NPNF* 2.2, p. 337).

As for the other writers I have mentioned, the personal associations we discover are somewhat more cosmopolitan in character. To be sure, as we shall see at the end of this chapter, Theodoret has firm and deep roots in his own locality; but he was also involved in the ecumenical disputes of the Nestorian controversy. Rufinus is more certainly cosmopolitan. Born about 345 in Concordia, he studied in Rome from 359 until he moved to Aquileia in 368 to embark upon the ascetic life with Jerome, among others. He left Aquileia for the East the same time as Jerome (373), but pressed on to Egypt, where he gained an acquaintance with the monks there and with the Alexandrian scholar Didymus the Blind. By 380 we find him ruling a monastery on the Mount of Olives in Jerusalem. The bitter quarrel with his old friend Jerome over Origen began during these years; and Rufinus returned to the West in 397, becoming bishop of Aquileia two years later. He fled from Alaric the Visigoth to Rome in 407 and died in Sicily three years later, the year Alaric sacked Rome.

The same sort of cosmopolitan pattern characterizes Palladius's life. A native of Galatia, in his early twenties (388) he went to Egypt, where he lived with the monks for a number of years and became a disciple of Macarius and of Evagrius Ponticus. About 400 he became bishop of Helenopolis in Bithynia, where he became a chief supporter of the unfortunate John Chrysostom. He pled Chrysostom's cause in Rome in 405, and suffered exile for his efforts the next year. By 412 he was able to return to his native Galatia, where he became bishop of Aspuna. He must have died shortly before the council of Ephesus in 431. Like Rufinus, he supplies a living link between East and West, the monasteries of Egypt and the patriarchal sees of Christendom. Even at the more cosmopolitan level, what strikes the student of the fourth- and fifth-century church is that its leaders were personally known to one another and in constant dialogue both for good and for ill.

As we shall see, miracles form a part of this personal setting for all the writers I shall examine. Whether on a local or an ecumenical level, Eusebius and the others were often eyewitnesses to the miracles they recounted. And at the least they were able to make their inquiries of those who preserved memories of the miraculous. To read Chrysostom's sermons is to gain the impression that miracles were safely guarded between the pages of Scripture and were no more an issue to be addressed in the church. But the impression is clearly erroneous, as even a cursory reading of the historians will demonstrate. We obviously have a puzzle on our hands, but it is not one I wish to address directly in this chapter. Instead, I want to begin by describing the sorts of miracles retailed by the historians without attempting to draw any large conclusions. Then I shall turn to three writers in order to examine how the miraculous is placed into a theological context. By looking at Athanasius's *Life of Antony*, several of Gregory of Nyssa's writings, and Theodoret's *History of the Monks of Syria*, we can, I think, gain some understanding of ways in which miracles were treated as part of the larger picture. To anticipate my conclusion, I shall wish to argue that it is no longer merely a question of the tail wagging the dog. Rather, it is a question of the tail not fitting the dog very well.

THE MIRACLES OF THE NEW COMMONWEALTH

The best-known miracle, of course, is the one that from a Christian point of view marked Constantine's victory over Maxentius at the Milvian Bridge in 312 as Christ's victory. Eusebius's account of the miracle sets it in the context of other omens and prodigies and of Maxentius's "putting confidence rather in the arts of sorcery than in the devotion of his subjects" (*EH* 9.9; *NPNF* 2.1, p. 363). Famine, pestilence, and war demonstrate the folly of the persecution and the vanity of Maxentius's confidence. In sending Constantine the vision of the cross "God, the great and celestial defender of the Christians . . . restored to us the bright and gracious sunlight of his providence in our behalf; so that in the deepest darkness a light of peace shone most wonderfully upon us from him, and made it manifest to all that God himself has always been the ruler of our affairs" (*EH* 9.8; *NPNF* 2.1, p. 363). The real miracle in the *History* is the new Exodus in which Maxentius's hosts are drowned in the Tiber. In the *Life of Constantine* Eusebius emphasizes Constantine's vision of the cross and his dream in which Christ commands him to make the *labarum*, the standard of the cross.[2] Wherever we place the emphasis and however we sort out the details of the different accounts, the story gives a miraculous beginning to the Christian commonwealth that gradually formed during the fourth century.[3]

In the Christian view, establishing the new commonwealth so auspiciously begun also involved miracles. Eusebius tells us of Constantine's building program. The discovery of Christ's tomb, buried beneath the "foul pollutions" of a pagan temple, is, according to words cited by Eusebius as Constantine's own, a miracle that "as far transcends the capacity of human reason as heavenly things are superior to human affairs" (*LC* 3.30; *NPNF* 2.1, p. 528). The miracle grows in the telling of it, and the later historians give credit to Constantine's mother, Helena, for the construction of the new basilica on the site of Christ's Resurrection. She also discovers three crosses and the title Pontius Pilate had placed over Christ's. The miraculous healing of a dying woman, perhaps a lady of rank, by one of the crosses dispels all doubt as to which one is Christ's.[4]

Sozomen, one of the historians who tells us of Helena's discovery of the true cross, continues his account of the beginning of the Christian commonwealth by describing Constantine's building of Constantinople. He singles out the Michaelium as "the most remarkable church." The place received its name "because it is believed that Michael the Divine archangel, once appeared there. And I also affirm that this is true, because I myself received the greatest benefits, and the experience of really helpful deeds on the part of many others proves this to be so." Sozomen goes on to tell several stories of miraculous healings, including one in which "a Divine Power" appeared to Aquilinus while he was lying in the church at night and commanded him to dip his foot in a concoction of honey, wine, and pepper. Though contrary to the usual medical prescriptions for "a bilious disorder," the miraculous remedy proved effective (Soz. 2.3; *NPNF* 2.2, p. 260).

Sozomen, of course, is writing more than a century after Eusebius; and it is tempting to suppose that the miraculous has grown in importance. There is a good deal of truth in the supposition, and we can scarcely doubt we are in the presence of a shift of sensibility. At the same time, we should not suppose that the shift is toward superstition and credulity. Instead, it seems to me a shift away from Eusebius's strong sense of the general and universal character of God's providence to an emphasis upon particular extraordinary events. Eusebius, of course, can also call attention to particular marvels, but they are not central for him in the same way that such events are for Sozomen. I note the shift of sensibility here not to explain it but more to call attention to it as a problem deserving further discussion.

If miracles function positively to establish the new commonwealth, they also function negatively to refute and to overthrow its enemies. The persecutors of the church come to a sticky end by suffering divine punishment.[5] God miraculously thwarts Julian the Apostate's attempt to rebuild the Jewish Temple in Jerusalem. An earthquake shatters the initial building attempts; and there follows fire, either from heaven or from the ground beneath the Temple site. Finally, crosses mysteriously appear on the clothing of the workmen.[6] We must remember how crucial the destruction of Jerusalem and the Temple was to early Christianity. It not only fulfilled Christ's prediction but also demonstrated the truth of the Christian message. Had Julian succeeded in rebuilding the Temple, he would have torn away a central plank in the Christian party platform.[7] Julian suffered punishment in yet another way. When the oracle at the shrine of Apollo in Daphne near Antioch failed to respond, the emperor attributed this to the presence nearby of the bones of the Christian martyr Babylas. He ordered the relics removed, and they were carried with great ceremony to a new shrine in Antioch itself. Immediately thereafter fire fell upon and utterly destroyed the pagan temple.[8]

Julian's death on his Persian campaign, of course, simply represents the culmination of God's displeasure. Indeed, according to Sozomen (6.2) earthquakes, floods, drought, and famine punctuated the apostate's reign as signs of this divine judgment. Julian's death needed no human messengers. Theodoret tells us that Julianus Sabbas, while praying earnestly in his monastery, "suddenly checked his tears, broke into an ecstasy of delight," and announced that "the enemy of the vineyard of the Lord, has paid the penalty of the wrongs he has done to Him; he lies dead" (*EH* 3.19; *NPNF* 2.3; p. 105). According to Sozomen, Didymus the Blind in Alexandria fell asleep because of too much fasting, and in an ecstasy (Soz. 6.2; *NPNF* 2.2, p. 347):

> he beheld white horses traversing the air, and heard a voice saying to those who were riding thereon, "Go and tell Didymus that Julian has been slain just at this hour; let him communicate this intelligence to Athanasius, the bishop, and let him arise and eat."[9]

It is Theodoret who says that Julian's last words were, "Thou hast won, O Galilean."

These miracles that represent God's punishment of the church's enemies are obviously based upon actual events, elaborated and woven into Christian convictions about God's purposes. And the same judgment strikes us when we read accounts of the way in which Christians went about the work of destroying paganism. Rufinus tells the story of how about the time of Nicaea (325) a simple Christian, who "knew only Christ and him crucified" (1 Cor 2:2), converted a philosopher, who was "astounded at the power of his words" (*EH* 1.3). Sozomen repeats the story, but adds "a similar miracle" accomplished by Alexander of Constantinople, who silences a philosopher by commanding him in the name of Jesus Christ not to speak. Sozomen raises the question "whether it is a greater miracle that a man, and he a philosopher, should so easily be silenced by a word, or that a stone-wall should be cleft by the power of a word, which miracle I have heard some attribute to Julian, surnamed the Chaldean" (Soz. 1.18; *NPNF* 2.2, p. 254). In a similar way the historians after

Eusebius tell how Christians destroyed pagan temples, sometimes without the addition of the miraculous.[10] On other occasions the miraculous enters the picture.

When Theophilus, the patriarch of Alexandria, destroyed the Serapeum in 386, a riot followed. But the work was successful, and mysterious hieroglyphs were found in the form of crosses (Soc. 5.16–17; *NPNF* 2.2; p. 126f.). Sozomen adds that during the riot the pagans took over the Serapeum as a fortress, where they tortured and killed Christians they had managed to seize. The governor, however, issued an order commanding that the temples be destroyed but that amnesty be granted the pagans. This act resulted in the capitulation of the Serapeum to the Christians, and the night before its surrender a pagan named Olympius "heard the voice of one singing hallelujah" (Soz. 7.15; *NPNF* 2.2, p. 386). The only miracle Theodoret tells in his account of the destruction of the Serapeum is that when Theophilus had the head of Serapis cut off, "multitudes of mice" ran out (*EH* 5.22; *NPNF* 2.3, p. 148). Sozomen tells another story about Alexandria concerning pagans who claimed that the failure of the Nile to rise one year was caused by the imperial prohibition of sacrifice to the river. Unimpressed by a petition they sent him, the emperor replied that he hoped the river would cease to flow "if it delights in sacrifices, or if blood must be mingled with the waters that derive their source from the paradise of God"(Soz. 7.20; *NPNF* 2.2, p. 391). A little later the Nile overflowed its banks, rather too much. This provoked many conversions to the church.

If we turn from the general picture of how the Christian commonwealth made its marvelous conquest of Rome to particular champions of that commonwealth, we find the same pattern of wonderful events becoming still more wonderful. Sozomen tells the story of how Basil the Great in the midst of his confrontations with the Arianizing emperor Valens withheld a miracle. Valens's son was mortally ill, and he sent messengers for Basil. As soon as the bishop arrived, the child began to get better. But when Valens refused to acknowledge orthodoxy by having heretics join Basil in his prayers, the child died (Soz. 6.16; *NPNF* 2.2, p. 356). Socrates's version of the story makes the death of the child the direct product of Basil's refusal to perform a miracle for a heretic (Soc. 4.26; *NPNF* 2.2, p. 111). What is most interesting is that the historians' narratives appear dependent upon Gregory of Nazianzen's *Panegyric on Basil*, where we read that had Valens not "blended salt water with the fresh, by trusting to the heterodox at the same time that he summoned Basil, the child would have recovered his health and been preserved for his father's arms" (*Pan. on Basil* 54; *NPNF* 2.7, p. 412).[11] The wonder is there all along, but it has grown in the telling.[12]

Palladius describes John Chrysostom more as a martyr for holiness than as a champion of orthodoxy, but the struggle he narrates is more than a merely human one. Indeed, it is the war with Satan; and Chrysostom's enemies are demonic. Chrysostom himself addresses the Synod of the Oak and says (*Dial.* 8; ACW 45, p. 52):

> As I see it, I shall endure many tribulations and I shall depart this life. For I know the cunning of Satan; he can no longer put up with the annoyance of my invectives against him.

When the troops led Chrysostom away for his final exile, a flame appeared amidst his bishop's throne and finding "the expounder of the Word" gone, consumed the basilica in retribution upon his enemies (*Dial.* 10; ACW 45, p. 67f.). Immediately before the bishop's death Basilicus, the martyr of Comana, appeared to him in a vision and said "Have courage, brother, tomorrow we shall be together" (*Dial.* 11; ACW 45, p. 73). Miraculous may be too strong an adjective, but Palladius's narrative certainly breathes the atmosphere of another world. It is Sozomen who adds a truly miraculous story. A woman who had failed to renounce her heresy either because of Chrysostom's words or by her husband's importunities attempted to avoid communicating by substituting her own piece of bread. But it turned to stone in her mouth, and she was compelled to seek forgiveness. The stone "is still preserved in the treasury of the church of Constantinople" (Soz. 8.5; *NPNF* 2.2, p. 403).

Sozomen tells stories of other bishops of Chrysostom's time. Donatus of Euroea in Epirus slays an enormous dragon by making the sign of the cross and spitting. He is buried by a stream which "God caused to rise from the ground in answer to his prayer." Theotimus of Tomi in Scythia foils barbarians by making himself invisible and by freezing a barbarian's outstretched arm in midair. Epiphanius of Cyprus, the heresiologist, is responsible for a mysterious gift of money from a stranger who replenishes the church's treasury. Two beggars play a trick on him to gain money, one of them feigning death in order to get funds for burial. Epiphanius consoles the supposed bereaved beggar and gives the money. But when he leaves, the beggar finds that his companion is in fact dead. Demons are expelled and diseases healed at Epiphanius's tomb (Soz. 7.26f.; *NPNF* 2.2, p. 395f.).

Socrates tells similar episcopal stories. Silvanus, the bishop of Troas, encounters a major problem in his city about the year 431. A cargo ship built on the shore proves incapable of being launched. The people form the idea that a demon is holding the ship back and implore Silvanus's help, trusting in his patronage. After prayer he has only to touch one rope before the ship runs successfully out to sea (Soc. 7.37; *NPNF* 2.2, p. 174). About the same time the failure of a miracle in Crete produces many conversions to Christianity. A self-styled Moses promises to lead the Jews through the sea "into the land of promise." He persuades many to renounce their work and possessions and on an appointed day leads them to a cliff on the island, where some are foolish enough to jump to their deaths. The Christian merchants and fishermen of the district manage to save many of the Jews either by rescuing them from the sea or by persuading them not to jump (Soc. 7.38; *NPNF* 2.2, p. 174f.). Some of Socrates' most appealing stories concern Paul, the Novatian bishop of Constantinople. His prayers preserve the Novatian church from a devastating fire that rages for two days and nights (in 433) and that destroys much of the city (Soc. 7.39; *NPNF* 2.2, p. 175). He also confounds a Jewish imposter who makes money by being repeatedly baptized. When he leads the Jew to the font, "a certain invisible power of God" makes the water suddenly disappear. Suspecting faulty plumbing, the bishop tries again with the same result. And then the fraud becomes evident (Soc. 7.17; *NPNF* 2.2, p. 161). The miracle may not defend orthodoxy, but it does testify to Paul's saintliness.

In an extended sense the Christian commonwealth could be thought to include lands outside the Roman Empire. In any case, we do find miracle stories associated with the mission of the church in the time of Constantine. Rufinus first tells the story of Frumentius; but Socrates and Sozomen repeat it almost word for word, while Theodoret simply makes explicit the resemblance of the story to the tales of Joseph and Daniel in Scripture.[13] A philosopher named Meropius sails for India with a company of people including two youthful kinsmen, Edesius and Frumentius. When the Indians kill them, they spare the two boys, who become slaves of the Indian king. Edesius is cupbearer, and Frumentius takes charge of the king's records. They are so efficient in their tasks that upon the king's death they become regents for his infant son. Frumentius fosters Christianity by seeking out Roman Christians who have traveled to India and by building a church. When the new king comes of age, the two Romans return home, Edesius to Tyre and Frumentius to Alexandria, where he consults with Athanasius, recently named bishop. Frumentius returns to India with episcopal authority in order to preach the Gospel, foster the new church, and perform apostolic miracles of healing.

The new commonwealth also bursts the limits of the Roman Empire by the miraculous conversion of the Iberians (on the east shore of the Black Sea). Again our historians tell pretty much the same story. The Iberians capture a nameless but devout Christian woman, who succeeds in healing the king's seriously ill infant son. She attributes the marvel to Christ, refuses the king's gifts, and asks him to acknowledge Christ. On his hunt the next day the king and his companions encounter a mist and thick darkness that cause them to lose their way. When prayers to his own gods prove unavailing, he invokes the captive girl's God with immediate results. The king and his queen then become preachers of Christ and decide to build a church. The building founders when one of the columns proves impossible to raise, but the slave girl saves the day once more. She goes to the building site and prays. The king arrives in the morning to discover the girl, with the column miraculously suspended in the air over its base. The column soon descends, the church is completed, and the king sends an embassy to Constantine "requesting that henceforth they might be in alliance with the Romans, and receive from them a bishop and consecrated clergy, since they sincerely believed in Christ" (Soc. 1.20; *NPNF* 2.2, p. 25). Theodoret omits the last of the miracles and says that the slave girl was able to draw a plan for the church. The miracle is that of a female architect (Theodoret *EH* 1.23; *NPNF* 2.3, p. 59).

The Martyrs and Their Bones

So far I have been describing the miraculous in its direct association with the new commonwealth either in terms of how the church triumphed in Rome and in India and Iberia or in terms of how bishops in the cities of the Empire defended that commonwealth and acted as patrons of its members. In turning to the tales of wonders performed by martyrs, in death as well as in life, and in the next section by monks, we shall not be altogether abandoning the central theme of the triumph of the church. At the same time, emphasis begins to shift to how patrons who hold their status because of special gifts of power exercise that power on behalf of their clients. In a profound sense the martyrs and monks belong together. After 312 martyrdom was no longer possible, at least generally speaking; but the monks understood their vocation as continuous with that of the martyrs. Moreover, the rapid spread in the fourth and fifth centuries of the cult of the saints, together with an increasing emphasis upon their relics, meant that the martyrs were, if anything, a stronger presence and power in death than they had been in life.

Eusebius, who lived through the Diocletian persecution, gives us the earliest and most sober account of the martyrs. The very unexpectedness of the persecution, following a period of toleration and rapid growth for the church, implies that it looms large in Christian consciousness. Indeed, the Coptic church still dates the years by counting them from the Diocletian persecution. Eusebius's account of *The Martyrs of Palestine* fulfilled his promise in *Ecclesiastical History* to make known to posterity the martyrdoms "which I myself witnessed" (*EH* 8.13.7; *NPNF* 2.1, p. 334).[14] The events that Eusebius narrates serve a double function. They are "manifest signs and glorious proofs of the divine doctrine," but also display the martyrs' "marvellous virtues as a constant vision before our eyes" (Cureton, p. 2).

The demonstrative function of the martyrdoms translates into the victory of the martyrs over Satan. And Satan primarily stands for pagan idolatry. The apparent defeat of the martyrs is really their victory (Cureton, p. 16):

> And all this wonderful spectacle did the glorious Epiphanius exhibit, as it were in a theatre: for they who were the martyr's oppressors became like corrupt demons, and suffered within themselves great pain; being also themselves tortured in their own persons, as he was, on account of his endurance in the doctrine of his Lord. And while they stood in bitter pains, they gnashed upon him with their teeth, burning in their minds against him, and trying to force him to tell them whence he came, and who he was . . . and commanding him to sacrifice and comply with the edict. But he looked upon them all as evil demons, and regarded them as corrupt devils.

The only answer Epiphanius gives is his confession of Christ. We are witnessing a judicial trial, but the victory belongs to the martyr who is condemned to be cast into the sea. A "prodigy" confirms this reading of the story; for after Epiphanius was killed by being thrown into the sea with stones bound to his feet, there was a fierce storm and an earthquake in Caesarea. The waves rolled the martyr's body before the gate of the city, and the whole city went out to see the marvel (Cureton, p. 17).

Eusebius tells another miracle story that implies the same demonstrative point. Again in Caesarea in the sixth year of the persecution several new martyrs won their crowns. Then "there happened in the midst of the city a prodigy which will scarcely be believed." Some of the columns of the city's porticos "emitted spots as it were of blood, while the market-places and the streets became sprinkled and wet as with water, although not a single drop had fallen from the heavens." The people concluded that "the stones shed tears and the ground wept." The prodigy, then, "rebuked all these godless folk." Eusebius concludes by admitting that what he has related may seem "a fable devoid of truth," but he insists upon its truth by appealing to eyewitnesses. The martyrs' "struggles and conflicts against error" were a victory (Cureton, p. 33f.).

The martyrs not only demonstrated the truth of Christianity, they also established for Christians an example to be followed. In his introduction Eusebius expresses his wonder "at their all-enduring courage, at their confession under many forms, and at the wholesome alacrity of their souls, the elevation of their minds, the open profession of their faith, the clearness of their reason, the patience of their condition, and the truth of their religion." Their endurance is spiritual in character and finds its summation in their love of God and his Christ, a love that is returned to them for their strengthening. Eusebius cites Paul's words in Romans (8:35ff.) that deny anything can separate us from the love of Christ and affirm that, though slaughtered like sheep, we are "more than conquerors through him who loved us." A miracle makes the same point and holds up the same example. Diocletian orders that Romanus's tongue be cut out. "Nevertheless, when that member by which he spoke was taken away, still was his true love not severed from his God; neither was his intellectual tongue restrained from preaching." And Romanus began to speak miraculously (Cureton, p. 8).

Eusebius regards the stories he tells as what are important. The martyrs' praises have not been "noted by monuments of stone, nor by statues variegated with painting . . . but by the word of truth spoken before God" (Cureton, p. 1). What matters is their confession and not their monuments.[15] Nevertheless, Eusebius does not mean to dismiss the martyrs' graves. The bodies of Pamphilus and his companions were placed inside the churches "and so consigned to a never-to-be-forgotten memorial in the temples of the house of prayer, that they might be honoured of their brethren who are with God" (Cureton, p. 45). Eusebius is not speaking of a novel custom. He even derides the pagan supposition that Christians might worship as gods their martyrs "lying in their sepulchers" (*EH* 8.6.7; *NPNF* 2.1, p. 328). The supposition can scarcely be explained if the Christians did not venerate the graves of their saints.[16]

Sozomen is the writer most preoccupied with the relics of the martyrs, and in the century or more that separates him from Eusebius we certainly find a shift of emphasis. Indeed, Sozomen ends his history with the triumphant discovery of the relics of Zechariah the Prophet (and according to the title of 9.17 of Stephen the Martyr). Despite having been buried so many years, the prophet "appeared sound; his hair was closely shorn, his nose was straight; his beard moderately grown, his head quite short, his eyes rather sunken, and concealed by the eyebrows" (Soz. 9.17; *NPNF* 2.2, p. 427). These are Sozomen's last words, and other passages in the history betray the same interest in relics. God revealed in a dream the place of the relics of Habakkuk and Micah (Soz. 7.29; *NPNF* 2.2, p. 397). More prosaically, some heretical monks told Mardonius, one of the emperor Valens's officials, the location of John the Baptist's head. An imperial chariot carried the relic as far as the district of Chalcedon, but here the mules stopped and refused to go further. Later Theodosius removed the head to Constantinople, where he built "a magnificent temple" for it. But only with difficulty did he persuade "a holy virgin, Matrona, who had been the servant and guardian of the relic," to part with it (Soz. 7.21; *NPNF* 2.2, p. 391).

Somewhat later, in the reign of Theodosius II, the relics of the Forty Martyrs of Sebaste were discovered. Sozomen's account credits a triple dream of the Empress Pulcheria with the discovery, and once more we find a transition from private to public care of the relics. Somehow a woman named Eusebia had secured the relics and enshrined them in the garden of her house outside the walls of Constantinople. On her death she left the property to some monks on the condition that they secretly bury her there with the relics. The property changed hands again, and Caesarius, the new owner, built a shrine for the martyr Thyrsus that obscured the other relics. These are some of the details that Sozomen recounts, but what is fascinating about his story is the way it reflects the private character of the cult of the saints as late as the first part of the fifth century. Several transitions have taken place. The story of the martyrs has yielded pride of place to their tombs; emphasis has been placed on the relics themselves; control of the relics is gradually transferred to the public domain, represented in Sozomen's stories by the emperor. And we shall not be surprised to find that the relics work miracles.

WONDERWORKING MONKS

If the martyrs, whether still living or dead, represent one locus of the miraculous in the early church, the living saints of monasticism, which as a movement really began only in the fourth century, represent another. When we examine sources such as *The Sayings of the Fathers*, *The Lausiac History*, and John Cassian's *Institutes* and *Conferences*, the most obvious conclusion to draw is that the monastic life is a battle with Satan. It is their success in this warfare that makes the monks examples for all Christians to emulate and sources of power that benefit those who turn to them for help. We have already encountered the first of these two themes in the context of catechetical instruction and the meaning of baptism. And there can be little doubt that figures like Basil the Great and John Chrysostom held the monks up as examples not of a special form of life but of the kind of victory over Satan that ought in principle to be won by all baptized Christians.

It is in this spirit that we can read many of these stories. In one sense, the defeat of Satan is the victory over paganism and its idolatrous worship of demons. One of "the old men in the Thebaid," who was the son of a pagan priest, told of how he once followed his father into the temple, where he went to sacrifice to the idol. He saw Satan on his throne receiving the reports of demons who had been sent on various wicked missions. The last demon reported that he had spent forty years in the desert attacking a single monk and had finally succeeded in making him lust. Satan crowned the demon with his own crown and said: "You have been brave, and done a great deed." The priest's son pondered this and decided to embrace the monastic life (*SF* 5.39; LCC 12, p. 73f.). The victory over Satan is the renunciation of idolatry, but the interest of the story is clearly in another sort of victory, a moral one.

Satan stands for vice and for the temptations that can prevent the monk from keeping to the kind of asceticism that, at least in principle, ought to lead to virtue. The battle is a moral and spiritual one, and the monk's example is to be followed as far as possible. One of the most appealing stories in *The Sayings of the Fathers* concerns Abba Apollos and the demon of lust. A brother came to an old man and confessed to lust, and finding only a rebuke, he "started on his way back to the world." Abba Apollos intervened, stopped the brother, and by prayer transferred the demon of lust from him to the old man. Everyone learned the lesson of God's mercy and found strength to continue the battle against Satan (*SF* 5.4; LCC 12, p. 60ff.). Indeed, continuing the battle may be the point. Abba John the Short successfully prayed to the Lord to take away his passions and told an old man that he was at rest. The old man said to him: "Go, ask the Lord to stir a new war in you. Fighting is good for the soul" (*SF* 7.8; LCC 12, p. 84).[17]

Sometimes our sources convey the impression that the battle becomes an end in itself, and even the ascetical practices such as fasting begin to look like feats of endurance that have their own meaning quite apart from the moral virtue toward which they should lead. Palladius, however, tells one story that not only shows how the defeat of Satan can be a moral triumph but also how it can benefit others. A virgin of Alexandria, though she was "exceedingly rich," refused to part with any of her money. She did keep promising to appoint one of her nieces her heir, but this was clearly a subterfuge. "For this is one way the devil deceives us, by contriving to make us fight to excess in the guise of loving one's relatives." There was a priest and superior of the poorhouse for cripples named Macarius that decided to cure the virgin of her greed. Plausible because he had been a gem engraver, Macarius went to the virgin and offered to let her buy for five hundred coins a far more valuable collection of precious stones. He spent the money for the poor in his hospital; and when the rich virgin demanded to see the jewels, he took her there. Pointing out "the crippled and inflamed women," he said: "Look, here are your hyacinths!" He showed her the men in the hospital and said: "Behold your emeralds! If they do not please you, take your money back!" The rich virgin understood and repented (*LH* 6; ACW 34, p. 37ff.).

This is a story not only of virtue but of public benefaction. The same point can be made of many of the miracle stories. For example, Palladius tells us that Macarius of Alexandria "cured so many demon-ridden people that numbers fail." He anointed a noble virgin from Thessalonica with holy oil for twenty days and so healed her paralysis. And (LH 18; ACW 34, p. 64f.):

> Before my very eyes a young boy possessed by an evil spirit was brought to him. He put one hand on his head and the other over his heart, and he prayed so intently that he caused the boy to be suspended in the air. The boy swelled up like a wineskin and became so inflamed that he became afflicted with erysipelas. Suddenly crying out he emitted water through all his sense organs, and he returned once more to his former size. Macarius handed him back to his father then, after anointing the boy with holy oil and pouring water on him. He enjoined him not to partake of meat or wine for forty days, and thus he cured him.

Palladius was instrumental in persuading Macarius to effect another wonderful cure. A priest of the village "whose head was all eaten away by the disease of cancer" found himself rejected by Macarius because, though a priest, he was "indulging his lust." By repenting and renouncing the exercise of his priesthood, the man persuaded Macarius to lay his hand on him. In a few days he was cured; hair even grew back on his head (LH 18; ACW 34, p. 63f.). Palladius also tells the story of how a hyena brought her blind puppy to Macarius, who put spittle on its eyes, prayed, and healed the animal (LH 18; ACW 34, p. 66). Macarius clearly bestowed a blessing on all of nature around him.

Even stories that do not at first seem to fit the theme of the wonderworking monk as a source of powerful blessing, as it seems to me, belong under this rubric. When Evagrius substitutes the sign of the cross for his lost key and opens the church door, his miracle simply establishes his credentials (LH 38; ACW 34, p. 114).[18] The same point can be made of the demonstration of Abba John's obedience by his patient watering of a dried stick for three years with the miraculous result of a green tree and fruit (SF 14.3; LCC 12, p. 150).[19] Marcarius of Egypt raises a dead man not to vindicate himself but to prove the Christian belief in the Resurrection (LH 17; ACW 34, p. 57).[20] More common, however, are stories of exorcisms and healings like those I have already described.[21]

One final class of miracles has to do with benefits to the community that are not connected with healing and exorcism. Abba Pior succeeds in providing water in the wilderness (LH 39; ACW 34, p. 114f.). The return of a hidden, penitent deacon enables the Nile to rise (*SF* 5.26; LCC 12, p. 67). An old monk near Mount Sinai prays and rain falls (*SF* 12.14; LCC 12, p. 143). The miracle of the loaves enables a monk to feed the poor (*SF* 13.15; LCC 12, p. 148f.). In many ways, then, the monk begins to seem more important as a special kind of patron, bringing blessing to his clients. Emphasis has shifted from his role as a paradigm of holiness and virtue to his social function as a wonderworker.

Perhaps this is what bothers John Cassian. In the preface to the *Institutes*, written early in the fifth century, he defines his aim in helping establish monasticism in Gaul and says (*NPNF* 2.11, p. 200):

> Nor certainly shall I try to weave a tale of God's miracles and signs, although we have not only heard of many such among our elders, and those past belief, but have also seen them fulfilled under our very eyes; yet, leaving out all these things which minister to the reader nothing but astonishment and no instruction in the perfect life, I shall try . . . faithfully to explain only their institutions and the rules of their monasteries . . . since my purpose is to say a few words not about God's miracles, but about the way to improve our character, and the attainment of the perfect life.

What worries Cassian is clearly not the miracles themselves, but the possibility they will detract from what he regards as the point of monasticism, progress in the perfect life of Christian virtue. He takes up the subject in more detail in *Conference* 15. He recognizes the wonderworking power given to some monks, but insists that it is dangerous. It can lead to vainglory and a forgetfulness that the power is Christ's. It is better "to cure the weaknesses of one's own soul than those of the body of another" (*NPNF* 2.11, p. 449). "For he can perform all the miracles which Christ wrought, without danger of being puffed up, who follows the gentle Lord not in the grandeur of His miracles, but in the virtues of patience and humility" (p. 448).

Several questions have begun to emerge in this brief survey of wonderworking in the church. Are the miracles to be treated as signs of virtue and of Christ's victory, or are they to be treated as valuable for themselves because they support the social fabric of the Christian commonwealth? Are the martyrs and the monks paradigms of the Christian life, or are they a special class of patrons capable of conferring remarkable benefactions? There may, indeed, be other and better ways of phrasing these questions. Nevertheless, what strikes me as surprising about the evidence of the historians and the monastic literature I have examined is that very rarely are the miracles related to the Christian message in any obvious way. They certainly reflect the triumph of the church in a variety of ways—in the Empire as a whole, in adjacent lands, in the cities of the Empire. But what is missing is the attempt, so clearly evidenced in the works I examined in the first three chapters, to place miracles in a theological framework. Let me conclude this chapter by examining what I should regard as three attempts to do this, and let me suggest that what we shall discover is not merely the danger of the tail wagging the dog but that of the tail no longer fitting the dog.

ATHANASIUS'S LIFE OF ANTONY

When Athanasius fled Alexandria for the third time in 355, he took refuge with the monks in the Egyptian desert and remained with them until Julian became emperor in 361 and allowed the exiled bishops to return to their sees. He most likely took the opportunity to forge a firm alliance between the monks and the patriarchate in Alexandria, an alliance that persisted and grew during the fourth and fifth centuries. While he was in the desert, the anchorite Antony died at an advanced age, probably in 356. Shortly afterward Athanasius responded to a request from some unnamed monks for information about Antony by writing *The Life of Antony*. It is against this background that we can argue that one purpose of the work was to mobilize the spiritual resources of monasticism for the support of orthodoxy and the orthodox hierarchy in Alexandria. This theme becomes explicit when Athanasius, after describing Antony as orthodox from every conceivable point of view, tells how he came to Alexandria to bear public witness against the Arians (*LA* 68–70; CWS, p. 81ff.).[22]

The more obvious purpose of *The Life of Antony*, however, is to present Antony as an example to be followed (*LA* intr.; CWS, p. 29):

> Since you have asked me about the career of the blessed Antony . . . so that you also might lead yourselves in imitation of him—I received your directive with ready good will. For simply to remember Antony is a great profit and assistance for me also. I know that even in hearing, along with marveling at the man, you will want also to emulate his purpose, for Antony's way of life provides monks with a sufficient picture for ascetic practice.

Augustine must not have been the only Christian to read *The Life of Antony* and embrace its example.[23] The model Athanasius describes is in some respects elitist, and we begin to find the sense that the monastic life is a higher form of the Christian life. Nonetheless, the ideal remains, I think, one toward which all are expected to aspire. Athanasius concludes his book by asking the monks to read it "to the other brothers" and "if the need arises, . . . to the pagans as well, so they may understand by this means that our Lord Jesus Christ is God and Son of God—and, additionally, that the Christians who are sincerely devoted to him and truly believe in him not only prove that the demons, whom the Greeks consider gods, are not gods, but also trample and chase them away as deceivers and corrupters of mankind" (*LA* 94; CWS, p. 99).

Antony, then, supplies a model of how the Christian shares in Christ's victory over Satan. And it is the war with demons that represents the fundamental dramatic action of *The Life*. The demons attack Antony through "foul thoughts" and the deceptive vision of a beautiful woman (*LA* 5; CWS, p. 34). As Antony says, the demons "pattern their phantasms after our thoughts" (*LA* 42; CWS, p. 63). Or they whip him and rush against him in the form of wild beasts (*LA* 9; CWS, p. 38). Sometimes the battle takes the form of actual wild beasts driven by Satan against Antony (*LA* 52; CWS, p. 70). Sometimes it takes place in the air (*LA* 65; CWS, p. 78f.). The demons tempt Antony by the mirages of a silver dish or of gold (*LA* 11–12; CWS, p. 40). The war with Satan is far from abstract, but the weapons Antony uses are the ones we should expect. The demons "are afraid of the ascetics on several counts—for their fasting, the vigils, the prayers, the meekness and gentleness, the contempt for money, the lack of vanity, the humility, the love of the poor, the almsgiving, the freedom from wrath, and most of all for their devotion to Christ" (*LA* 30; CWS, p. 54). The weapons are not only ascetic but also moral and spiritual. They are also texts from Scripture, which Antony hurls at his demonic foes just as Christ defeated Satan by quoting Scripture against him.[24]

Athanasius notes that during the persecution Antony went to Alexandria, hoping to complete his triumph over Satan by suffering martyrdom. But, even though the prefect noted him, he refused to take any action. Antony grieved at not attaining the gift of martyrdom, "but the Lord was protecting him to benefit us and others, so that he might be a teacher to many in the discipline that he had learned from the Scriptures. For simply by seeing his conduct, many aspired to become imitators of his way of life" (*LA* 46; CWS, p. 66). Nevertheless, the benefits Antony confers go beyond the teaching he gives by precept and example; for Antony is a wonderworker who expels demons and effects cures. Athanasius tells many stories about what happened (*LA* 48, 56–64, 71; CWS, pp. 67, 73ff., 83). Most of them are the sort with which we are by now familiar. But he also tells how Antony received in a vision the news of Ammon's death (*LA* 60; CWS, p. 76). And he recounts one story in which Antony saves a caravan by miraculously producing water from the ground (*LA* 54; CWS, p. 71). If we add to these blessings what Antony accomplished in his encounters with heretics, philosophers, and rulers, we find an important dimension of Antony's life that does not quite fit the picture of someone who is merely a teacher and an exemplar of Christian virtue (*LA* 72–82; CWS, p. 83ff.).

Athanasius appears to recognize the difficulty. It is not that he fails to take the miracles seriously or that he disbelieves them. But he repeatedly insists that Antony himself ascribed the miracles to God and the Saviour.[25] For example, a young girl had a horrible disease; her tears and other bodily excretions turned to worms when they fell to the ground. Her parents, who had heard of Antony and who had "faith in the Lord who had healed the woman troubled with an issue of blood," sought help. Antony denied them entrance, but said to the monks who had brought them (*LA* 58; CWS, p. 74f.):

> "Go away, and you will find that she has been healed, unless she is dead. For this good deed is not mine, that she should come to me, a pitiable man; rather, her healing is from the Savior who works his mercy everywhere for those who call on him. So also in this case the Lord has granted her prayer and his benevolence has shown me that he will cure the ailment of the child where she is." And indeed the wonder took place, and going out they found the parents exulting and the child completely healthy.

Athanasius appears to diminish Antony's role in the miracle. And the same conclusion attaches to his observation that Antony did not in fact heal everyone who came to him (*LA* 56; CWS, p. 73). Finally, Athanasius, in turning from Antony's miracles to his visions and his success in spiritual warfare, speaks of these as "still more wonderful things" than the obvious wonders (*LA* 65; CWS, p. 78).

My suggestion is that Athanasius senses that the miracles stand slightly to one side of his major purpose in portraying Antony as a model of Christian virtue. He achieves that purpose partly by emphasizing Antony's success in the war with Satan, and partly by interpreting that success as the triumph of the mind's governance over the body and its passions. Antony triumphs over Satan by "thinking about Christ and considering the excellence won through him, and the intellectual part of the soul" (*LA* 5; CWS, p. 34). Athanasius's narrative implies the same set of themes, deriving in large part from a standard philosophical understanding of virtue. When Antony emerges from the fortress where he has struggled in the ascetic life for twenty years, those who see him are astonished at the excellent health of his body. He is neither too thin nor too fat; and this bloom of bodily health reflects the state of his soul, which was "one of purity, for it was not constricted by grief, nor relaxed by pleasure, nor affected by either laughter or dejection. . . . He maintained utter equilibrium, like one guided by reason and steadfast in that which accords with nature" (*LA* 14; CWS, p. 42). Even in advanced old age and immediately before his death Antony remains in the peak of health. His eyes are "undimmed and sound" (cf. Deut 34:7). He had all his teeth (though "worn down to the gum") and "retained health in his feet and hands, and generally he seemed brighter and of more energetic strength than those who make use of baths and a variety of foods and clothing" (*LA* 93; CWS, p. 98).

If Antony's appearance implies a Christianized understanding of virtue, his words in the long discourse he gives make it explicit this is what Athanasius has in mind. Just as in *On the Incarnation* Athanasius places Christ's victory over Satan in the more sophisticated context of a doctrine of salvation influenced by the commonplaces of Greek philosophy, so here Antony's struggle with Satan comes to be understood in the light of similar philosophical commonplaces revolving around the notion of virtue. The renunciation the monk must make is a surrendering of "these things through virtue." The possessions we may take with us to our true kingdom are "prudence, justice, temperance, courage, understanding, love, concern for the poor, faith in Christ, freedom from anger, hospitality" (*LA* 17; CWS, p. 44).[26] Since Christ has told us "the Kingdom of God is within you" (Lk 17:21), all that virtue requires "is our willing, since it is in us, and arises from us. For virtue exists when the soul maintains its intellectual part according to nature." Making the soul straight in this way is the contest we have against, say, anger and desire; and the contest is, as well, one against the demons (*LA* 20–21; CWS, p. 46f.).

Antony, toward the end of his discourse, points out what is probably Athanasius's own conviction. "We ought not to boast about expelling demons, nor become proud on account of healings performed." This is because the signs are the Savior's work, and he has told us not to rejoice because the demons are subject to us, but because our names are written in heaven (Lk 10:20). "The fact that the names are written in heaven is a witness to our virtue and manner of life, but the ability to expel demons is itself a gift from the Savior, who bestowed it." Those who boast in signs rather than in virtue are like the wonderworkers whom Christ rejects, though they have worked marvels in his name (Mt 7:22). The theme I have noted in the narrative also appears in Antony's discourse (*LA* 38; CWS, p. 59f.). The conclusion I should suggest is that Athanasius seeks to define Antony's life as a paradigm of virtue by interpreting the contest with Satan in terms of late antique conventions about virtue. But in doing this he recognizes that the miracles Antony works do not quite fit the pattern that occupies center stage.

GREGORY OF NYSSA: FAMILY AND FAITH

Several of Gregory's shorter works supply evidence that uncovers, I think, the same sort of gap I have suggested may be found in *The Life of Antony*. Here the tension is not merely between miracles and the Christian faith, but is between Gregory's commitment to his own fatherland and to faith in the heavenly Jerusalem. The works I want to consider briefly are his *Praise of Theodore the Martyr*, delivered on the 7th of February, 381, at the martyr's shrine in Euchaita; his three *Sermons on the Forty Martyrs of Sebaste*, the first two of which were delivered on the 9th and 10th of March, 383, at the shrine in Sebaste, and the third of which was delivered four years earlier at Caesarea in Cappadocia; the *Panegyric on Gregory Thaumaturgus*, probably delivered sometime after 386; and the *Life of Macrina*, written shortly after her death in December of 379.

It is his sister Macrina who discerns the fundamental tension in Gregory's life. When he goes to be with her as she is dying, Gregory complains about the hardships he has been obliged to endure because of his involvement in church affairs. Macrina rebukes him by pointing out that what he regards as a misfortune is really a gift for which he ought to be thankful. Their father gained a fame that did not extend beyond the law courts of his fatherland, and even as a teacher he was content with a reputation that did not extend beyond Pontus. Gregory, however, is "a name to be reckoned with" in cities, peoples, and nations. Churches all over the world seek his help. "Do you not see the grace?" says Macrina. "Do you not understand the cause of such remarkable goods, that your parents' prayers have lifted you on high, while you have little or no disposition for such eminence?" (*LM* 21; SC 178, p. 210f.).[27] Despite his commitment to the wider church Gregory remains devoted to his fatherland and to its shrines and miracles.

The shrine of Theodore the Martyr stands in sharp contrast to most burial places. People ordinarily feel revulsion at dead bodies and tend to avoid graves. But Theodore's remains are the magnet that draws a joyful throng to celebrate his victory. The skill of the artists has adorned the church so that we can read "as in a book" the story of Christ's glorious athlete (*TM*, PG 46.737CD).[28] It is a question of a people rehearsing the lore that constitutes for them what they are. Gregory addresses the Forty Martyrs as "my fathers." They are the "fatherland" of his parents (*FM* 1, PG 46.752B). What he means is that his parents are buried with the relics of the Forty Martyrs. He has his own "share in the gift." The proximity of his parents' bodies to the martyrs assures them of "boldly confident" (*euparresiaston*) advocates at the day of resurrection (*FM*, PG 46.784B).[29] The stories of the martyrs are full of marvels. Theodore's jailor hears festal singing and sees a bright light; but when he enters Theodore's cell, he finds all the prisoners quiet and asleep in the dark (*TM, PG* 46.745B). The Forty Martyrs are soldiers, and before their arrest they had duplicated Elijah's miracle by calling down rain to save an army perishing of thirst (*FM* 2, *PG* 46.760AB). But the true marvels occur in the martyrs' final struggle. The Forty perish of the cold on a frozen lake, bound together by chains. They are a magnificent crown or a glorious necklace or twinkling stars linked together in the heavens. They are "Christ's soldiers, the Holy Spirit's infantry, the champions of faith, towers protecting the divine city" (*FM* 2, *PG* 46.761AB).

Still more important than these past marvels, however, is the persistence of the martyrs' power. Gregory addresses Theodore as "our invisible friend." He prays that as a kinsman and fellow citizen Theodore may be an ambassador "on behalf of our fatherland to the universal King." As Theodore has helped in the past by frustrating the invasion of the Scythians, so Gregory asks him to help in the future (*TM, PG* 46.748). The Forty Martyrs healed a lame soldier who spent the night in their shrine. Gregory is an eyewitness, and he also tells of his own experience. He had come reluctantly at his mother's bidding to join in the celebration of the Forty Martyrs' feast and was sleeping in the garden near the saints' relics. He dreamed and had a vision of himself trying to enter the garden to join the celebration. But the door was barred by soldiers brandishing their spears. The vision leads him to repentance for his failure to take his faith seriously. "I have spoken of these matters to give us confidence that the martyrs are alive. They are God's bodyguard, and enthroned with him they benefit and adorn our church today" (*FM* 3, *PG* 46.784f.).

The same association of the miraculous with the lore of his fatherland characterizes Gregory's account of Gregory Thaumaturgus. He begins his panegyric by making a rhetorical contrast between the stock content of an encomium and what he wishes to make the basis of his praise of Gregory. "For us there is only one fatherland to be honored, paradise, the first hearth of the human race, and only one city, the heavenly one built of living stones" (*GT, PG* 46.896B). The rhetoric reveals, however, that Gregory takes great pride in the fact that the wonderworker's city is, in fact, Neocaesarea, a city bound up with Gregory's own family history. In a sense, then, the miracles Gregory tells about Gregory Thaumaturgus are part of the lore he grew up with. The saint's career really begins with a vision in which John the Evangelist and the Virgin Mary reveal to him the orthodox doctrine of the Trinity (*GT, PG* 46.909). Empowered by this vision he goes to Neocaesarea, where he expels the demons from a pagan temple, thus incurring the wrath of the temple guardian. Relenting, he gives Satan written permission to return to the temple. But this great power makes the temple guardian wonder, and his conversion is completed when Gregory miraculously moves an enormous stone by prayer (*GT*, *PG* 46.916f.). Soon the entire city becomes Christian, and Gregory's miracles continue. He does "apostolic wonders," drying up a lake to stop a lawsuit between two brothers and diverting a river by planting his staff in its way (*GT*, *PG* 46.924, 928). When "two Hebrews" try to trick him by pretending that one is dead and in need of burial, he turns the trick on them by turning the feigned death into a real one (*GT*, *PG* 46.940).[30] His prayers give the martyrs courage during persecution and deliver a deacon who finds himself in peril in demon-infested baths that collapse (*GT*, *PG* 46.944, 952).

The miracle of Gregory of Nyssa's sister Macrina's life, if less astonishing than that of Gregory Thaumaturgus's career, is no less marvelous. And Gregory is an "eyewitness of her marvels" (*LM* 1; SC 178, p. 140). Even her birth was surrounded by miracle, since her mother three times dreamed that the virgin martyr Thecla was giving her a second Thecla.[31] And a triple vision of Gregory's own signals her death; he sees himself holding the relics of the martyrs (*LM* 15, 19; SC 178, pp. 192, 202). The ceremonies around Macrina's corpse are those of a martyr's festival (*LM* 33; SC 178, p. 248). She is buried with her parents and the relics of the Forty Martyrs (*LM* 34; SC 178, p. 252). Her cross and her ring seem treated as precious relics (*LM* 30; SC 178, p. 240). Gregory tells us about two miracles worked by Macrina. She healed herself of breast cancer (*LM* 31; SC 178, p. 242), and she cured the diseased eyes of a soldier's daughter (*LM* 36–38; SC 178, p. 256ff.). Because he realizes that people judge events by the limits of their own experience and are apt to doubt what goes beyond it, Gregory says he has omitted many of Macrina's deeds—healings and exorcisms, predictions of the future (*LM* 39; SC 178, p. 264).

The miraculous for Gregory is bound up with his own family heritage in many ways, but there are also indications in the works I am examining that he seeks to place this lore in the larger context of Christ's victory over Satan and of an understanding of virtue not unlike that found in Athanasius's *Life of Antony*. Theodore the Martyr, though he is "a poor soldier, newly conscripted," is one "whom Paul armed, whom the angels anointed for the contest, whom Christ crowned after he won the victory" (*TM*, *PG* 46.740D). The true warfare of the Forty Martyrs is with Satan (*FM* 2, *PG* 46.761C). They win the victory over Satan that those first contestants, Adam and Eve, lost (*FM* 2, *PG* 46.764). Gregory Thaumaturgus is an athlete or a noble soldier, warring against Satan (*GT*, *PG* 46.913). Macrina is an "invincible athlete" (*LM* 14; SC 178, p. 190). She has won "the crown of righteousness" by fighting "the good fight" (2 Tim 4:7f.; *LM* 19; SC 178, p. 204).

The theme of the contest with Satan shifts attention from the benefactions of the saints to their exemplary function. And it is in this context that Gregory can speak of the life of virtue. Indeed, the introduction to his *Panegyric on Gregory Thaumaturgus* suggests that this is where he wishes to place emphasis. "His virtuous life" is like a beacon for us when we embark upon our own journey "towards the good" (*GT, PG* 46.893C). Gregory of Nyssa describes Gregory's education as a training in virtue and as what makes possible his "apostolic wonders." Like Abraham leaving his home and Moses abandoning the wisdom of the Egyptians and entering the dark cloud of God's presence, Gregory embraces the contemplative life.[32] This is what enables him to be not only a model but also a teacher of virtue. The miracle of moving the stone shows the power of God's servant to move lifeless things, but his words show God's power to move living humans to conversion (*GT, PG* 46.920A). Similarly, what is most powerful about Macrina is her teaching and the fact that despite her nearness to death "her mind retained unimpeded its contemplation of transcendent realities" (*LM* 18; SC 178, p. 200).

Once more I have the sense that Gregory betrays a tension between the wonders he recounts and the theological framework in which he tries to set them. The tension, moreover, seems to me related to that between his deep commitment to his fatherland and the gift of his involvement in the wider church. Pontus and the heavenly Jerusalem tend to rub against one another. The ending of the *Panegyric on Gregory Thaumaturgus*, like that of the *Life of Macrina*, reflects this tension (*GT, PG* 46.957D):

> There are many other miracles of the great Gregory that have been preserved in memory to this day. But I have spared unbelieving ears by not adding them to what I have written, so that people who treat the truth as a lie because of the greatness of what is told may suffer no harm. To Christ, who works such wonders through his servants, be given, as is right, glory, honor, and worship, now and always and forever. Amen.

To be sure, the obvious meaning of his words has to do with the issue of the credibility of miracles. But, I think, to read between the lines is to understand that Gregory himself betrays a degree of uneasiness that can have nothing to do with his own doubt of the miracles. Instead, the problem is the deeper one of a sense, whether conscious or unconscious, of a disparity between the miracles of his fatherland and the sophisticated theology of his maturity in the faith.

THEODORET OF CYRRHUS AND THE MONKS OF SYRIA

A History of the Monks of Syria tells us much of what we know of Theodoret's life. He and his parents before him were deeply involved with the monks near Antioch, to whom they constantly resorted as patrons. Theodoret's mother first met Peter the Galatian because she sought a cure for a disease that had afflicted one of her eyes. She got more than she bargained for, since Peter not only cured her body by making the sign of the cross on her eye, but also healed her soul by persuading her to abandon her jewels and cosmetics (*MS* 9.5ff.; CS 88, p. 83f.). From that moment she frequently and successfully sought Peter's help. Nor did she limit her attention to him. She also supplied Macedonius with ground barley. It was Macedonius that Theodoret's father besought to overcome his wife's barrenness. After three years the monk's promise was fulfilled, and Theodoret was born (*MS* 13.3, 16f.; CS 88, pp. 101, 105f.).

Theodoret, then, was a child of promise. He remembers his association with Macedonius, who used to exhort him (*MS* 13.18; CS 88, p. 107):

> "You were born, my child, with much toil: I spent many nights begging this alone of God, that your parents should earn the name they received after your birth. So live a life worthy of this toil. Before you were born, you were offered up in promise. Offerings to God are revered by all, and are not to be touched by the multitude: so it is fitting that you do not admit the base impulses of the soul, but perform, speak, and desire those things alone that serve God, the giver of the laws of virtue."

The miracle of his birth is a gift to be employed in a life of dedication to God and of virtue. Theodoret remembered other monks whom he visited with his mother. Peter the Galatian gave him half his girdle, which Theodoret often wore as a child and which cured him of diseases (*MS* 9.15; CS 88, p. 87). Once Aphrahat took him into his cell, leaving his mother outside but giving both mother and child his blessing (*MS* 8.15; CS 88, p. 79). More often than not Theodoret knew the monks whose stories he tells. As a bishop he was solicitous of their welfare and even sought on occasion to moderate the rigors of their asceticism.[33] He also sought their assistance, and James of Cyrrhestica lent his miraculous power to Theodoret's struggle to purge his diocese of Marcionite heretics (*MS* 21.15ff.; CS 88, p. 139ff.).

Theodoret emphasizes miracles of healing and exorcism, and he notes that these can be worked not only by the saints while alive but also by their relics.[34] But he also tells of other sorts of miracles. Monks slay serpents (*MS*

2.6, 3.7f.; CS 88, pp. 26, 40). They cause springs to well up (*MS* 2.7–8, 10.7; CS 88, pp. 27, 91). Symeon Stylites, "in imitation of the Master, who told the paralytic to carry his bed," heals a paralytic (*MS* 26.16f.; CS 88, p. 168). Symeon the Elder "like the Apostles and Prophets" calls down miraculous judgment on a thief (*MS* 6.5; CS 88, p. 64f.). James of Nisibis causes a large boulder to explode beside an unjust judge, forcing him to reverse his decision (*MS* 1.6; CS 88, p. 14f.). And Theodoret tells the story of the false dead man as a miracle of James of Nisibis (*MS* 1.8; CS 88, p. 15f.)[35] With some frequency Theodoret compares the miracles to those of Moses, Elijah, Elisha, Christ, or the apostles. In all these respects we are on ground by now familiar.

Several of Theodoret's stories underline the fact that the monks act as patrons for the village population around them.[36] Abraham, for example, by protecting from the tax collectors the people of the village he settles in as a stranger, succeeds in becoming their patron (*MS* 17.3; CS 88, p. 121). In another story Letoius, who was a member of the council in Antioch and the master of a village, is too demanding of the peasants' crops. He visits the monk Maesymas, and when he refuses to moderate his demands, finds his chariot wheels clogged "as if fastened with iron and lead." Only when he relents and pleads for forgiveness is he able to drive off (*MS* 14.4; CS 88, p. 111f.) In one sense Theodoret's emphasis is upon the monks as heroes and their deeds as benefactions. This is certainly the picture of his society that emerges from the pages of his history. In his prologue Theodoret speaks of the monks as exceptional in their asceticism and prayer; they "have deemed fasting a Sybaritic nourishment, . . . a life of prayer and psalmody a pleasure measureless and insatiable" Consequently, "who would not rightly admire them? Rather, who could extol them as they merit?" (*MS* prol.7; CS 88, p. 7).

I am suggesting that the theme of the monks as examples and paradigms of virtue has suffered something of an eclipse. To be sure, Theodoret at least implies the theme that takes pride of place in Athanasius's *Life of Antony*. He speaks by analogy of witnessing athletic contests in order "to draw benefit with the eyes" and "impel the beholder to attain" what they praise (*MS* prol.1; CS 88, p. 3). But the implication of these words is not explicit either in the prologue or in the work as a whole. At the same time Theodoret does attempt to place his narratives in the religious and theological framework we have encountered in the writings of Athanasius and of Gregory of Nyssa. The familiar metaphors of the athlete and the soldier of Christ struggling against Satan appear throughout the history. Zeno "departed like some Olympic victor from the place of contest" (*MS* 12.7; CS 88, p. 99). And in the prologue Theodoret says that he is not portraying "their bodily features . . . , but we sketch the forms of invisible souls and display unseen wars and secret struggles." The armor of God of which Paul speaks (Eph 6:13ff.) is necessary for this war (*MS* prol.3–4; CS 88, p. 4f.).

It is the Epilogue to the work, *On Divine Love*, that represents Theodoret's fullest attempt to integrate the stories he has told with a sophisticated theology. Our deepest yearning is for God. And once we have "received the goad of divine love" the more we yearn and the more we draw our fill. The desire for God "does not admit the laws of satiety" (*MS* epil.4; CS 88, p. 193). Moses, the bride in the Song of Solomon, and Paul all teach this lesson, as does Peter's triple affirmation of love for his risen Lord (*MS* epil.14f.; CS 88, p. 199):

> Therefore he who has conceived divine love despises all earthly things together and tramples on all the pleasures of the body. He looks down upon wealth and glory and honor from men; he thinks that the royal purple is no different from spiders' webs; he likens the stones that are precious to pebbles on the bank. . . . Virtue, or philosophy, is an abiding good. It overcomes the hands of the robber, the tongue of the slanderer, and the showers of darts and spears of the enemy; it does not become the victim of fever, nor the plaything of a storm, nor the casualty of shipwreck. Time does not remove its power, but increases its power.

What seems remarkable about these words is that they drive in two directions. On the one hand, they conjure up the notion of the Christian life as a progress in love toward God and a perpetual movement toward the good that is itself the attainment of virtue, an attaining that can never attain or stand still. On the other hand, Theodoret's words quickly move to the power of virtue. What virtue does seems as important as what it is.

This is a way of characterizing the tension in Theodoret's attitude toward the Christian faith. He takes seriously the theological *lingua franca* that tends to equate Christianity with the acquisition of virtue, but his own concern is with the power of Christianity.[37] And this means that the miracles he recounts are of central importance to him, perhaps more than is true of Athanasius and Gregory of Nyssa. In the prologue he singles out the problem of the miracles and their credibility in a way reminiscent of Gregory (*MS* prol.10; CS 88, p. 8):

> I ask those who will read this *Religious History* or *Ascetic Life* . . . not to disbelieve what is said if they hear something beyond their own power, nor to measure the virtue of these men by themselves, but to recognize clearly that God is wont to measure the gifts of the

all-holy Spirit by the resolve of the pious and gives greater gifts to those with more perfect resolve.

Theodoret goes on to insist that the miracles are worked by the Spirit through human agency "drawing the faithless to a knowledge of God by the mighty working of prodigies." What is true of Moses, Joshua, Elijah, Elisha, and the apostles remains true of the monks. "Grace is ever-flowing: it elects the worthy and through them as through springs pours forth the streams of beneficence." Let me suggest that Theodoret, unlike Gregory, does not find himself tempted to share the disbelief of those he imagines. If this is so, then the tension between the theological framework he has inherited and repeats in the epilogue and his own commitment to a heroic Christianity of benefaction is not really evident to him. The miracles do not necessarily stand in contradiction to the idea of divine love, but the relationship of the two has become more difficult to understand.

CONCLUSION

John Chrysostom's opinion that miracles ceased after the apostolic age is certainly a minority view. There can be no doubt that the miraculous is an important dimension of the church in the fourth and fifth centuries. At first sight the miracles we have examined seem somehow different from those of Christ in the New Testament. There may be some truth to this reaction, but it seems to be superficial. Exorcisms and miracles of healing continue in the imperial church, and precedents may be found in Scripture for miracles in the natural world and for divine punishments. Christ turned water to wine, stilled a storm, and walked on the water. And the apostles struck down Ananias and Sapphira, had shadows and handkerchiefs that healed people, and miraculously opened prison doors. Moreover, we must add the miracles of the Old Testament, especially those of Moses, Elijah, and Elisha. The writers we have examined are quite conscious of these parallels and do not, on the whole, sense any difference between the miracles of Scripture and those of their own day. It may well be that this strikes us as odd only because we are so familiar with the biblical miracles that they have been robbed of their remarkable character. I remember meeting an undergraduate once who decided to read the New Testament for the first time. He was utterly astonished at the miracle stories and could not believe they belonged in a book claimed as the basis for much of modern Christianity.

The real difference, I think, between what we found in the first three chapters and what we have encountered in this one is that with the miracles of the imperial church we have entered a living social setting. The miracles establish the Christian commonwealth, and they function to support it. Moreover, they tend to find two specific contexts, the relics of the saints and the holy men and women of the desert. The martyr buried in his tomb is the "invisible friend" who bestows blessings on those who come to him for aid. And in much the same way the monk becomes a spiritual patron of all who wish to be his clients. Indeed, in the case of the holy man we are able to see at times an actual social and economic relationship at work. The miracles in these contexts no longer function merely as signs of spiritual truths or as deeds that act out the meaning of the Christian faith. Instead, they are powerful benefactions that often seem to have very little to do with the Christian faith. It occurs to me that many analogies help make sense of the phenomenon. What does celebrating the Fourth of July or Thanksgiving have to do directly with the Gospel? Or if someone were to examine modern Christianity a thousand years from now, what would he make of the Christmas fair or the entertainments of the young people's fellowship? A tension begins to emerge between the Christian message and the social setting in which it appears. And in the imperial church the miracles seem to me more clearly located in that social setting than in the message. In other words, I am not entirely convinced that Athanasius, Gregory of Nyssa, and Theodoret have been successful in tying the miracles and the social setting in which they function to the Gospel as they understand it.

In a sense, we can turn these conclusions into a set of problems worth examining somewhat further. And we can add other problems to the list. At times it looks as though miracles have grown by the telling; can we trace this in any way? How can we explain what seems to be a movement from the martyrs' stories to their relics as a focus of attention? There also appears to be a tendency to take relics out of private hands and put them in the public domain. Both with the martyrs and with the monks I sense a shift from underlining their exemplary function to an interest in them as patrons and benefactors. The writers toward the end of the period I have been examining appear to be more comfortable with the idea of special acts of God than were the earlier ones. All these questions and preliminary observations suggest that the problem of miracles is partly one of the tail wagging the dog, but partly, as I have suggested, of the dog and the tail not quite belonging together. In chapter 5 I wish to examine the issues that have been raised from the point of view of the social setting of miracles. In chapter 6 my preoccupation will be with the theological problems that are raised.

5

Hope in the Community

 One preliminary conclusion I should wish to draw from the evidence examined up to this point is that a gap begins to emerge between the meaning given Christ's miracles by the interpreters and homilists of the fourth and fifth centuries and the emphasis we more often than not find upon the miraculous, particularly in relation to the cult of the saints and to the holy man. In the first three chapters it is almost as though the miracles function so completely as signs of a spiritual and moral message that they cease to have any importance in themselves. In chapter 4, however, we discovered a real preoccupation with the miraculous power of the Gospel expressed not only in miracles of healing and exorcism but also in miracles designed to impress and dazzle their witnesses by the manipulation of natural phenomena.

If we grant the existence of the gap for which I have argued, then it is not surprising that the sort of view presented by Edward Gibbon in the eighteenth century has tended to prevail in the assessments given of the post-Constantinian church. In chapter 28 Gibbon describes the destruction of "the Pagan Religion" under Theodosius the Great and correlates it with the rise of the cult of the saints and an emphasis upon the miraculous:

> The sublime and simple theology of the primitive Christians was gradually corrupted; and the Monarchy of heaven, already clouded by metaphysical subtleties, was degraded by the introduction of a popular mythology, which tended to restore the reign of polytheism.

... it must ingenuously be confessed, that the ministers of the Catholic church imitated the profane model, which they were impatient to destroy. The most respectable bishops had persuaded themselves that the ignorant rustics would more cheerfully renounce the superstitions of Paganism, if they found some resemblance, some compensation, in the bosom of Christianity. The religion of Constantine achieved, in less than a century, the final conquest of the Roman empire: but the victors themselves were insensibly subdued by the arts of their vanquished rivals.[1]

Gibbon regards the development I have described in chapter 4 as a corruption of early Christianity and attributes that corruption to the triumph of popular superstition, a triumph that really represents the victory of paganism over Christianity. In one form or another this view has tended to dominate discussion of the fourth- and fifth-century church.

It is the great merit of Peter Brown's work to have demonstrated that Gibbon's view is in crucial respects misguided. To be sure, the cult of the saints rises to prominence and becomes central to Christianity in the century after Constantine. Moreover, the great importance of the holy man in certain areas is also the product of the same period. Nevertheless, Brown argues convincingly that these developments cannot be understood as the triumph of popular superstition or of the old paganism. This dimension of Gibbon's view rests upon certain assumptions of the Enlightenment that can be seen most clearly in the work of Hume. The "two-tiered model" that opposes popular and official piety is largely the product of an Enlightenment equation of "superstition" with a popular sensibility.[2] Brown successfully demonstrates that the evidence must be read another way. What we discover is a struggle over who shall control the relics of the saints, and the church gradually succeeds in winning the battle and ensuring that the cult of the saints be public and not private. Moreover, at least at the level of the cult of the saints we cannot argue for any triumph of paganism. On the contrary, the ancient sensibility that abhorred dead bodies stands in stark contrast to the Christian reversal of that sensibility. Dead bodies find their resting place in the churches and in the heart of the ancient city instead of being relegated to places outside the city walls.

In this chapter I wish to examine the miraculous in its social context in the fourth and fifth centuries. And I shall hope to follow the conclusions reached by Peter Brown without in any way minimizing the degree to which I am dependent upon his work. In one respect, however, I wish to make a slightly different point, though it in no way contradicts Brown's conclusions. To return to Gibbon's view, it seems to me that the truth that lies behind his view is that there is a gap between the miraculous and the usual way of understanding the Christian message. But the gap is not between superstition and pure religion, between popular and official piety, or between a paganized Christianity and the Gospel of Christ. Instead, the gap is between the social and institutional development of the church and dominant themes in Christian theology during the period I am studying. To put the point as clearly as possible, I wish to argue that the miraculous correlates with the Christian community, while the theological themes I have in mind correlate with a Christianized version of the late antique quest for virtue. The deeper issue, then, has to do not so much with miracles in and of themselves, but with the tension between the realities of the Christian community and attempts to articulate the Gospel that constitutes it.

THE BATTLE WITH PAGANISM

In one sense there can be no difficulty in understanding that Christianity excluded the old paganism. The exclusive religious loyalty that had characterized ancient Judaism continued to define Christianity. One could not be a Christian and retain any other religious loyalty. At the same time, many practices that can be called religious were not necessarily tied to the pagan cults as they were practiced in public. For example, an ancient Christian may not have entirely understood that wearing an amulet or observing unlucky days was necessarily incompatible with Christianity. There were even Christians who found no difficulty in resorting to magicians and necromancers, or who employed spells and charms. We have already discovered the uncompromising view of most Christians toward this persisting underbrush of religion. Eusebius, Chrysostom, Augustine, and Cyril of Alexandria all condemn the use of amulets, the practice of sorcery, the consultation of astrologers, and the whole of what we should call ancient magic.[3] The underbrush is pagan and must be cut down together with the more obvious and public manifestations of the old religions.[4]

We should expect to find this polemic against magic in the canons that have survived from the ancient church, and in some degree this expectation proves correct. What is surprising is that we find so little evidence. A synod met in Elvira in Spain, probably in 305 or 306. Hosius of Cordoba was present, and the major task of the synod seems to have been how to deal with the lapsed after the Diocletian persecution. Several of the canons prohibit magical practices.[5] Anyone who kills someone by magic (*per maleficium*) can never be restored to communion (canon 6). Lighting candles in daytime in the cemeteries brings excommunication (canon 34). Women must not spend the night in cemeteries (canon 35). Farmers must

not permit Jews to bless their crops (canon 49). No Christian may attend
the public pagan sacrifices (canon 59).

A few years later (314) a synod convened in Ancrya. Canon 24 reads:

> Those who foretell the future, and follow pagan customs, or admit
> into their houses people (magicians) in order to discover magical
> remedies, or to perform expiations, must be sentenced to a five
> years' penance, to three years of *substratio*, and to two years of
> attendance at prayers without the sacrifice (non-communicating
> attendance).[6]

The canon conforms to what the preachers of the fourth and fifth century
argued, and the identification of magic and paganism is made clear. The
same judgment obtains of the evidence from the synod of Laodicea, held at
some time between 343 and 381.[7] Several canons prohibit Christians from
following Jewish practices (canons 29 and 38), worshipping angels (canon
35), accepting festal gifts from Jews or heretics (canon 37), and sharing in
pagan feasts (canon 39). But the most interesting canon (36) prohibits the
clergy from being "magicians, conjurors, mathematicians, or astrologers"
and from making amulets. Moreover, all who wear such amulets are to be
excommunicated.[8] Only one other canon needs to be added as evidence,
and it takes us to a rather different setting. The second synod of Arles,
which met in 443 or 452, instructs the bishops to forbid "unbelievers in his
diocese to light torches or trees in honour of fountains or rocks."[9] This
canon (23) presupposes that bishops will have some control over pagans in
their dioceses and also reflects a barbarian paganism rather than the old
idolatry of Greece and Rome.

The evidence is clear but in one respect puzzling. People do not make
laws unless what is proscribed is a present danger. And so it cannot be
doubted that Christians, and even clergy, often sought to bring magic into
the church. Of course, this conclusion depends upon identifying what may
have seemed to many the harmless use of amulets and charms with
paganism. The polemic against magic is real. On the other hand, it is
surprising to find so little evidence of canonical legislation in the context of
the polemic. I am not sure how to explain this peculiarity. Perhaps the
identification between paganism and magic was so firm and so univer-
sally accepted that legislation against it was unnecessary. It was as obvious
that Christianity excluded private paganism as that it excluded the public
cults. Or perhaps it was a question of leaving to the state the legal prohibition of paganism. And we can certainly see in the Theodosian Codex the
gradual development of a total prohibition of pagan practices.

The specifically Christian polemic is easier to see in the homiletical literature already examined, and I should like to add to that evidence one further consideration. In 385 Monica joined her son in Milan. Augustine tells us that she had been accustomed "to take meal-cakes and bread and wine to the shrines of the saints on their memorial days," but found herself prohibited from doing this in Milan. Ambrose had forbidden the custom "both for fear that to some they might be occasions for drunkenness and also because they [such ceremonies] bore so close a resemblance to the superstitious rites which the pagans held in honour of their dead" (*Conf.* 6.2; PC, p. 112f.).[10] It is easy to imagine the complexity of the issue raised. Burial customs are virtually elemental in character and tend to persist regardless of the religious structures in which they are placed. To find the polemic against paganism extended to the prohibition of long-standing burial customs is to see how carefully the church sought to protect itself from paganism. It seems to me impossible to reconcile the polemic with any acquiescence in a covert paganism on the part of the church's leadership.

The attitude of the state toward paganism was, obviously, a more complicated matter. Constantine's decision in 312 to patronize the church can by no means be equated with a decision to declare Christianity the only or even the official religion of the Empire. The following edict to be dated in 319 characterizes Constantine's attitude:

> We forbid soothsayers and priests and persons accustomed to serve that rite to approach a private home or under pretext of friendship to cross the threshold of another; and punishment will threaten them if they disregard the statute. You, however, who think this profits you, go to the public altars and shrines and celebrate the ceremonies of your custom; for we do not forbid the services of a bygone usage to be conducted in open view.[11]

The operative distinction is that between private and public. What was difficult in practice was to see where that line should be drawn. It was not until 391, when Theodosius the Great (379–95) issued the first of a number of edicts prohibiting paganism altogether, that the state finally adopted the same line as the church.[12]

With these facts in mind it becomes necessary to question whether the imperial attacks on magic during the period before 391 are to be regarded as motivated by Christianity or should be understood in the light of similar earlier repressions of magic and religion from the time of Augustus onward. Ammianus Marcellinus, who was probably a pagan and certainly an admirer and companion of Julian the Apostate, tells us a good deal about the witch-hunting mentality of the fourth century. Only a few years before Constantius's death and the succession of Julian to the principate (361), Ammianus speaks of "many abominable acts" for which Constantius was responsible (Amm. Marc. 16.8.2; LCL 1, p. 233):

> ... if anyone consulted a soothsayer about the squeaking of a shrew-mouse, the meeting with a weasel on the way, or any like portent, or used some old wife's charm to relieve pain (a thing which even medical authority allows), he was indicted (from what source he could not guess), was hailed into court, and suffered death as the penalty.

Ammianus explains this as a consequence of Constantius's insecurity. And clearly enough the emperor is equating magic with treason, perhaps not entirely without justification (Amm. Marc. 19.12.9). He goes too far, however, at least in Ammianus's view, when he executes someone who simply wears "an amulet against the quartan ague or any other complaint, or was accused by the testimony of the evil-disposed of passing by a grave in the evening, on the ground that he was a dealer in poisons, or a gatherer of the horrors of tombs and the vain illusions of the ghosts that walk there" (Amm. Marc. 19.12.14; LCL 1, p. 541). Ammianus tells similar stories of Valens (364–378) and Valentinian (364–375), including an account of how a magical table was used to discover the name of Valens's successor (Amm. Marc. 29.1.28ff.; cf. 29.1.5ff., 29.1.41f., 29.2.1ff., 30.5.11).

It is difficult to fault Ammianus's assessment of these events. The charge of magic or sorcery has little to do with religion and reflects an insecure government's preoccupation with subversion. Sometimes the imperial reaction seems justified, but more often it appears to reflect the uncertainty of power. The same phenomenon appears in what we know of church affairs during the fourth century. Accusations of practicing magic are fairly common in the church disputes of the day. Occasionally, in this context, the religious issue may have been serious. But in every case other factors appear more operative. For example, in 341 the Arianizing synod of Antioch considered Eusebius of Emesa as a replacement for Athanasius in Alexandria. But, according to Socrates, Eusebius instead went to his native city as bishop, where he was accused of being an astrologer and was obliged to flee the city (Soc. 2.9). Later he returned to Emesa but was this time accused of being a Sabellian. Heresy somehow seems a more important issue than astrology. The same conclusion attaches to Socrates' account of a number of depositions that took place at the instigation of Acacius of Caesarea about 360. The Acacian party temporarily gained the upper hand with the emperor, Constantius, and did so by an alliance with the neo-Arians. There is no need to examine the political details in order to conclude that the Acacians succeeded in deposing their enemies. And they did so on the basis of a wide variety of charges: admitting a deacon to communion who had been convicted of fornication, ordaining as deacon a priest of Hercules who practiced magic, dressing in a way unbecoming a bishop (Soc. 2.42f.).

The best example of how accusations of magic could function as an excuse for eliminating ecclesiastical rivals is the case of Athanasius. At the synod of Tyre in 335 the Arians charged Athanasius with a number of misdeeds having nothing to do with orthodoxy. One of the charges was that he had cut off the hand of a bishop named Arsenius and used the hand for magical purposes (Soc. 1.27ff.). The charge was proved false when Athanasius's supporters were able to produce Arsenius, hand and all, at the synod. What we are encountering is the attempt to draw boundaries and define structures of political power. In the fourth century the Empire is attempting to define itself and does so by repudiating sorcery and magic as subversive. Similarly, the struggle in the church to define orthodoxy leads to an analogous rejection of magic. In the process it looks as though the terms were sometimes reversed. Suspicion of subversion led to the conclusion that magic was being practiced.[13]

I am suggesting that, although part of the church's struggle against pagan magic must be understood as a genuine religious confrontation, part of it must be seen as a factor of the church's attempt to define itself during the fourth century. To repudiate even the hint of pagan practices is to ensure that the church will not be subverted by alien ideas and forces. In order for this conclusion to make sense I must add one further consideration. We have already seen ways in which the church supplied an alternative to the popular practices to which converts were accustomed. Instead of an amulet to ward off disease, Augustine recommends the Gospel book. Chrysostom says that the sign of the cross is far more powerful than any amulet. And Hilarion, according to Jerome, by prayer was able to overcome the power of magic used to force love or to win races.[14] Clearly what bothers Christians about magic is not the supernatural but rather the religious context in which the magic appears.

If I am correct, it follows that the issue as it appeared in the social context of post-Constantinian Christianity is not so much the miraculous as the religious context in which it was to function. It may be possible to distinguish between perceptions of the miraculous that spring from biblical and Jewish roots and perceptions found in Graeco-Roman traditions.[15] But whatever differences may be found must be located within a common mentality that presupposes a supernatural explanation for what commands our wonder. We may find it difficult to distinguish an amulet from the sign of the cross or a relic, but that is simply because we tend to see all three as examples of magic. For the Christian in the fourth century the difference is obvious. The amulet belongs in the context of paganism; the cross, in that of the Gospel. Some ambiguity remains, as we can see by Ambrose's prohibition of feasts at the graves of saints; Christian practices must be purged of even the suspicion of paganism. But the real problem for the fourth- and fifth-century church is not the acceptance of the miraculous but its firm location in the life of the Christian community.[16] For this reason we must now turn to the cult of the saints and to the role of holy men in the church.

SPECIAL PLACES

The harnassing of the miraculous to the church is, I think, part of a larger development. The Christianizing of the Roman Empire took place on a number of different levels. The state itself gradually came to define itself as, at least in principle, Christian.[17] This, of course, left open the question of precisely how the emperor was related to the church; and the ambiguity eventually resolved itself quite differently in the Latin West and in Byzantium. On another level, the church itself sought to establish its own structures in doctrine, in polity, and in liturgy.[18] In all these ways most Christians thought that a process of sacralization was taking place. In a sense, heaven had come down to earth in order to transform it; and the Empire itself was part of this new sacral order. The organization of the cult of the saints was not only a part of the larger enterprise but was central to it. If we can see the community of the imperial church defining itself negatively by rejecting paganism in all its form, we can see it doing so positively by establishing throughout the Mediterranean holy places where supernatural power appeared at the heart of the Christian community.

Let me begin by describing Theodoret's view of the cult of the saints in Book 8 of his *The Cure of Pagan Maladies*, an apologetic work probably written before he became bishop of Cyrrhus in 423.[19] The incarnate Son of God, who presided over their contests, has given the apostles and martyrs the prize for their victory (*Cure* 8.10; SC 57, p. 313):

> The noble souls of the victors traverse heaven, united with the chorus of incorporeal [angels]. A single grave for each does not guard their bodies hidden. Instead, the cities and villages to which they have been distributed call them the saviours and healers of bodies and souls and honor them as guardians and protectors. They use them as ambassadors to the Lord of the universe and through them receive divine gifts. Though the body is divided, the grace has remained undivided; and that small and very tiny relic

has a power equal to the martyr even if he had never in any way been divided.

Theodoret goes on to defend the powerful patronage of the saints' relics against the pagans. The objection he must counter is the pagan abhorrence of dead bodies, and his argument depends upon pointing out a contradiction in the pagan attitude. Though they pretend a horror of corpses, they actually honor the tombs of their heroes.

Theodoret's argument leads him to define paganism as a perverse mirror image of Christianity. And by Christianity he means the cult of the saints. "Our Lord has established his dead in the place of your gods" (*Cure* 8.69; SC 57, p. 335). The parallel Theodoret draws between paganism and the cult of the saints functions to contrast the two and reflects the conventions of a Christian apologetic that can be traced back to Justin Martyr in the second century. The continuities between paganism and Christianity make pagan objections absurd, while the discontinuities prove Christianity alone true and superior to paganism. With respect to the cult of the saints, it is important to note that Theodoret treats it as a central feature of Christianity. To understand the cult is to understand the Gospel. Obviously, this is only one aspect of Theodoret's view. As we have seen, he also attaches great importance to the function of the holy man as a locus of the Gospel's power. But his discussion in Book 8 of *The Cure* shows that the cult of the saints, far from deriving from paganism, represents a substitute for it, truth replacing a lie.

Theodoret's view also reflects the fact that by the middle of the fifth century the cult of the saints had been organized throughout the Christian Empire, and is is to that development I now wish to turn. Of course, it is clear that from early times great care was taken to preserve the bodies of saints and martyrs. The cult of the saints did not begin in the fourth century. Nevertheless, we have already discovered a shift in sensibility in the period after the Constantinian revolution. Emphasis upon the martyrs' examples yields to a preoccupation with the present power of their patronage, which is connected with their relics. Moreover, we also find a tendency to take relics out of private hands and place them under the control of the church's hierarchy.[20]

Though he is speaking particularly of Ambrose's management of the cult of the saints in Milan, Peter Brown uses a metaphor that enables us to imagine what happened throughout the church in the fourth and early fifth centuries. Ambrose was "like an electrician who rewires an antiquated wiring system: more power could pass through stronger, better-insulated wires toward the bishop as leader of the community."[21] Of course, in seeking to reconstruct what happened we are faced with the problem fundamental to reconstructing the history of the early church. Most of the pieces of the puzzle are lost. We must not only imagine the relation of one piece to the others but also what the missing pieces were like. In the following discussion I want to suggest that we find sufficient evidence to argue that what Theodoret describes in the first quarter of the fifth century is the product of the careful organizing work of bishops and emperors during the century after Constantine.

One place to begin is with the work of Damasus, who was bishop of Rome from 366 until his death in 385. The story is not altogether an edifying one. What made his election as pope possible was the victory of his supporters that left a hundred and thirty-seven corpses in the basilica of Santa Maria Maggiore, where the election was held.[22] Damasus proved to be powerful and succeeded in organizing and strengthening the early papacy. He built a number of churches, including San Lorenzo in Damaso, where the papal archives were housed, basilicas dedicated to the apostles on the Appian Way, and the Basilica of Saints Mark and Marcellianus. He was so successful in raising money from wealthy women that his enemies called him "the matrons' ear-tickler."[23] What is relevant to my discussion is the fact that he took an interest in the catacombs, organized the relics of the saints, and placed near many of them marble tablets inscribed with verses he composed. His friend Furius Dionysius Filocalus devised a new lettering for these inscriptions, many of which are still preserved.

One of the most interesting of these inscriptions is the one Damasus made for his own tomb:

> He who stilled the fierce waves of the sea by walking thereon, He who makes the dying seeds of the earth to live, He who could loose for Lazarus his chains of death and give back again to the world above her brother to his sister Martha after three days and nights, He, I believe, will make me Damasus arise from my ashes.[24]

Here we are in the world of thought we encountered in the first three chapters. The miracles of Christ are treated as signs that assure the general resurrection of those who believe in him. When we turn, however, to the inscriptions Damasus wrote for the saints and martyrs, we enter the world of the cult of the saints. Sixtus II was bishop of Rome in 258, when he was martyred. The judgment of Damasus's inscription is "Christ who awards the prize of life shows the merits of the shepherd: He himself keeps safe the number of the flock."[25] The words, of course, refer to Sixtus's leadership during a time of persecution; but Damasus's use of the present tense implies that the merits of the shepherd are still effectual.

Many of the other inscriptions do little more than commemorate the martyrs and their stories; but the one Damasus composed for Cornelius, who was bishop of Rome from 251 to 253, clarifies the aim of Damasus's work:

> Behold now that a way of descent has been made and the darkness put to flight, you see the monument of Cornelius and his conse-crated grave. The watchful care of Damasus in his sickness has completed this work, that there might be a better mode of access, and that the help of the saint might be procured for the people, and that if you prevail to pour forth prayers from a pure heart, Damasus may rise stronger, though it is not love of light that keeps him here, but rather care for his work.[26]

The text implies that Damasus has moved Cornelius's body so that it may rest with the other early bishops of Rome. The "rewiring," to use Peter Brown's metaphor, makes access to the relics easier; and the specific power thought available through Cornelius's relics has to do with healing Damasus's illness.

We can turn our attention from Rome to Milan and the work of Ambrose. He and Augustine both tell us of the discovery of the relics of Protasius and Gervasius in 386, the year after Damasus's death. Augus-tine tells us that a vision given Ambrose revealed to him "the place where the bodies of the martyrs Protasius and Gervasius were hidden." He then had the bodies carried with honor to his new basilica. On the way the relics expelled demons from several possessed people, and a blind man received sight (*Conf.* 9.7; PC, p. 191).[27] Ambrose's letter to his sister tells the same story and includes his account of two sermons he delivered to the people at the time. The first of these seizes upon words that had just been read in the church: "The heavens are telling the glory of God" (Ps 19:1). Ambrose identifies "the heavens" with the relics of "men of heav-enly conversation, . . . the trophies of a heavenly mind." Heaven has, as it were, come to earth in the relics of the saints (Amb. Ep. 22; *NPNF* 2.10, p. 437). Milan, "barren of martyrs hitherto," has now found her own patrons. No longer must Milan depend upon martyrs' "carried off" from other places.

Ambrose describes the function of these hometown martyrs quite clearly. It is not just that a source of healing power has appeared, nor that "the miracles of old time are renewed, when through the coming of the Lord Jesus grace was more largely shed forth upon the earth."[28] Still more the Lord has stirred up the martyrs when the church needs "greater protec-tion." They are "champions . . . who are able to defend, but desire not to attack." What Ambrose certainly means is that the relics will help him in resisting the Empress Justina's attempt to take over one of the church's basilicas for the Arians. The miracle of the discovery of the martyrs resembles the way Elisha opened Gehazi's eyes to see the invisible host of angels fighting for them (2 Kings 6:16). "We had patrons and knew it not" (Amb. Ep. 22; *NPNF* 2.10, p. 438).

Damasus and Ambrose sought to make the patronage of the saints more available to their people, and their success is witnessed by Prudentius in a collection of poems called *Crowns of Martyrdom*. Prudentius was born in 348 in Spain, where he eventually became a prefect governing two cities. A trip to Rome taken during the first years of the fifth century provided his inspiration for the second half of the *Crowns of Martyrdom*, while the focus of attention in the first half is upon Spanish martyrs. Prudentius, at least in these poems, is a kind of Christian Horace, writing patriotic poetry to celebrate the Christian commonwealth. The reader is always conscious of the community in festival at the martyr's shrine. The earth of Spain drank the blood of the martyrs of Calagurris (*CM* 1; LCL 2, p. 99):

> . . . and now its people throng to visit the ground that was coloured with their holy blood, making petitions with voice and heart and gifts; and dwellers in the outside world too come here, for report has run through all lands publishing the news that here are patrons of the whole earth whose favour they may seek by prayer.

The patronage of the martyrs is available not only to their fellow citizens but also to those who come to the shrine on pilgrimage.

Although Prudentius tells us the stories of the saints his poems commemorate, what really counts is their present function as guardians of the community. The story of the two martyrs of Calagurris is lost. "We are denied the facts about these matters, the very tradition is destroyed." This is because "long ago a reviling soldier of the guard" destroyed the records, hoping to obliterate the memory of the martyrs (*CM* 1; LCL 2, p. 105). Nothing is really lost, however, since the saints are the guardians of the community. "We" venerate the bones of Saint Eulalia, "while she, set at the feet of God, views all our doings, our song wins her favour, and she cherishes her people" (*CM* 3; LCL 2, p. 157). The favor of the saints manifests itself in gifts of healing (*CM* 1; LCL 2, p. 101), but also in the grace of forgiveness. Celebrating the festival and bowing down before the relics in joy brings "the favour of Christ, that our burdened souls may feel the relief of forgiveness" (*CM* 5; LCL 2, p. 203).

For Prudentius the cult of the saints is not only civic in a local sense but also, perhaps paradoxically, personal and civic in a cosmopolitan sense. On his way to Rome the poet finds the shrine of Cassian on the Via Aemilia in northern Italy. The verger tells him that Cassian was a teacher, martyred for his faith by the boys he taught, who slew him with their pens. And he assures Prudentius that Cassian will hear his prayers (*CM* 9; LCL 2, p. 229):

> I obeyed, clasping the tomb and shedding tears, warming the altar with my lips, the stone with my breast. Then I reviewed all my private distresses, and murmured my desires and fears, with a prayer for the home I had left behind me in the uncertainty of fortune, and my hope, now faltering, of happiness to come. I was heard. I visited Rome, and found all things issue happily. I returned home and now proclaim the praise of Cassian.

Prudentius sees no contradiction between this very personal function of the saints and their patronage of a Christian Empire. In his poem on Saint Lawrence he gives the martyr a long speech in which Rome receives the sacred mission of fostering Christianity so that "the Christian name might bind with one tie all lands everywhere" (*CM* 2; LCL 2, p. 133ff.). The point of view is more fully elaborated in Prudentius's long poem replying to Symmachus's address asking for the restoration of the altar of victory, and it represents the usual view of Christians at the beginning of the fifth century.

Paulinus of Nola supplies us with evidence very like that of Prudentius's poems. He was born in Bordeaux in the middle of the fourth century and was educated as a member of the Gallic aristocracy. Probably through the influence of his friend and tutor Ausonius, he became governor of Campania in 379. It was then that he first encountered St. Felix of Nola, and began his full conversion to Christianity by slow and almost imperceptible degrees. He was baptized in 389 in Bordeaux; and some six years later, already a priest and soon to be bishop, he settled in Nola, where he established a monastery and tended St. Felix's shrine. He soon became well known in Christian circles and corresponded with people like Augustine, Rufinus, Jerome, and Sulpicius Severus. With Paulinus we enter the world of the great leaders of the church in the early fifth century, and yet the piety we find does not differ from that embraced by the more modest Prudentius.

A cycle of Paulinus's poems called the *Natalicia* celebrates the feast of St. Felix (14 January). These poems, written from 395 to 408, tell the story of Felix, describe the buildings Paulinus constructed at Nola, and supply us with information about the saint's function as patron and guardian. Paulinus insists that Felix's "mind so powerful in its holiness dwells in the highest heaven," but he also argues that his "power is felt equally throughout the earth" (Poem 12; ACW 40, p. 73). What Paulinus means is that the power of Felix, while it uses his relics, is to be identified with the martyr himself, who is Christ's "dear friend" (Poem 15; ACW 40, p. 82). There is greater power in "dead saints than in wicked men alive." Felix is certainly dead and buried. But while the "dwellers in heaven enjoy the mind of Felix, . . . we benefit from his body" (Poem 18; ACW 40, p. 117f.).

Paulinus wants to attribute the power of Felix to the saint himself and not to his relics as such. But he takes quite seriously the relics as instruments mediating that heavenly power to those on earth. The shrine at Nola is part of a universal system of power. The translation of relics has enabled those "areas of earth . . . without martyrs" to share in this system. That is why Constantine took Andrew from Greece and Timothy from Asia and placed them in his new capital. In this way "the sacred ashes" have been scattered like "life-giving seeds" throughout the world. "Wherever a drop of dew has fallen on men in the shape of a particle of bone, the tiny gift from a consecrated body, holy grace has brought forth fountains in that place, and the drops of ashes have begotten rivers of life" (Poem 19; ACW 40, p. 142f.).[29]

Whether we think of this system as electrical or as an irrigation system, it clearly stands at the heart of the ecumenical Christian community. At the same time, the universal function of the cult of the saints by no means undermines its local and personal power. Paulinus treats Felix as his own special guardian. Felix converted him, guided his career, and brought him back to Nola. "You laid the foundations of your servant's future resting-place when you implanted a commission in the silence of my heart" (Poem 21; ACW 40, p. 184f.). Moreover, the shrine holds the place of honor for Nola and its civic life (Poem 14; ACW 40, p. 80):

> Now the golden threshold is adorned with snow-white curtains, and the altars crowned with crowds of lanterns. The fragrant lamps burn with waxed wicks of paper, and are ablaze night and day, so that the night shines with the brightness of day, and the day, too, is bright with heavenly glory, gleaming the more since its light is redoubled by the countless lamps.

Felix is Nola's "saintly citizen" and "heavenly patron" (Poem 13; ACW 40, p. 76). Paulinus conjures up an Arcadian landscape. The local farmers bring not only their sick children but their animals to be healed at the shrine (Poem 18; ACW 40, p. 121). And the miracles Paulinus recounts convey the same impression. Felix finds lost oxen (Poem 18) and arranges to have a fat porker and a heifer butchered to provide meat for the poor (Poem 20). He provides exorcism for those possessed by demons (Poems

23 and 26), protects his servants from fire and water (Poem 26), and heals a punctured eye (Poem 23). Though part of a larger network of holy power, the shrine at Nola takes care of its own.

Thus far I have spoken only of the West and of bishops there who were concerned to organize the cult of the saints. But we have already encountered another dimension of this enterprise. Paulinus tells us that Constantine removed the relics of Andrew and Timothy to Constantinople; and we have learned from Sozomen that Theodosius the Great brought John the Baptist's head to the capital, while his grandson Theodosius II presided over the discovery of the relics of the Forty Martyrs of Sebaste.[30] The court of Theodosius II, according to Socrates (7.22; *NPNF* 2.2, p. 164), was "little different from a monastery." Theodosius had succeeded to the throne upon his father Arcadius's death in 408. He was only seven years old, and in 414 his older sister Pulcheria succeeded Anthemius as regent. Pulcheria was almost certainly the real power in the imperial court even after her brother took authority into his own hands. She and her sisters Arcadia and Marina took vows of virginity, and Theodosius himself willingly participated in the piety of the court.[31]

Relics figure prominently in a series of episodes revolving around the empress Theodosius, married in 421. Originally named Athenais and the daughter of an Athenian pagan philosopher, she took the name Eudocia. She and Theodosius had a daughter named Eudoxia; and in 437 a marriage took place between Eudoxia and the Western emperor Valentinian III, the son of Galla Placidia. The complicated political situation need not detain us, but at the time of the marriage one of the officials representing the West in Constantinople was a former urban prefect named Volusian. His niece, Melania the Younger, traveled from Jerusalem to Constantinople in order to convert him to Christianity. Let me tell the story by following her biography.[32] She was the granddaughter of the woman by the same name who had been the friend of Rufinus and Paulinus of Nola. Driven from the West partly by the barbarian invasions and partly by the desire to see the holy places in the East, Melania and her companions finally arrived in Jerusalem, where she established a monastery and an oratory in which she placed relics of Zechariah, Stephen, the Forty Martyrs, "and others, whose names God knows" (*LMY* 48, p. 61). Her asceticism was astonishing and included the fashioning of a small wooden chest in which she was so confined she could neither turn nor stretch out (*LMY* 32, p. 49).

It was this saintly Melania that arrived in Constantinople at the time of Eudoxia's marriage to Valentinian III. She was encouraged along the way by visits to the shrines of Leontius in Tripoli and of Euphemia in Chalcedon (*LMY* 52–53). She found her uncle seriously ill, but managed to save him body and soul. Her task accomplished, she stayed in Constantinople forty days, meeting and edifying the imperial family. She persuaded Theodosius to allow his empress Eudocia to visit the holy places in Jerusalem, and returned there herself to make everything ready. After a triumphant reception in Antioch Eudocia arrived in Jerusalem in time for the festival during which Melania deposited relics in her newly built martyrion. Eudocia sprained her ankle, but Melania's prayers while seated by the relics of the holy martyrs effected an immediate cure (LMY 59, p. 71). While in Jerusalem Eudocia acquired a number of relics, including the chains with which Herod had bound Peter. She sent these relics to her daughter in the West, and Eudoxia built the church in Rome now called St. Peter ad vincula.[33] Eudocia's visit to Jerusalem in 438 was not her last. In 443 an obscure political crisis that involved her rightly or wrongly in the suspicion of adultery resolved itself when she removed to Jerusalem, where she spent the last sixteen years of her life in piety and good works.

To return to Constantinople, it was during or shortly after the reign of Theodosius II that the relics of the first martyr Stephen were transferred to Constantinople. Sozomen's history ends with a chapter entitled "Discovery of the Relics of Zechariah the Prophet, and of Stephen the Proto-Martyr" (Soz. 9.17; NPNF 2.2, p. 427). But the chapter itself makes no mention of Stephen. The various legends that survive explain how Stephen's body was miraculously discovered and equally miraculously brought to the capital.[34] Pulcheria, Theodosius's powerful sister, prepared the way for the most important and interesting of the relics in Constantinople. When Theodosius died in 450 she married his successor Marcian and reigned with him until her own death in 453. She built three churches dedicated to the Virgin, one of which was founded at Blachernae shortly before her death. It was the church destined to receive the Virgin's robe in the reign of Marcian's successor. The robe became the palladium of Constantinople.[35]

Let me conclude this brief discussion of the organization of the cult of the saints during the fourth and fifth centuries by turning to Jerusalem. The story of Eudocia shows that the holy city was a rich source of relics. And we have already encountered Constantine's and Helena's work in constructing a basilica at the site of the Resurrection and the story of Helena's discovery of the true cross. The sources that survive enable us to see something of how the holy places in Jerusalem and the relics of the true cross gradually assumed importance during the fourth century. It seems reasonably clear that the cross itself was not originally a central feature of the cult that grew up in Jerusalem. The Constantinian basilica was oriented toward the empty tomb, and the Calvary was eccentric to the dominant orientation of the buildings. Moreover, the catechetical homilies of Cyril of Jerusalem, probably delivered in that basilica in 350, confirm the impression that the true cross, however important, had not yet gained the central place it was destined to occupy.

In three of his homilies Cyril refers to the true cross. Homily 4 is a brief exposition of the ten major tenets of the Christian faith and follows the order of the creed. Cyril refers to "this blessed Golgotha, in which we are now assembled for the sake of Him who was here crucified" as a refutation of any denial that Christ was "truly crucified for our sins." He does go on to say that "the whole world has since been filled with pieces of the wood of the Cross," but his emphasis is upon the true cross as proof of the reality of Christ's crucifixion (*NPNF* 2.7, p. 21). In speaking of Christ's ascension Cyril begins by arguing that we should not be ashamed of making constant use of the sign of the cross, since "He who was here crucified is in heaven above. . . . He who was crucified on Golgotha here, has ascended into heaven from the Mount of Olives on the East" (*NPNF* 2.7, p. 22). As he says in homily 10, the "holy wood of the Cross bears witness, seen among us to this day, and from this place now almost filling the whole world, by means of those who in faith receive portions from it" (*NPNF* 2.7, p. 63). What matters to Cyril is the witness of the true cross to Christ, and even the slivers of its wood distributed throughout the world function merely as signs that the preaching of the cross has triumphed everywhere. Cyril is our earliest witness to relics of the true cross outside Jerusalem, but he places no emphasis upon this interesting development.

Homily 13, in which Cyril explains the words "crucified and buried," confirm the conclusion I should draw from his allusions in homilies 4 and 10. The cross "is no illusion." If Cyril were to deny the reality of Christ's Passion, "here is Golgotha to confute me, near where we are now assembled; the wood of the Cross confutes me, which was afterwards distributed piecemeal from hence to all the world" (*NPNF* 2.7, p. 83). Later in the homily he returns to the same theme. "The Lord was crucified; thou hast received the testimonies. Thou seest this spot of Golgotha!" (*NPNF* 2.7, p. 88). Moreover, Golgotha is "the very centre of the earth"; and when Christ stretched out his hands on Golgotha, he did so in order to "embrace the ends of the world." We may add one final piece of evidence in the form of a letter Cyril wrote the emperor Constantius in 351 to report to him the miraculous manifestation of "a gigantic cross formed of light" that appeared above Golgotha. This good omen will encourage Constantius to march forward under the victorious banner of the cross. And Cyril contrasts the heavenly epiphany of the cross with the wood of the true cross. The new sign is "not from the earth any more, but from the heavens" (LCC 4, p. 195).

The discovery of the true cross and Cyril's references to it do not yet presuppose the cult that will surround it by the end of the fourth century. What appears incidental when Cyril is preaching in 350 takes on central importance by the time Egeria arrives as a pilgrim in Jerusalem for Holy Week and Easter of 383.[36] She describes the ceremony of the Veneration of the Cross. The bishop and the deacons carefully guard the cross during the ritual to avoid repeating a sacrilege that once took place when someone, instead of kissing the cross, took a small piece of it away in his teeth (SC 21, p. 234). Not only do we find this emphasis upon the true cross in Jerusalem by the end of the fourth century, shortly after we discover slivers from the cross venerated in the West. Paulinus of Nola wrote two letters (31 and 32) to Sulpicius Severus in 402 or 403 and in 404, sending him by the first a piece of the true cross that had been brought him from Jerusalem by Melania the Elder.

Paulinus's two letters make it abundantly clear that fifty years after Cyril's catechetical homilies the cult of the true cross is well established. The bishop of Jerusalem alone has the right to give away "these tiny fragments of sacred wood from the same cross . . . made available to win great graces of faith and blessings" (Ep. 31.6; ACW 36, p. 132). Paulinus has heard that Severus is looking for relics to place in the new basilica he is about to dedicate (Ep. 31.1; ACW 36, p. 126):

> So from your loving brethren, who long to associate with you in every good, receive this gift which is great in small compass. In this almost indivisible particle of a small sliver take up the protection of your immediate safety, and the guarantee of your eternal salvation. Let not your faith shrink because the eyes of the body behold evidence so small; let it look with the inner eye on the whole power of the cross in this tiny segment. Once you think that you behold the wood on which our Salvation, the Lord of majesty, was hanged with nails whilst the world trembled, you, too, must tremble, but you must also rejoice.

Paulinus treats the relic in a sacramental fashion. It is an outward and visible sign, and spiritual imagination alone can discern its true significance. At the same time, he takes it seriously as a relic. And he expects Severus to place it in his new basilica with the relics of martyrs or to keep it with him "available for your daily protection and healing" (Ep. 32.7f.; ACW 36, p. 142).

Let me suggest that the evidence I have briefly examined is paradigmatic of what happened more generally in the fourth and early fifth centuries. Relics and the tombs of the saints were obviously current before the Constantinian revolution, but what is new is the way in which the church orchestrates them and puts them in a central place for the life of Christian communities. It is the work of organization that is novel; and, as we should expect, there may be found a few foot-dragging reactions in the evidence that has been preserved for us. About 383 Gregory of Nyssa wrote a letter attacking what he implies is a novel emphasis on the spiritual value of making pilgrimages to the holy places in Jerusalem (*NPNF* 2.5, p. 382f.). What bothers him, of course, is not the cult of the saints as such, but rather the custom of pilgrimages and the veneration of places rather than people. A pilgrim cannot possibly escape the temptations of immorality that attend him in Jerusalem. In particular, a woman is in grave danger. "How will it be possible for one passing through such smoke to escape without smarting eyes?" Even if there were no moral danger, it is false to suppose that changing place effects "any drawing nearer unto God." What matters is the moral and spiritual condition of "the inner man." Gregory finds it hard to reconcile certain aspects of the cult of saints and relics with his commitment to Christian virtue, even though we have seen that he is fully committed to the shrines of the martyrs in his homeland.

A second hesitating reaction that pulls up short of even a token resistance to the cult of the saints betrays itself in one of Augustine's most interesting shorter works. Probably in 421 Paulinus of Nola wrote Augustine about a question that had arisen in Nola. A wealthy widow named Flora successfully requested that her son be buried near the shrine of Saint Felix, but afterward raised the question of what advantage this practice held. Paulinus shared her perplexity and asked Augustine his opinion, which he gives in the brief treatise *The Care to be Taken for the Dead*. It is as though a practice not in itself unusual suddenly forces itself into the consciousness of Paulinus and Augustine and so demands explanation. Augustine poses the question in terms of whether our care of the dead can in any way benefit them, particularly in view of the fact that Paul (2 Cor 5:10) clearly states that we shall be judged by what we have done "in the body" (*CD* 1.2; FC 27, p. 352).

Augustine's answer is no—and yes. On the one hand, our fate at the day of judgment depends on what we have done before death. And all the care we take for our dead is "more of a solace for the living than an aid for the dead" (*CD* 2; FC, p. 355). Moreover, no failure to provide decent burial can interfere with God's power to raise the dead. On the other hand, proper burial shows our respects for bodies that have been used by souls "as organs and vessels for all good works in a holy manner." And it demonstrates our belief in the resurrection (*CD* 3; FC, p. 356). Still more, burying someone near a saint is an effective, although not the only, way to commend him to the saints "as if to patrons" (*CD* 4; LF, p. 358). "Truly, the fact that one is buried in a memorial of a martyr seems to me to benefit the dead only in this respect, namely, that in commending the dead to the patronage of the martyr the desire for supplicating in his behalf is increased" (CD 18; LF, p. 383). What Augustine means is that our prayers enable the merits of the martyr to assist the dead in ways that come short of giving them salvation.[37]

In the course of his argument Augustine raises the difficult question of how the patronage of the saints is exercised in response to our prayers. He explores the analogies of people, dead and living, who have appeared to others in dreams and visions to help them. The dead have no knowledge of our affairs and take no part in them, though they may hear of them from the recently dead or from angels (CD 14; LF, p. 375f.). On the other hand, the martyrs do intervene, as St. Felix did to defend Nola from the barbarians. Nevertheless (CD 16; LF, p. 378):

> One must not think, then, that any of the dead can intervene in the affairs of the living merely because the martyrs are present for the healing or the aiding of certain ones. Rather, one should think this: The martyrs through divine power take part in the affairs of the living, but the dead of themselves have no power to intervene in the affairs of the living.

Getting this far in the argument, however, does not resolve the question fully. How the divine power works, says Augustine, "surpasses the powers of my intelligence." Perhaps God gives the martyrs this power directly. Perhaps it is simply a question of the martyrs praying they know not what for and of the angels giving specific answers to their prayers. Augustine's arguments in the treatise seem rather muddled and inconclusive. He does not deny the value of the cult of the saints, but simply finds himself hard pressed to explain it in any satisfactory theoretical way. One senses a certain uneasiness that is dissipated only by appealing to God's sovereignty.[38]

Some years before Augustine's response to Paulinus the most direct attack upon the cult of the saints we know of had taken place in Gaul. Vigilantius, originally from Spain and an acquaintance of Sulpicius Severus and Paulinus of Nola, with the approval of several Gallic bishops attacked a number of practices, most of which revolved around the new asceticism that was spreading into the West at the end of the fourth century. Vigilantius opposed vigils lasting all night, the use of Alleluia apart from Easter, sending alms to Jerusalem, the increasing emphasis upon clerical celibacy, and the excessive value that ascetics placed upon fasting. It is in the context of a suspicion of asceticism that Vigilantius also rejects the cult of the saints (AV 4; NPFN 2.6, p. 418):

What need is there for you not only to pay such honour, not to say adoration, to the thing, whatever it may be, which you carry about in a little vessel and worship? . . . Why do you kiss and adore a bit of powder wrapped up in a cloth? . . . Under the cloak of religion we see what is all but a heathen ceremony introduced into the churches: while the sun is still shining, heaps of tapers are lighted, and everywhere a paltry bit of powder, wrapped up in a costly cloth, is kissed and worshipped.[39]

We cannot know the extent of Vigilantius's influence; his was the losing cause, and we know of his views only because they were important enough to attract Jerome's attention.

Jerome had met Vigilantius in 395, when he came to Bethlehem with a letter of introduction from Paulinus of Nola. Jerome was not impressed, and it seems certain that Vigilantius shied away from Jerome because he was out of favor with John, the bishop of Jerusalem. At the end of 404 a priest in Aquitaine named Riparius wrote Jerome complaining about Vigilantius's campaign against asceticism and relics, but it was not until 406 that Jerome received the necessary writings and evidence enabling him to write one of his most vitriolic broadsides.[40] Dissolute, insane, possessed by demons, and supplying Gaul's lack of a monster, Vigilantius ("Wide-awake") should be called "Sleepyhead" and scarcely deserves refutation. Jerome's arguments, however, do appear in the course of his scathing attack. In the first place, Christians do not worship the saints and their relics; they are simply venerated. Second, Vigilantius implicitly condemns the emperors Constantius and Arcadius for transferring relics to Constantinople and the bishop of Rome for celebrating the Eucharist over the bones of Peter and Paul. A third and more positive point is that if the prayers of the martyrs were efficacious while they were alive, how much more effective will they be now that the martyrs are crowned with victory. It is absurd to suppose they are confined to their tombs as to prisons (*AV* 5–8; *NPNF* 2.6, p. 418ff.). Finally, Vigilantius's argument that the miracles wrought by the martyrs are for unbelievers and not for believers may be dismissed because it shifts the question away from the power of the relics to the issue of for whom it operates (*AV* 10; *NPNF* 2.6, p. 421).

Not only does Jerome's point of view prevail, it is also apparent that Vigilantius's voice is very much that of a minority. We find no evidence of any widespread opposition to the cult of the saints and its organization during the century and a half after Constantine. To be sure, there is enough uneasiness to make it clear that novelty attaches to the orchestration of the cult and to the central importance it acquires. But saints' tombs and relics were not themselves novel. The saints become more than examples to be followed, and emphasis comes to be placed upon them as patrons and guardians of the city, the Empire, and the individual Christian. Their relics become special places where heaven is made available on earth.

SPECIAL PEOPLE

The other major locus of the holy and the miraculous in the period I am examining is, of course, the living saints, the ascetics and monks who populated the desert of Egypt and spread throughout the Empire. In contrast to the special places and things, these special people constantly sparked controversy. What I should like to suggest is that one way of understanding the debates over Priscillian, Origenism, and Pelagius is to see the holy man as a problematic figure, particularly in the West. Theodoret's account of the monks of Syria does, of course, show us how the holy man could function in the East in the middle of the fifth century. And we must remember that monasticism had spread to the West by the turn of the fifth century through the work of men like Ambrose, Augustine, John Cassian, and Martin of Tours. There were holy people throughout the Empire, and miracles were often associated with them. Moreover, as we have already seen, the holy man tends to become more than an example of virtue for all to follow. Instead, he becomes a source of power and patronage, an exceptional person. The monastic life by the end of the fourth century becomes a special form of life; and, following Evagrius Ponticus, John Cassian treats the life of the contemplative hermit as a higher form of monasticism than the cenobitic life that is its preparation.

We have already encountered Western opposition to what must have seemed a strange Oriental version of Christianity. And even in the East we find evidence of a lively debate. In one form the question is simply that of how to tell a legitimate holy man from a charlatan. In another form it is the deeper worry as to whether there should be special holy people at all. Let me begin by supplying a brief narrative of the various controversies that in one way or another raise the question in its two forms. As we shall see, the issue at stake is not always obvious. Debates about asceticism, theology, and the moral and spiritual character of the figures involved are at the front of the stage. And perhaps many of those engaged in controversy remained unaware of the deeper, underlying issue. Nevertheless, I wish to suggest that what is at stake is that special people are hard to control and pose serious problems for the community however much they may function as its patrons.

In 380 a synod took place at Saragossa in Spain, presumably to resolve a controversy over the teaching and practice of Priscillian. Even Sulpicius

Severus admits that Priscillian "was instructed, a man of noble birth, of great riches, bold, restless, eloquent, learned through much reading, very ready at debate and discussion" (*SH* 46; *NPNF* 2.11, p. 119). According to Severus, Priscillian had revived gnosticism and practiced magical arts. He was also accused by some of being a Manichee. The synod of Saragossa did not, however, take these charges with utter seriousness; and its canons came short of a full condemnation of Priscillian, who in 381, a few months after the council, became bishop of Avila in Lusitania.[41] The second of the Priscillianist tractates found in the Würzburg codex refutes the charges made against Priscillian and his followers and enables us to see the issues that were at stake. One of these is theological, and Priscillian is attacked for taking a monarchian view of the Trinity and a docetic view of Christ. A second theme has to do with moral teaching, and the Priscillianists must refute the conflicting charges that they deny salvation to married Christians and teach immoral practices. Finally, the charges of Manicheism and of practicing magic appear.[42]

The synod of Saragossa by no means settled the Priscillian question, and Priscillian set out with several followers for Rome to appeal to Damasus. On the way they found themselves expelled from Bordeaux but befriended by some nearby aristocrats named Delphidius and Euchrotia. Euchrotia was the Christian, and she and her daughter Procula accompanied Priscillian's company to Rome. We must imagine a fairly impressive retinue, a renowned charismatic leader and a wealthy and aristocratic band of followers. Damasus, however, refused to see them, just as later Siricius refused to see Paulinus of Nola when he went to Rome.[43] Ambrose gave the same treatment to the Priscillianists in Milan. To make a long and complicated story short, the emperor Maximus, who was eliminated as a usurper by Theodosius the Great somewhat later (388), tried to settle the dispute by summoning a synod to Bordeaux. Priscillian appealed from the synod's condemnation to the civil court. This was a mistake, since Maximus felt the necessity of proving himself a zealous defender of the church. Priscillian was condemned on the capital charge of sorcery, probably in the summer of 386, and was eventually executed. Many were horrified at this outcome, partly because the state had interfered in ecclesiastical matters and partly because this was the first time anyone had been executed for heresy. As we shall see later, Martin of Tours was particularly distressed by what happened.

Many years later Jerome saw what the real issue had been in the dispute over Priscillian. In 414 or 415 a wealthy lay supporter of Pelagius named Ctesiphon wrote Jerome on behalf of Pelagius, apparently hoping at least to stir him to a friendly debate.[44] The letter backfired and provoked Jerome to a bitter attack upon Pelagius, whom Jerome lumps together with other wicked leaders such as Simon Magus, Montanus, and more recently, Priscillian and the Origenists. Jerome describes Priscillian as "an enthusiastic votary of Zoroaster and a magian before he became a bishop" (Ep. 133.4; *NPNF* 2.6, p. 275). He also says that Priscillian's "infamy makes him as bad as Manichaeus, and whose disciples profess a high esteem for you." In other words, Ctesiphon's Pelagian loyalties make him a fellow traveler with the Priscillianists. Jerome then clarifies what troubles him. Priscillian's disciples "are rash enough to claim for themselves the twofold credit of perfection and wisdom. Yet they shut themselves up alone with women" (Ep. 133.3; *NPNF* 2.6, p. 273f.). The elitism of the Priscillians is the real problem. Priscillian put himself in the place of Christ and, more to the point, in the place of the church.

Jerome himself had been at the storm center of controversies like the one over Priscillian for most of his career. Shortly after the Council of Constantinople, in 382 or 383, Jerome took up employment with Damasus in Rome. He soon became known as a champion of the new asceticism, with its roots in the Christian East. It is probably for this reason that upon Damasus's death in 385 he was disgraced and was obliged to leave Rome for Bethlehem.[45] He nonetheless kept abreast of developments in Rome, and early in 393 he received a letter from friends in Rome complaining about the views of someone named Jovinian. It was probably Pammachius, a Roman aristocrat and senator and the son-in-law of Jerome's companion Paula, who took the lead and who succeeded in having Jovinian condemned in Rome and Milan. Most of what we know of the affair derives from Jerome's treatise against Jovinian. In some respects Jerome's response is disappointing. He seizes upon Jovinian's rejection of the new asceticism without attempting to penetrate more deeply into his views.[46] Jerome is horrified that Jovinian would deny the superior value of virginity by arguing that the married, the widowed, and the virgins stand on equal footing. He also rejects Jovinian's attack on excessive fasting, failing to see that what Jovinian really means is that extreme forms of asceticism in no way confer superior status on the Christians who practice them. And Jerome says little about two of Jovinian's other theses: no one after a true and faithful baptism can fall prey to Satan; all will have equal bliss in heaven. What is not clear in Jerome's refutation is transparent in the views he attacks. Jovinian rejects the new asceticism precisely because it exalts some people over others. He refuses to think of holiness in terms of special people, and the issue that seems implicit in Priscillianism becomes explicit. For Jovinian the issue is not merely whether a holy person is legitimately holy, but rather that any notion of special people undermines the proper Christian insistence upon the holy people of God.

In the same year that Jerome refuted Jovinian (393) the zealous—or fanatical—bishop of Salamis in Cyprus, Epiphanius, took his battle against Origen and those who espoused his views to Palestine. He sent a band of monks to demand of Rufinus and Jerome that they repudiate Origen and his opinions. Both men had been attracted to Origen, and Jerome had translated some of his homilies into Latin; and both were leading monasteries in Palestine, Rufinus on the Mount of Olives and Jerome in Bethlehem. They were also friends of long standing. Rufinus refused to be forced by the mob, while Jerome agreed to condemn Origen. By September of 393 Epiphanius took his campaign further and confronted John, the bishop of Jerusalem, who refused to be moved. The lines were drawn, and the dispute raged for four years.

According to Jerome's letter *Against John of Jerusalem* the points in Origen's writings that Epiphanius insisted should be condemned were: (1) as the Son cannot see the Father, so the Holy Spirit cannot see the Son, (2) souls preexisted and later were shut up in the body as in a prison, (3) the devil and demons will repent and be saved, (4) the coats of skin given Adam and Eve after the Fall are their bodies, (5) there is no bodily resurrection, (6) paradise is not historically true, (7) the waters above and below the earth are angels and demons, (8) humanity lost the image and likeness of God after the Fall (Cf. *AJJ* 7; *NPNF* 2.6, p. 428). It is easy to see that the debate revolves around Origen's allegorical exegesis of Scripture and the doctrines that are its product. The controversy, in other words, is on the surface theological.

That more is involved becomes clear when we turn to the second act of the drama. In 397 at Easter a reconciliation of Jerome to John and to Rufinus took place, probably thanks to the good offices of Theophilus, the bishop of Alexandria and at that time a supporter of the Origenists. Two years later, however, Theophilus turned coat and condemned the Origenists. It is difficult to know exactly what to make of this. Part of what was involved was a scandal in Alexandria that centered upon the aged Isidore, a strong Origenist and a close friend and associate of Theophilus. The scandal precipitated a breach between Theophilus and Isidore. In addition, a dispute had arisen in the monasteries of Egypt between the "Origenist" monks and the "anthropomorphite" monks. This second party insisted upon a literal reading of Scripture and disavowed any use of Greek philosophy. The feud probably reflects not only the antipathy of the unlearned for the learned but also the tension between Coptic and Greek speaking monks.[47]

Clearly "Origenism" is more than a theological problem. It involves how one was to think of the monastic life. Theophilus, having condemned Origenism with words, sent his troops round the monasteries, burned books, and arrested suspicious monks. The leaders of the Origenist monks,

the Tall Brothers, fled to Jerusalem, hoping to find support from John. But
Theophilus wrote to the bishops of Palestine and Cyprus in such a way as
to make it impossible for them to befriend the Tall Brothers. Jerome
preserves the letter for us, and it reads in part (Ep. 92; *NPNF* 2.6, p. 185f.):

> We have personally visited the monasteries of Nitria and find that
> the Origenistic heresy has made great ravages among them. It is
> accompanied by a strange fanaticism: men even maim themselves
> or cut out their tongues to show how they despise the body. . . . The
> Origenists have tried to coerce me; they have even stirred up the
> heathen by denouncing the destruction of the Serapeum. . . . They
> have tried to murder me.

Theophilus's letter also includes a list of eight charges against Origen that
are similar to but not identical with the charges Jerome tells us had been
debated earlier in Jerusalem. The letter was effective and obliged the Tall
Brothers to seek help in Constantinople, where John Chrysostom gave
them refuge but not communion. The story ends with the synod of the Oak
in 403, Chrysostom's vindication, and his second banishment and death.
And within the larger story there is the sad controversy and irrevocable
breach between Jerome and Rufinus.

I am obliged to admit that it takes some reading between the lines to
draw the conclusion I wish to suggest, but I am convinced that the
Origenist controversy falls into the same pattern as the disputes we have
already mentioned and that it is also tied to the Pelagian controversy.[48] It
is not difficult to see that Origenism equates with an extreme form of
asceticism and with a theosophical and speculative understanding of spiritual contemplation. What is less clear is that elitism is an issue. The
strongest hint that this is so, however, may be found in the writings of
John Cassian. He follows his teacher, Evagrius Ponticus, who was probably
the most important Origenist monk, but who died in 399 on the eve of the
controversy. Evagrius distinguishes between the active and the contemplative life, regarding the first as a preparation for the second and superior
stage. The distinction correlates with that between the monk and the
anchorite. According to Cassian, in principle long training in the common
life of the monastery prepares the exceptional monk for the solitary life of
contemplation. The pattern clearly presupposes a small elite of contempla-
tives, who leave the many behind. This point of view was most likely
central to Origenism and the controversy must have called it into question.
If this is so, we find a simple explanation for a fundamental ambiguity in
Cassian's perspective. He does not abandon the Evagrian party platform,
but he repeatedly raises the question whether it is really practicable.[49]

Let me complete this survey of controversies by saying just a word about the last but best known of them. Pelagius was in Rome at the beginning of the fifth century and had established a reputation as a charismatic spiritual leader. He gained the support of elements of the old Roman aristocracy and of such Christian notables as Paulinus of Nola and Melania the Younger.[50] When Alaric the Visigoth moved toward Rome, which he sacked in 410, Pelagius and others fled, first, to Africa and Sicily, and then to Palestine. Augustine was at first reluctant to oppose Pelagius and to believe that he held the opinions he was accused of teaching. In 411, then, a synod in Carthage condemned one of Pelagius's disciples, Caelestius. Moreover, in 415 Pelagius was cleared of charges brought against him in Palestine. But by 416 the African bishops had condemned Pelagius as well as Caelestius. Soon afterward they persuaded Pope Innocent I to excommunicate the two; and despite a certain amount of confusion, this excommunication was confirmed by Pope Zosimus in 418. Julian of Eclanum then took up Pelagius's cause only to be condemned by the Council of Ephesus in 431. The debate continued in Gaul throughout the fifth and early sixth centuries, and no resolution was achieved until the Second Council of Orange in 529.

It is beyond my purpose to enter the details of the story, nor do I wish to discuss the obvious theological issues of the Pelagian controversy: the Fall, original sin, grace. The issue that is germane to the argument is the elitism of Pelagius's party platform.[51] Nothing makes this more apparent than Pelagius's letter to Demetrias, written from Palestine in 413. Demetrias, a young girl of the aristocratic Anician family, had fled with her mother and grandmother to North Africa after Rome was sacked in 410. Three years later, influenced by Augustine and Alypius, she broke off preparations for an illustrious marriage and decided to take a vow of virginity. Her family did not thwart her, but did seek guidance from both Jerome and Pelagius. Pelagius's letter is his response, outlining the kind of discipline that will be appropriate for Demetrias and at the same time expounding his basic platform.

Pelagius's concluding exhortation indicates the character both of his advice and of the theology on which it is based (Burns, p. 54f.):

> Apply the strength of your whole mind to achieving a full perfection of life now. Prepare a heavenly life for its heavenly reward. The virgin's holiness should shine for all like the most splendid star. . . . The way to goodness will be easier for you since your soul does not have evil customs to hold it back. . . . You need only drive the vices away, not drive them out. How much easier not to acquire them than to get rid of them once they are acquired.

The exhortation is based upon Pelagius's view that human nature has the capacity for moral perfection. But what is more interesting is that he clearly believes that only the few are willing to employ this capacity. Demetrias is clearly able to be one of the few. Her renunciation of marriage and wealth reveals that "she is not satisfied with the ordinary way, with a way of life that loses its value in being shared with many companions. She searches for something new and untried; she demands something singular and outstanding. She wants her way of life to be no less extraordinary than her conversion" (Burns, p. 40).

My discussion has moved far afield from the holy man as a locus of the miraculous, and yet the troubling issue that runs through the controversies I have described is by no means unrelated to the question of miracles. Many if not most of the holy people we have encountered were wonderworkers, but what makes them often problematic is not their working of marvels but the possibility that they will constitute an elite which can compete with the community. Of course, the danger is not inevitable. Theodoret's evidence proves that. Nevertheless, particularly in the West the nervousness we have encountered as a response to charismatic spiritual leaders springs from a suspicion that such people are subversive of the community and of the ecclesiastical structures that organized and guided it. In other words, the problem once again is not the miracles but who controls them. And control of the cult of the saints was possible in a way that did not obtain with respect to the holy man.

Let me conclude this chapter by turning to Sulpicius Severus's defense of a particular holy man, Martin of Tours. And let me argue that what we find in Severus's writings is a last ditch attempt to defend the holy man as a locus of the holy and of the miraculous by distinguishing the true holy man from the false. Severus was an aristocrat, born in Gaul about 360 and educated in Bordeaux, which was probably where he met Paulinus of Nola. Like Paulinus he withdrew from society and embraced the ascetical life, settling on one of his estates at Primuliacum in Aquitaine. A letter written by Paulinus to Severus in 397 acknowledges the receipt of the *Life of Martin*, which Severus seems to have completed shortly before Martin's death, also in 397 (Ep. 11.11; ACW 35, p. 100). Three letters of Severus, written this year and the next, and the *Dialogues*, written at some point before Severus's death around 420 or 424, complete the account given in the *Life*. Although Severus does not give us a narrative biography, the *Life* divides Martin's career into three unequal parts—his career as a soldier (1–4), his work under the patronage of Hilary of Poitiers beginning about 360 (5–8), and his activity as bishop of Tours from 372 until his death in 397 (9–27).[52]

Severus presents Martin "as an example to others," and hopes that those who read the *Life* will be "roused to the pursuit of true knowledge, and heavenly warfare, and divine virtue." Martin replaces Hector as a paradigm of the powerful warrior and Socrates as the model of the sage and philosopher (*LMar* 1; *NPNF* 2.11, p. 3f.). The book, then, is meant to be propaganda for the ascetical life to which Severus is committed. And he is pleased that, largely thanks to Paulinus, it has received universal acclaim (*Dials.* 1.23; *NPNF* 2.11, p. 35). Martin's example consists in the first instance of a true asceticism, involving fasting, watching, and prayer (*LMar* 26). His life in this respect is a martyrdom, and his ascetical sufferings give him the honor of martyrdom even though the times in which he lived prevented him from literal martyrdom (Ep. 2; *NPNF* 2.11, p. 20f.).

Gaul, whose natives are embarrassed by their tendency to gluttony and by the ways in which they fall short of the spiritual ideals of the monks in the Egyptian desert (*Dials.* 1.4, 8), can be proud of Martin. He surpasses "the recluses of the desert" (*Dials.* 1.24; *NPNF* 2.11, p. 36):

> For they, at freedom from every hindrance, with heaven only and the angels as witnesses, were clearly instructed to perform admirable deeds; he, on the other hand, in the midst of crowds and intercourse with human beings—among quarrelsome clerics, and among furious bishops, while he was harassed with almost daily scandals on all sides, nevertheless stood absolutely firm with unconquerable virtue against all these things, and performed such wonders as not even those accomplished of whom we have heard that they are, or at one time were, in the wilderness.

We begin to see that Martin is for Severus more than an example of virtue. Indeed, his asceticism enables him to work marvels. It disengages him from society and so gives him power over it. This is how we should understand Severus's stories that portray Martin as independent and even scornful of civil and ecclesiastical authorities.[53]

Martin's extreme asceticism alienates him from society, but also gives him his authority and his power. He is able to be a powerful patron for those who seek his aid both by his virtuous deeds, such as dividing his cloak with the beggar (*LMar* 3), and, more importantly, by the "signs and miracles" Christ works in him as his servant (*Dials.* 1.2; *NPNF* 2.11, p. 24). Martin holds miraculous conversations with angels and saints, has power over Satan and demons, has the gift of healing people and animals, and even raises the dead.[54] His miracles also function to overthrow paganism.[55] Severus is at pains to assure us that these miracles are "truly apostolical" (*LMar* 7; *NPNF* 2.11, p. 8). One miracle makes the point vivid. One

Easter the deacon Cato reported that his fishing had been unsuccessful, but Martin sent him back and told him to let down his line. The deacon miraculously "drew out, in a very small net, an enormous pike." Severus has his "Gallic friend" comment (*Dials.* 3.10; *NPNF* 2.11, p. 50):

> Truly that disciple of Christ, imitating the miracles performed by the Saviour, and which he, by way of example, set before the view of his saints, showed Christ also working in him, who, glorifying his own holy follower everywhere, conferred upon that one man the gifts of various graces.

Martin's exceptional powers are the gift of Christ, and they seem to take precedence over his character as an example of virtue.

What makes Severus's account different from Theodoret's descriptions of the monks of Syria is not the view he takes of the holy man as a source of miraculous power and patronage but the fact that Severus is on the defensive.[56] He takes a dim view of the bishops of the church. Martin's consecration seems almost an embarrassment, and the saint himself is supposed to have said "that such an abundance of power was by no means granted him while he was a bishop, as he remembered to have possessed before he obtained that office." For example, he raised two people from the dead before he was a bishop, but only one afterward (*Dials.* 2.4; *NPNF* 2.11, p. 39f.). Several times Severus refers to people who disbelieve the stories about Martin or who speak of "lies in that book of yours."[57] Martin became bishop of Tours over the opposition of people who said that his "person was contemptible, that he was unworthy of the episcopate, that he was a man despicable in countenance, that his clothing was mean, and his hair disgusting" (*LMar* 9; *NPNF* 2.11, p. 8). One of Martin's priests, inspired by Satan to be a Judas to his bishop, attacked him as "now entirely sunk into dotage by means of his baseless superstitions, and ridiculous fancies about visions" (*Dials.* 3.15; *NPNF* 2.11, p. 53).

Severus preserves these hostile reactions in order to refute them, but they show that Martin and his followers were problematic to many of their contemporaries. A large part of the reason for this is that Martin had sympathized with Priscillian and had dissociated himself from the bishops that condemned him.[58] Even though he communicated with these bishops after Priscillian's execution, he regretted doing so (*Dials.* 3.13; *NPNF* 2.11, p. 52):

> Therefore, from that time forward, he carefully guarded against being mixed up in communion with the party of Ithacius. But when it happened that he cured some of the possessed more slowly and

with less grace than usual, he at once confessed to us with tears that he felt a diminution of his power on account of the evil of that communion in which he had taken part for a moment, through necessity, and not with a cordial spirit. He lived sixteen years after this, but never again did he attend a synod, and kept carefully aloof from all assemblies of bishops.[59]

Part of Severus's task, then, is to defend Martin against the charge that he was a fellow traveler with Priscillian. But the issue is clearly larger than this. This explains why Severus appears bemused by the Origenist controversy (*Dials.* 1.6–7).[60]

The issue as Severus sees it is to distinguish the true holy man, who works apostolic miracles through the grace of Christ, and charlatans, who disguise themselves as Christ's servants. Severus makes the point by describing how Martin rejects a demonic vision in which Satan appears to him "surrounded by a purple light" and "clothed also in a royal robe, and with a crown of precious stones and gold encircling his head." The devil claims to be Christ, but Martin notes the absence of the marks of the Passion. The devil vanishes, leaving behind "a disgusting smell." Martin's rejection of this "false prophet" is associated with stories of other false prophets who appeared in his time (*LMar* 24; *NPNF* 2.11, p. 15f.). It is the true holy man who acts as a locus for the holy and the miraculous. Severus, obviously, does not insist upon this as an alternative to the cult of the saints, since we know from Paulinus's letters that he was concerned to house relics in the church he built at Primuliacum. Nevertheless, one story he tells of Martin suggests that he gives the holy man a place prior to the cult of the saints. With the exception of one casual reference to the shrine of Cyprian (*Dials.* 1.3), the only place Severus mentions relics is in *Life of Martin* 11. There he tells how Martin, suspicious of a shrine near his monastery, prays that the Lord will reveal who is buried there. The shade appears and confesses he was a robber. Martin, then, orders the altar removed, and "thus he delivered the people from the error of that superstition" (*NPNF* 2.11, p. 9). We cannot generalize and argue that Severus opposes the cult of the saints. But we can say that his chief concern is to defend, against strong opposition, the centrality of the wonderworking saint.

CONCLUSION

It seems to me inescapable that in the course of the fourth century two novelties appear in the Christian church, the cult of the saints and the role of the holy person as patron. In one sense, of course, neither phenomenon is altogether new. There had been martyrs' shrines before Constantine, as there had been ascetics and even monks. The novelty attaches not so much to the phenomena themselves as to the way in which they came to be organized and placed at center stage. One way of imagining this is to think of the automobile. Of course, there were automobiles before the Second World War; but the central impact of the invention has occurred only since then and in such a way that our modern culture is in many ways dominated by the automobile. Similarly, there were shrines and relics before Constantine but no cult of the saints in a full sense. And there were monks before Constantine but not a monastic movement with a central impact upon Christianity. We might also think of a later time in Christian history and of the rise of private penance in the medieval church, a development that places something with earlier roots in a place of central importance.

It is difficult to explain just why the two novelties I have sought to describe appeared in the fourth century. But it seems reasonably apparent that they are to be placed in the context of what could be called the Christianization of the Roman Empire. Christians before Constantine had thought of the Gospel as something capable of transforming culture. Now that capacity could be exercised, and there must have been many who rejoiced that the kingdom of this world could be made the kingdom of Christ. Certainly, people like Eusebius of Caesarea, Athanasius, Basil the Great, and John Chrysostom were determined to make the Roman world a sacral order. The church and the Empire were integral parts of this new commonwealth, and bishops and emperors alike went about organizing it. It is in this context that we must see the two chief loci of the miraculous in the fourth and fifth centuries. The wonders wrought by saints, dead and living, functioned to maintain the community. There seems to have been widespread agreement that the cult of the saints deserved a central place in the new commonwealth. The opposition we hear is faint and ineffective. In contrast, particularly in the West, the living saint and wonderworker proved far more problematic.[61] Granted that saints could benefit the community by their powerful gifts, it was also obvious that their very alienation from society could make them an exclusive elite and an authority competitive with that of the hierarchy.

In any case, I have sought to argue that the miraculous represents a heavenly power brought down to earth and tied to the life of the community. This explains why miracles as such are never the real question. We do find evidence that people disbelieve miracles, but it is always *these* miracles they refuse to accept. No one raises the modern question how there can be miracles at all. Instead, the issue is one of legitimacy; and what makes a miracle authentic is the way it is harnessed to the life of the community. Granted this point, it immediately becomes clear that we have encountered a gap between miracles in their social setting and the way they are treated in much of the theology of the patristic church. The contrast between the treatment given miracles in the evidence examined in the first three chapters and the conclusions reached in this and the preceding chapter supplies, then, the difficulty I wish to examine in chapter 6.

6

Divine and Human Freedom

 When Cardinal Newman published his *Apologia pro Vita Sua* in 1864, several strangers told him that his conversion at the age of fifteen, as he described it, had not been truly Evangelical. Newman agreed and admitted that "he had ever been wanting in those special Evangelical experiences which, like the grip of a hand or other prescribed signs of a secret society, are the sure tokens of a member." He had also previously confessed that he had never experienced Evangelical conversion in "its stages of conviction of sin, terror, despair, news of the free and full salvation, apprehension of Christ, sense of pardon, assurance of salvation, joy and peace, and so on to final perseverance."[1] Newman's comments raise the interesting and perplexing question of the relationship between religious experience and conventional stereotypes in which it comes to be described in a given age. Are the usual themes that attach to accounts of Evangelical conversions accurate descriptions of a common experience? Or are the experiences the product of expectations set up by widely accepted conventions?

I certainly do not pretend to be able to answer these questions, but they are questions that are as applicable to the fourth century as to Evangelicalism in the nineteenth century. What I mean is that the dominant Christian Platonism of the fourth century had generated a set of themes that gave a normative definition to conversion and to the Christian life. The conventions are most easily discerned in the writings of Augustine, not least because he is uncomfortable with them and finds his own experience in tension with the expectation of his age. I refer specifically to the passage that opens *The Confessions*. After citing two verses from Psalms (145:3 and 147:5), Augustine continues (*Conf.* 1.1; PC, p. 21):

> Man is one of your creatures, Lord, and his instinct is to praise you. He bears about him the mark of death, the sign of his own sin, to remind him that you *thwart the proud* (1 Pet 5:5). But still, since he is a part of your creation, he wishes to praise you. The thought of you stirs him so deeply that he cannot be content unless he praises you, because you made us for yourself and our hearts find no peace until they rest in you.

The human soul, made in the image of God, naturally yearns for God. Death and sin tend to stifle this yearning. Nevertheless, with God's help the Christian can embark upon a process of moral and spiritual purification that will ultimately lead to the perfect peace found in the satisfaction of his yearning in the full contemplation of God.

In this chapter I wish to attempt to describe the basic pattern more fully and to argue that Augustine does not so much reject it as transform it into something new. My argument will be that the pattern of the soul's purification in order to achieve its destiny in the vision of God represents a fundamental structure that is elaborated in complex ways, that is brought into some relationship with the resurrection of the body and the corporate character of the Christian life, and that represents a Christianization of what I have called the late antique quest for virtue. I shall suggest that Gregory of Nyssa, Ambrose, John Chrysostom, and Basil the Great supply us with representative ways in which the basic pattern is understood and elaborated. And I shall conclude that human freedom, assisted by the persuasion of God's love, occupies center stage. In the final section of the chapter I will turn to Augustine's transformation of the pattern and to his insistence that God's sovereign grace alone bestows freedom. This transformation tends to purge Christianity of the basic assumptions of the late antique quest for virtue, but it also tends to cohere more readily with the community piety described in chapter 5.

GREGORY OF NYSSA AND CHRISTIAN VIRTUE

It was probably shortly after 390 and toward the end of his life that Gregory wrote the *De instituto Christiano*. He tells us that he is writing "some small seeds of instruction, selecting them from the writings previously given me by the Spirit, but also making use in many passages of the very words of the Scriptures as proof of what I say and for the clarification of my own view about it" (*DIC* 42, 17ff.)[2] We can understand the treatise as Gregory's final legacy to monasticism, but also as a summary of his mature understanding of Christian destiny in general. The treatise is, to be sure, addressed to what appears to be a large community of monks; and its second half directly addresses how the monks should live "their common life, how the superiors should direct the philosophical chorus, and what exercises those who want to climb the peak of highest virtue should undertake in order to prepare their souls to become worthy receptacles of the Holy Ghost." Nevertheless, I should argue that Gregory supposes that all are capable of ascending the "peak of highest virtue" and that the "goal" and "path" he speaks of in this first part of the treatise is, in principle, Christian rather than specifically monastic (*DIC* 41, 10ff.).[3] At any rate, I wish to use the *De instituto Christiano* as the basis of my discussion, appealing occasionally to other of Gregory's writings.

Gregory begins his treatise by asserting that human beings have the capacity of seeing their own soul and in its nature "God's love towards us and the will of his creative power." He explains what he means by speaking of "the impulse of desire for what is fine and best, united with human essence and nature, and the impassible and blessed love for that spiritual and blessed image of which humanity is the copy, united with human nature." In other words, a clear vision of the soul enables us to discern our basic yearning for God. Such a vision, however, depends upon freeing ourselves from "bodily understanding" and from "the bondage of the passions" (*DIC* 40, 1ff.).[4] The contemplative "goal" presupposes the "path" of achieving moral virtue by overcoming the passions.

Gregory usually speaks of the struggle with the passions by employing what were originally Stoic conventions, but which by his time had become a part not only of much Platonist thought but also an integral dimension of Christian Platonism. The soul or mind is the governing principle of the body; and the passions of the body or the lower part of the soul, when not controlled by the soul, result in the "disease" of vice. The passions "are not the soul, but only like warts growing out of the soul's thinking part" (*OSR*; *NPNF* 2.5, p. 440). The task of the soul is to heal the person by removing these "warts." Purging the passions, however, by no means implies that we must eliminate our emotions. Rather, "according to the use which our free will puts them to, these emotions of the soul become the instruments of virtue or of vice" (*OSR*; *NPNF* 2.5, p. 442). The soul must transform lust to love and anger to courage. And it does so through its power of free choice. "Therefore, when he commands us to imitate our heavenly Father (Mt 5:48), he commands us to cleanse ourselves of earthly passions, the purging of which is effected not by changing place but by free choice alone" (*DPC*; 140, 2ff.).

It is the more positive side of this process of actualizing the soul's governing power that engages Gregory's interest in *De instituto Christiano*. The laws that forbid yoking an ox and an ass, mixing wool and linen, and sowing a field with two kinds of seed (Deut 22:10; Lev 19:19) are "enigmas" that mean that "vice and virtue must not be planted together in the same soul" (*DIC*; 56, 14ff). The single-mindedness of the good soldier or the good farmer is analogous to the Christian's single-minded pursuit of virtue. The pursuit requires hard labor and discipline, and the virtues are inseparably interlocked. Simplicity, obedience, faith, hope, righteousness, ministry, humility, gentleness, meekness, joy, love, and prayer are linked so as to be different aspects of "the summit of our longing" (*DIC*; 77, 15ff.). Only by rejecting sin absolutely and by achieving virtue can the person "who yearns to become Christ's bride become like Christ's beauty through virtue as far as he is able" (*DIC*; 50, 2ff.). Virginity stands for the perfection demanded. "For the aim of the soul that honors virginity is nearness to God and becoming the bride of Christ" (*DIC*; 49, 18ff.).[5]

If the "path" to virtue tends to be described by showing how the soul's free choice can purge the Christian of vice and lead him to the summit of virtue, the "goal" of virtue tends to be thought of as a "likeness to God so far as possible." Stoicizing conventions yield to a Platonizing understanding of human destiny, and Gregory alludes to Plato's definition of human destiny in *Theaetetus* 176 B.[6] At the same time, Gregory's description of the goal makes full appeal to Scripture. St. Paul's description of love in 1 Corinthians 13 leads him to say that without love, even if a person has made great progress, there can be no assurance he will not fall. Only love can supply a firm establishment in virtue. Moreover, this perfect attainment of virtue is the "new creation" of which Paul speaks (Gal 6:15; 2 Cor 5:17). Paul (*DIC*; 61, 17ff.):

> calls the new creation the indwelling of the Holy Spirit in a pure and blameless soul, when it is delivered from all vice and wickedness and shame. For when the soul hates sinning, makes itself God's own as far as it can by its virtuous conduct, and when it is transformed in its life and receives into itself the grace of the Spirit, then it becomes entirely new and is recreated.

The phrase "makes itself God's own as far as it can" alludes, I think, to the Platonic definition from the *Theaetetus*. Gregory has Christianized the definition by making it clear that the soul's perfected relationship to God is moral and spiritual rather than one implying any identity of nature.

Nothing establishes this point more securely than the fact that Gregory consistently identifies our "likeness to God" with his doctrine of the image of God. The whole of his treatise *On the Making of Man* treats the image as an ideal located in God's creative purpose for humanity and in the realization of that purpose in the age to come. What we are in principle by creation we shall become in fact in the new order of things. Moreover, in the *De professione Christiana* Gregory defines "Christianity" as "the imitation of the divine nature," proving the definition by an appeal to Genesis 1:27 (*DPC*; 136, 7ff.). Imitations, of course, can be false. And Gregory uses the story of a trained monkey in Alexandria that successfully imitates a human dancer and actor until someone throws it some food and it reverts to simian behavior. In contrast, our imitation of God is a true embracing of divine moral virtues (*DPC*; 131, 11ff. and 138, 14ff.). More particularly, Christians become like God by becoming like Christ. Some of Christ's characteristics exceed our nature, and these we "venerate and worship." But others we can comprehend, and these "we imitate" (*DP*; 178, 9ff.). When Paul refers to Christ as "the image of the invisible God" (Col 1:15), he alludes to the Incarnation by which the divine Christ "through love of humanity became the image of the invisible God" (*DP*; 195, 1f.). Just as artists seek to imitate a model, so we must paint our lives so that they resemble the image in the human Christ: "Each one of us is the painter of his own life; free choice is the artist of this skill; and the colors for fashioning the image are the virtues" (*DP*; 196, 2ff.). By our freedom we imitate the human Christ and so become God's image and "like God as far as possible."[7]

Free choice is central to Gregory's account of the path by which we move toward our destiny in the image of God, and his emphasis raises the question of his treatment of grace. We need to remember that for Gregory there can be no real contrast between grace and nature, and so human freedom is not only a natural capacity but also a gift of God's grace. Still more, he argues that baptism supplies a grace that initiates the Christian life. In *De instituto Christiano* Gregory employs the parable of the talents (Luke 19:13ff.) to make the point. Christ gives us "talents" at our baptism, but it is up to us to make proper use of what we have received (*DIC*; 44, 27ff.):

> for the soul that has been reborn by God's power must be brought up to the measure of its spiritual stature in the Spirit, watered abundantly both by the sweat of virtue and by what grace supplies.

Gregory goes on to describe this process as growth into the body of Christ (Eph 4:13ff.) and as a transformation "by the renewal of your mind" (Rom 12:2). This formation to which Gregory refers, whether it is thought of as education or as the natural development of a human being, reflects Greek notions of *paideia*.[8] But it also must be understood in the light of the common patristic understanding of the relation of providence and freedom, an understanding that owes a great debt to Greek philosophical thought and that had been most clearly formulated by Origen.

Providence is a general and universal divine operation, but it has differing effects depending upon how it is freely received. We cannot blame the sun for causing us to fall into a ditch. Instead, it is "the failure to participate in the light that causes the person who does not see to fall into the ditch" (*LMo* 76; CWS, p. 71). Consequently, it is a person's wrong use of providence that causes the divine operation to have a punitive effect: "Each man makes his own plagues when through his own free will he inclines toward these painful experiences" (*LMo* 86; CWS, p. 74). By our misuse of God's love we bring punishment upon ourselves, but the punishment is not merely retributive. It is always a *paideusis*, a word that in Greek means both "punishment" and "education." At another level, then, God always teaches us to learn by our mistakes. And here, grace or providence acts as a response to our actions. More positively, when we make some progress in virtue, God's providence also comes to our assistance. Grace, in other words, cooperates with freedom and constantly seeks to persuade us toward perfection.

At one point in the *De instituto Christiano* Gregory summarizes the basic pattern of his thought (*DIC*; 85, 9ff.):

> . . . those who are Christ's and who do the truth through faith and toiling for virtue, receive goods beyond their nature from the grace of the Spirit. They bear fruit with a joy that cannot be spoken and accomplish without toil guileless and changeless love, faith that cannot be moved, peace that cannot fail, true goodness, and everything else through which the soul by becoming better than itself and stronger than the wickedness of the Enemy makes itself a pure dwelling place for the worshipful and Holy Spirit. Through him the soul receives the deathless peace of Christ, is joined by peace to him, and cleaves to the Lord.

The path of the Christian life is a process of growth that involves the simultaneous activity of human freedom and divine providence. Three further implications may be found. First, the process takes place in stages, which Gregory can describe in a number of different ways.[9] But the union with Christ he describes represents his reworking of Origen's contemplative ideal. He differs from Origen in thinking that the perfection of this ideal takes us beyond ourselves. Furthermore, the union with Christ, mystical because it is the transcending as well as the fulfilling of our nature,

involves Gregory's notion of *epektasy* or perpetual progress in the good.
The mystical union, which takes the soul beyond itself, is really a "stable
motion" (*LMo* 243; CWS, p. 117) and represents the perfection of the soul's
free movement toward the good. Second, the fact that Gregory speaks in
the plural in the passage I have just cited implies his concern for the
corporate character of human nature and of the spiritual life. The common life of the monastery points toward the common destiny in which all
people become members of Christ's body. Finally, Gregory's use of the
adjective "deathless" implies that he is reworking Origen's understanding
of the spiritual life not only by giving it a corporate dimension and by
relating it more firmly to the sacraments of the church but also by seeking
to bring it into harmony with the doctrine of the resurrection. Elsewhere,
Gregory treats the physical dimension of Redemption as the transfiguration of the entire created order.

   Needless to say, much more should be said about the ways in which
Gregory Christianizes the late antique quest for virtue. By insisting that the
divine help we receive be understood in terms of Christian and Scriptural
themes, by thinking of the quest and of human nature in corporate terms,
and by placing the quest in some relation to the physical dimension of
Redemption, he significantly transforms the Greek conventions he uses. At
the same time, the sea changes thus effected cannot obscure the fact that
he is committed to the central importance of human freedom as a capacity for God. God created us free and gave us an instinctive yearning for
him. He never ceases his attempts to persuade us to cultivate that capacity;
but since his providence is never coercive, we have the duty and the
privilege of cultivating our freedom so that our restless hearts may find
rest in him.

AMBROSE AND CHRISTIAN VIRTUE

Ambrose reflects the same basic understanding of the Christian life that
may be found in Gregory's writings. I do not mean to ignore the important
respects in which they differ from one another. We do not find the ideas of
the *epektasy* or of the corporate character of human nature in Ambrose;
nor is it clear he has sought to think through the relation of human moral
and spiritual progress to human destiny in the resurrection of the body.
Moreover, Ambrose, while he shares with Gregory a dependence upon
Origen's thought, draws more directly upon Plotinus's thought. It would
be possible to examine these difference in more detail, but my purpose is
not to supply a detailed analysis either of Gregory or of Ambrose, but
simply to show that both writers reflect the fundamental convention ex-

pressed in Augustine's contention that God made us for himself and "our hearts find no peace until they rest in you."

The opening sentences of Ambrose's treatise on *Jacob and the Happy Life* make the point I wish to underline (*J* 1.1.1; FC 65, p. 119):

> Necessary for the training of all men is good discourse, full of prudence, while the mind given to reason excels in virtue and restrains its passions, for virtue is teachable. . . . Thus reason, given fuller consideration, may persuade us to the command laid down by good discourse. For man is not bound to obedience out of servile necessity, but by free will we either incline to virtue or lean to vice.

The human mind is meant to be the governing principle, and it is by ruling the passions and the body that the mind establishes virtue for the individual. In order to accomplish this task the mind must freely elect to act upon its knowledge of what is right. In doing this the mind or soul shows its superiority over bodily pleasures and human weakness; and it finds its reward in the happiness of sharing "in the fellowship of many virtues, of all, if possible" (*J* 1.7.31; FC 65, p. 140). It is freedom that translates a knowledge of the good into the virtuous life.

Ambrose sets this pattern in the context of his understanding of Creation and the Fall: "When God created man and implanted in him moral laws and feelings, at that time He established the royal rule of the mind over man's emotions" (*J* 1.1.4; FC 65, p. 121). The Fall, however, corrupted human nature. "Don't you know that the guilt of Adam and Eve sold you into servitude? Don't you know that Christ did not buy you, but bought you back?" (*J* 1.3.12; FC 65, p. 127f.). Ambrose means that the Fall made all humanity slaves of Satan, subject to sin and death. He takes this servitude with utter seriousness, even though he does not treat it in such absolute terms as the later Augustine did. His emphasis is not so much on the human predicament as on the grace of Christ that "bought you back." Christ, that is, has not purchased us as slaves; rather, he has redeemed us from Satan and made us free. The grace of baptism frees the mind to exercise its governing capacity, but "we must work to keep the grace of God" (*J* 1.5.17; FC 65, p. 131).

Ambrose's emphasis upon freedom has affinities with Stoicism not only because he treats the mind as the governing principle but also because he insists that outward evils are matters of indifference. Indeed, the major theme of the *Jacob* is to show how Jacob's story proves that the happy life transcends the sufferings and failures of human life. "Further, the happy life is not diminished by such adversities as worldly troubles or sufferings of body but is confirmed by them" (*J* 1.6.23; FC 65, p. 134). The ideal

Ambrose wishes to describe is that of the free human being (J 2.3.12; FC 65, p. 153):

> The man who is subject to vices has sold himself to many masters, so that he is scarcely permitted to go out of servitude. But take the man who is the master over his own will, judge over his counsels, agent of his judgment, the man who restrains the longing of his bodily passions and does well what he does. . . . Such a man is assuredly a free man. For the man who does all things wisely and in complete accord with his will is the only free man. It is not accidental status that makes the slave, but shameful and foolish conduct.

This moral ideal, of course, is made possible by the freeing grace of baptism. But it is also attained with the constant help of God's grace which assists the individual's free efforts. "Can He exile from His paternal love and favor those whom He took up by way of adoption?" (J 1.6.26; FC 65, p. 136).

The path of the Christian life that Ambrose describes is not unlike Gregory's understanding of it, and even in the *Jacob* Ambrose sees the path as leading to the serenity that alone can produce vision. The story of how Jacob wrestled with God and saw him face to face (Gen. 32:22ff.) suggests this to Ambrose. That Jacob "lodged that night in the camp" (Gen 32:21) betokens a sleep standing for the fact that "perfect virtue possesses tranquillity and a calm steadfastness" (J 2.6.28; FC 65, p. 162). This is what prepares him for his wrestling with God (J 2.7.30; FC 65, p. 163f.):

> For whoever forsakes worldly things comes nearer to the image and likeness of God. What is it to wrestle with God, other than to enter upon the struggle for virtue, to contend with one who is stronger and to become a better imitator of God than the others are? Because Jacob's faith and devotion were unconquerable, the Lord revealed His hidden mysteries to him by touching the side of his thigh.

The mysteries are those of Christ's virgin birth, his cross, and the Jews' rejection of him. In the blindness of his old age Jacob's vision becomes still clearer. He tells the mysteries to his sons (Gen 49); and "undaunted by age . . . he could, when he wished, go out from this hovel of the body and enter into the realms of paradise that are above with vigor of mind, rejoicing in spirit as he gave the last instructions for his burial" (J 2.9.38; FC 65, p. 170).

The hint that we find in the *Jacob* of the contemplative goal of the

Christian life is made explicit and elaborated in Ambrose's *Isaac, or the Soul.* The two treatises are, however, quite coherent with one another. Ambrose continues to define the soul or mind as the governing principle of the body. And he recognizes that despite the excellence of its nature the soul "generally becomes subject to corruption through its irrationality [the lower part of the soul], so that it inclines to bodily pleasures and to willfulness, while it does not keep to moderation; or else it is deceived by the imagination, turns to matter, and is glued to the body." The flight of the soul, then, "is not to depart from the earth but to remain on earth, to hold to justice and temperance, to renounce the vices in material goods, not their use" (*I* 2.5; FC 65, p. 14). The establishment of virtue so frees the soul from bodily things that it can "rise" to the contemplation of God. Ambrose can describe this movement in what appears to be dualistic language (*I* 4.11; FC 65, p. 19):

> And so the good soul scorns visible and material things and does not linger over them or delay or tarry in despising them. Rather, she rises to things eternal and immaterial and filled with wonders, for she rises with pure thought from pious mind.

Ambrose certainly does not mean to oppose the soul to the body; it is simply that once the soul has established its governance of the body, it is prepared to move toward the contemplation of God.

The movement Ambrose describes can involve stages. Like Origen and Gregory of Nyssa he thinks of Solomon's three books as symbols of three successive dimensions of the Christian life. The moral instruction of Proverbs prepares the Christian for the natural teaching of Ecclesiastes, by which we learn to despise the world as vanity. Finally, the Song of Songs stands for the mystical dimension of the Christian life (*I* 4.23). The three senses can also appear in the Song of Songs itself (*I* 4.27), even though the emphasis of the last of Solomon's books is upon the mystical union between Christ and the soul. When the bride speaks of having "put off my garment" (Song 5:3), "she is not aware of the remnants of the flesh; now, like a spirit, she has divested herself of the connection with the body." She has removed the "garments of skins" with which God clothed Adam and Eve after the Fall (Gen 3:21). Once she has removed this "robe of corruption, the robe of the passions," she is no longer able to look back, but is ready to receive the love of the Word of God (*I* 6.52; FC 65, p. 42).

The *Isaac* is really an allegory based upon the Song of Songs, and Ambrose depends to a great degree upon the earlier work of Origen and Hippolytus. At an allegorical level the story of Isaac in Genesis corresponds to the meaning of the Song of Songs, and this common meaning has to do with the union of Christ with the church or with the soul. Ambrose's emphasis, of course, is upon the soul; and he thinks of the perfection of the soul as the spiritual and contemplative union of the Christian with Christ. The marriage of the Song of Songs is "a union of love" between the soul and Christ (*I* 8.73; FC 65, p. 58). This union depends in part upon the rebirth of those "in whom the image of Christ is formed"; and Ambrose almost certainly means the grace of baptism. But it also depends upon the soul's own efforts. The "seal" on the heart and the arm (Song 8:6) is Christ's double seal—"on the forehead that we may always confess Him, in the heart that we may always love Him, and a sign on the arm, that we may always do His work" (*I* 8.74; FC 65, p. 59).

The end of the *Isaac* (8.76–79) is really a long appeal to the soul to exercise its freedom so that it may fulfill its destiny by taking wing to the contemplative union of love with Christ. Ambrose's peroration is thick with citations from Scripture and with allusions to Plato's *Symposium* and *Phaedrus*. It can also be treated as a meditation upon Plotinus, *Enneads* 1.6.[10] Ambrose exhorts us to flee to the heavenly Jerusalem, "our real, true fatherland," not with our feet or with ships, chariots, or horses. Rather (*I* 8.79; FC 65, p. 64):

> . . . let us flee with the spirit and the eyes and feet that are within. Let us accustom our eyes to see what is bright and clear, to look upon the face of continence and moderation, and upon all the virtues. . . . And let each one look upon himself and his own conscience; let him cleanse that inner eye, so that it may contain no dirt. For what is seen ought not to be at variance with him who sees, because God has wished that we be conformed to the image of His Son. (Rom 8:29)

The soul, then, attains its destiny and perfect virtue by a process of formation or education. And the term of this process is conformity to the image of Christ.

The richness and diversity of the themes by which Gregory and Ambrose expound their visions of Christian virtue and the ways in which they differ from one another should not obscure the fact that both of them reflect a commonplace structure that is central to the patristic understanding of the Christian life. We have, indeed, encountered aspects of this structure in the earlier chapters of this book. Baptism is what frees the Christian to embark upon the quest for virtue, the destiny intended for humanity by God at Creation. The quest is an education, a *paideia*, that involves the persuasive teaching of God's providence and the free learning of human beings.[11] Central to the education is the assertion of the mind or soul's created capacity to govern the body and its passions. The warfare with Satan stands for this aspect of the matter.[12] The contemplation and knowledge of the good empowers the mind to govern the passions and so secure moral virtue. But contemplation also represents the product of moral virtue.[13] The acquisition of virtue begins to still our restless hearts, and they find perfect peace by being united in love with Christ. The pattern of the soul's purification and assimilation to Christ is, of course, thought to represent a proper reading of Scripture. At the same time, it appeals in various ways to the Greek philosophical tradition and particularly to Plato's understanding of love in the *Symposium* and the *Phaedrus* and to his definition of human destiny as "likeness to God as far as possible." And this philosophical tradition is integrated with the Christian theme of the image of God. Our creation in the image of God finds completion only in the perfection of the Christian life; and Redemption is the completion of Creation.

As a Christianized version of the late antique quest for virtue, the pattern I have been examining puts human freedom at center stage.[14] I should wish to add that Gregory and Ambrose represent the fourth-century flowering of a tradition that springs from the work of the Christian Platonists of Alexandria, particularly Origen. In a real sense, people like Gregory and Ambrose preserved Origen for the church. And by doing so they preserved his appeal to Christian freedom. For Origen the insistence upon freedom needs to be understood against the background of his times. He rejected the determinism of the gnostics and the astrologers; and he insisted that, despite appearances, God has given us the gift of freedom, a gift we can with his help use rightly in order to attain our destiny. In repeating Origen's gospel of freedom, Gregory and Ambrose were also repeating some of the implications of that gospel. Let me turn, then, to the views of God and of nature implied by the Origenizing understanding of freedom. And let me do so by examining Chrysostom's small treatise *On Providence* and Basil the Great's *Homilies on the Six Days of Creation*. Both these writers share the basic vision of freedom found in Gregory's and Ambrose's works.

CHRYSOSTOM'S ON PROVIDENCE

The most moving aspect of Chrysostom's treatise derives from the circumstances under which it was written. He wrote the work, almost as an extended letter, to his supporters in order to explain how his own exile should not tempt people to doubt God's providence. The work was written early in 407 from Cucusus, and Chrysostom died in exile in September of the same year. The treatise is medicine designed to cure erroneous opinions about God. And it is a treatment that cannot be applied "by constraint or force or when someone is unwilling to accept it and does not accept divine teachings" (OP 1.5; SC 79, p. 58). Chrysostom's insistence that his ideas can persuade but not coerce is in absolute congruence with his equal insistence that God always uses persuasion and never force. Obviously, the point marks a necessary correlation with a commitment to the importance of human freedom. Chrysostom's God suits the view of Christian virtue he shares with Gregory and Ambrose.

It is God's goodness that Chrysostom gives pride of place. And the doctrine of Creation is what chiefly establishes the primacy of this aspect of God's nature. As Creator, God is "the beginning and cause and fount of all good things" (OP 2.9; SC 79; p. 64). Moreover, we must go further and insist that all created things are good, "not only light but also darkness, not only fruits but also thorns." Even poisonous serpents, sea monsters, storms, and scorpions are good (OP 4.1–5; SC 79, p. 82f.). Chrysostom reflects Plato's opinion in the Timaeus that God created the world because he has no envy and his goodness prompts him to give life. But his primary appeal is to Genesis 1:31. ("And God saw everything that he had made, and behold, it was very good.") This "declaration" of the Creator is clearer proof of the goodness of Creation than "the works themselves" (OP 4.7; SC 79, p. 86). Chrysostom's judgment already suggests one way of handling the problem of evil. The fact that certain aspects of the created order seem to us evil has to do with our inadequate perception rather than with what they are in God's purpose.

The goodness of the Creator, moreover, is chiefly apparent in his dealings with humanity. What should provoke our amazement is not the fact or the way God created us but rather his absolute lack of any need of us. Yet to say that God does not need us by no means implies that he is sovereign and remote from us. Instead, Chrysostom uses the observation to show that God created us simply because of his love for humanity (OP 7.39; SC 79, p. 130). At one point he summarizes his argument by saying (OP 6.15; SC 79, p. 102):

> And so, when he [God] says that he loves like a father and more than a father (Ps 103:13; Mt 7:9ff.), like a mother and more than a mother (Isa 49:14f), like a young bridegroom and more than a young bridegroom (Isa 62:5), and that his love is as great as the distance between heaven and earth and more than that or as far as the east is from the west and more than that (Ps 103:11f.), he does not stop the images there. Instead, he goes on to demonstrate his love by using a much more lowly example.[15]

The example, says Chrysostom, is the story of how God teaches Jonah that mercy is greater than justice by killing the plant that gave Jonah shade (Jonah 4). God's merciful love of humanity finds expression in the fact that he created the entire universe for us (*OP* 7.4ff). "All this, my friend, is for you. For you are the arts; for you, human pursuits and cities and towns. Sleep is for you; death is for you; life is for you" (*OP* 7.33; SC 79, p. 126).

Chrysostom deliberately includes death in his list, since he wishes to argue that dispensations of God's providence that seem evil to us are really a part of his beneficent education of us. Our mortality teaches us humility; and death is "a fine teacher of philosophy, educating our understanding, bridling the passions of the soul, stilling the waves, and creating calm" (*OP* 7.37; SC 79, p. 128). God, of course, is the true teacher. And he has given us our immediate teacher "the implanted [moral] law" to act as a pilot does for a ship or a bridle for a horse (*OP* 8.1; SC 79, p. 132). Thus, both directly and indirectly God in his great love for us teaches and trains us for perfection. Even the punishments he sends are meant to prepare us for that kingdom whose good things cannot be described (*OP* 8.1–8; SC 79, p. 132ff.). The evils we suffer educate us. "The present life is a wrestling-school, a gymnasium, an arena, a forge, a dyeing vat of virtue" (*OP* 21.1; SC 79, p. 252).

Chrysostom can relate God's work as Creator and teacher to his sovereign power. Abraham's willingness to sacrifice Isaac (Gen 22) springs from his having "taken refuge in the power of the one who had promised, a power that is ineffable, highly skilfull and resourceful, shining through what opposes it, higher than the laws of nature, mightier than all things, brooking no opposition" (*OP* 10.12; SC 79, p. 158). It would be a mistake, however, to understand this passage as though Chrysostom were treating God's providence as in any way coercive. The "power" of God attaches not so much to his sovereignty in the present as to his ability to work his purposes out in the long run. The reason Abraham trusts in God is because he is confident that God will make good his promise in the end. God's promises find no immediate fulfillment. The righteous of the Old Testament know this, and that is why they remain steadfast in affliction. "They bore all things nobly, because they had as the greatest proof of what was to be, the power of the one who promised" (*OP* 11.1; SC 79, p. 178).

The power of God, then, belongs primarily to his work in creating the world and in completing his creative purpose in the age to come. He does not use his power to coerce us toward that consummation. Instead, God's providence is chiefly expressed in his persuasive love. And the cross of Christ is the chief sign of that love (*OP* 17.4; SC 79, p. 226):

> When he [John] wishes to describe his love, what does he speak of?
> Signs? wonders? miracles? Not at all. Rather, he brings forward the
> cross and says: "God so loved the world that he gave his only Son,
> that whoever believes in him should not perish but have eternal
> life." (John 3:16)

Chrysostom, of course, does not deny God's sovereignty; but his emphasis
is upon God's persuasive love. It is this that expresses God's providence,
and he thinks of providence in relation to the entire process that leads
from Creation to its redemptive consummation in the age to come. Moreover, God as the great teacher and physician guides the process without in
any way coercing it. His teaching takes account of our freedom to learn,
and his healing asks for the cooperation of the patient.

The chief problem of *On Providence* is to argue for this view of human
life in the face of circumstances that appear to contradict God's educative
love. Implicitly, Chrysostom's own fate appears to contradict his view of
God's providence. The resolution of the apparent contradiction has already
been suggested by what we have seen of Chrysostom's argument. The first
point has to do with the adjective "apparent." Chrysostom locates the
problem not in the nature or the activity of God, but in the limitations
imposed upon human knowledge of God. Two passages from Scripture are
especially important to Chrysostom in arguing this. Paul speaks of our
present knowledge as that "in a mirror and in an enigma"; and he contrasts his knowledge with the "face to face" knowledge of the age to come
(1 Cor 13:12). It is our present childlike vision that prevents us from
perceiving God's love (*OP* 2.14f.; SC 79, p. 68).[16] In another place (Rom 9–
11) Paul argues that despite appearances God's dealings with Jews and
Gentiles shows his mercy and requires us to exclaim: "O the depth of the
riches and wisdom and knowledge of God! How unsearchable are his
judgments and how inscrutable his ways!" (Rom 11:33; *OP* 2.1–11; SC 79,
p. 60 ff.).[17]

Chrysostom uses his basic understanding of Romans 9–11 as one of
Paul's arguments that God's mercy is inscrutable to interpret Paul's ques-
tion in Romans 9:20: "But who are you, a man, to answer back to God?
Will what is molded say to its molder, 'Why have you made me thus?' "
One might expect the verse to argue for God's absolute sovereignty. But
Chrysostom says (*OP* 2.16; SC 79, p. 70):

> Do you see how much obedience he demands, how much silence?
> For he does not say this to take away our free will. God forbid!
> Rather, he says it to show that the person who wants to ask these
> questions must be as silent as the nature of clay, which follows

where the artist leads, without contradicting, without busying itself with idle questions.

For Chrysostom the Pauline text exhorts us to remember that we cannot
always understand God's love. Far from teaching that we have no freedom
in the face of God's sovereignty, it tells us to use our freedom faithfully,
trusting in God without trying to fathom his purposes.

The inscrutability of God's providence leads Chrysostom to the second
theme that vindicates the view of God for which he has argued. Abraham's
example makes the point. From a human point of view he could not
understand how God could give him a son; and, still more, he could not
see justice in God's command that he sacrifice the son so marvelously
given him. But Abraham does not ask idle questions. Instead, he recognizes the limitations of his own understanding and places his confidence
in the future. Somehow God will fulfill his promises (*OP* 10.1–18; SC 79, p.
150ff.). Similarly, Joseph and David "wait for the end" (*OP* 10.40, 43; SC
79; p. 174f.). The moral is clear (*OP* 10.44; SC 79, p. 176):

> You also, then, my beloved, wait for the end. It will inevitably come
> to pass either here or in the age to come. Always give way to the
> incomprehensibility of God's providence, and do not say: "How will
> such great evils find a remedy?" Do not busy yourself in asking how
> God works his marvelous acts.

It is the union of the two themes that solves the problem Chrysostom has
posed. We cannot now fully understand God's loving providence, but we
can trust in the divine love that guides creation from beginning to end.

The schema Chrysostom elaborates leaves room for human freedom
and for the human quest for virtue. God's sovereignty attaches primarily to
the beginning and end of the process, and his activity between these two
points is persuasive and not coercive. In the time between Creation and the
age to come divine providence and human freedom are simultaneously at
work. The metaphor of the sailing ship, as we saw earlier, requires the
cooperation of the wind and the hoisting of the sails.[18] Like the wind,
God's providence is a general and universal activity. Its effect depends
upon how our freedom hoists its sails to meet providence.[19] Chrysostom
has found a portrait of God that fits his emphasis upon our obligation to
use freedom in the service of virtue. Neither he nor the other Fathers, who
share his view, draw the obvious implications of the view. But it is easy
enough to see that this theology requires some qualification of God's sovereignty. Granted that it can be described as a self-limitation, it nonetheless
seems necessary that by the very act of creation God abandons total con-

trol of the world. In giving humanity freedom God limits himself to the role of a teacher, persuading us to use our freedom in accord with his purposes. In this way, God's sovereignty is something that will be; and our submission to his will remains voluntary.

BASIL THE GREAT AND THE CREATED ORDER

A similar point can be made about how the majority opinion of the fathers in the fourth century treats the natural world. It, too, has a kind of freedom; and God's sovereignty over nature is primarily a way of discussing the end and the way in which God consummates his creative purpose in the age to come. Basil's *Homilies on the Six Days of Creation* enshrine this view of the matter, and I wish to argue that his view of nature accords with what we have seen of the Christian Platonist understanding of God and his providence. Once more, the view that is elaborated leaves room for human freedom, understood as our capacity to move toward virtue. We have already encountered aspects of this basic perspective in the earlier chapters of this book. The miracles of Christ are the product of his power as the agent of Creation, and so miracles are merely an "intensification" of God's creative power.[20] It is important to remember that the word "nature" (*physis*) in Greek has no one meaning, and is certainly not used to refer in any technical sense to an order of secondary causes. The word tends to retain its root meaning of "production" or "growth."[21] As a result, "nature," while it is the production of God, has its own powers of growth.

Basil delivered his *Homilies on the Six Days of Creation* in 370 shortly before becoming bishop of Caesarea. His debt to ancient philosophy and science is evident throughout the homilies, but his genius is to integrate his learning with a Christian perspective that translates it into a popular form. He explicitly rejects an allegorical interpretation of the Scriptural account of Creation. "So far as I am concerned, when I hear of grass, I understand grass . . . I accept everything as Scripture tells it; for I am not ashamed of the Gospel." (*HSD* 9.1; SC 26, p. 480; cf. Rom 1:16). At the same time he is quite capable of drawing morals from the text that edify his hearers. The crab supplies a cautionary example, teaching us not to harm our neighbor, and similarly the octopus warns against hypocrisy (*HSD* 7.3; SC 26, p. 404ff.). My concern, however, will be with what Basil says about the relationship of God to the created order.

God and the Creation are, of course, absolutely distinguished from one another. God is "the blessed nature, goodness without envy."[22] Like a potter whose art is not exhausted by making many pots, God's creative power is by no means limited to this world, but "exceeds boundless creativity." In contrast, the universe has a beginning. Basil rejects the Aristotelian notion of an eternal world, allying himself with other Christians and with the Platonists who would interpret the *Timaeus* this way. But the philosophical issue is really quite secondary. What Basil wishes to insist is that the Scriptural witness requires an absolute difference between God and the created order. God is beyond the intervals of time and space that characterize the universe he created. At the same time, his transcendence of the world is balanced by his providential care of it. "We must confess that the universe as a whole is held together by the power of the creator" (*HSD* 1.9; SC 26, p. 126).

When he speaks of the Creation as distinct from but dependent upon God, Basil can think of the beginning. This beginning, which is mentioned in the first verse of the Bible, suggests the timeless character of Creation, since the "beginning" or "first principle" (*arche*) is "without division and without interval." Just as the beginning of a road is not yet the road, so the beginning of time is not yet time. If it were, then we could keep on dividing time to infinity. The argument from infinite regress, in other words, requires us to distinguish "the beginning" from the creation that is begun. Basil concludes (*HSD* 1.6; SC 26, p. 112):

> Therefore, so that we might learn that the world was constituted in a timeless way simultaneously with God's will, it says: "In the beginning God made" (Gen 1:1). Other interpreters, giving the meaning more clearly, have said: "In a summary way [*en kephalaio*] God made," that is, all at once and in a little.

Basil seems to imply a creation before Creation. And it may well be that complicated philosophical ideas lie behind his argument. Yet, at one level, his idea is simply that God's creative will is the eternal purpose that lies behind or above Creation as we know it. He makes a similar point by noting that Genesis 1:5 speaks not of the "first" day, but of "one day." The phrase is used to preserve the relationship of time to eternity (*HSD* 2.8; SC 26, p. 182).

I want to understand Basil's argument to mean that God's creative intent is actualized in a process that extends from the beginning to the end. That is, Basil reads the account of Creation as the description of the initiation of this process. It is God's "beginning" that represents his eternal purpose, and the Genesis narrative shows how he starts to effect that purpose in time and space. When God commands the waters to be gathered (Gen 1:9), we must understand that "the voice of God is creative of nature, and the order given then to the creation supplies a future sequence for created things" (*HSD* 4.2; SC 26, p. 250). God's command in Genesis 1:20 coincides with the preparation of the waters to produce life (*HSD* 7.1;

SC 26, p. 392). The first step in actualizing the divine intent is to establish the universe with a set of potencies capable of being actualized.

This point finds support in Basil's interpretation of "Let the earth bring forth" (Gen 1:24). Let me cite the entire passage (*HSD* 5.10; SC 26, p. 320f.):

> This small command was immediately a great natural constitution (*physis*) and a skilful word, since quicker than our thought it accomplished the many thousands of particular qualities of plants. Even now that command, stored in the earth, urges it in each changing year to bring forth its own power to produce grasses, seeds, and trees. Just as tops continue to spin after the first blow that is given them, so the sequence of nature once it received its beginning by the first command moves forward for all future time until it meets the common perfecting of the universe.

The "creation" described in Genesis, then, is like starting tops. Once the motion has begun, the tops revolve themselves. And the natural process of growth that we observe in creation continues with the same kind of limited independence. Basil is describing a kind of law of nature implanted by God in the Creation.[23] But what he really means is a law of *growth*. That is, God has so constituted the universe that it is capable of growing and of doing so as he wishes. "The divine word is the nature of what comes to be" (*HSD* 8.1; SC 26, p. 430). And so the growth in one sense is produced by God's creative power. But at another level we need to take seriously Basil's words in the passage cited at the beginning of this paragraph. The divine command "urges" the creation to grow, but it also has its "own power" to do so.

Once we think of creation as a process of growth, it becomes possible to think of proper and improper growth. This makes sense for Basil only if we think of human beings, since "evil properly takes its principle from failures in our choices" (*HSD* 2.5; SC 26, p. 160). In other words, we cannot make moral judgments about what we see growing in the nonrational creation. Even poisonous plants have some function in the created order either by providing food to animals or by being given a medical use (*HSD* 5.4; SC 26, p. 292f.). Basil's tendency is to argue that all of nature grows harmoniously together, suggesting that whatever freedom nature has cannot be understood as a true and moral freedom. The harmony may not always be apparent to us, and sometimes created things function to frighten and to chastise us rather than to serve us or let us rejoice in their beauty (*HSD* 7.6; SC 26, p. 420f.). The independence of the lower creation is limited because it always functions as the arena in which human moral growth takes place. The world is a school in which rational souls are taught and where they learn the knowledge of God (*HSD* 1.6; SC 26, p. 110).

If from one point of view Basil thinks of creation as a process initiated by God, more importantly he thinks of it in terms of the completion of the process in the age to come. Basil raises the question of what "beauty" (*kalon*) God sees when he pronounces that what he has made is "good" (*kalon*). Beauty in the true sense of the word attaches not to any particular thing or even to the harmony of details with one another. Rather, beauty attaches to the finished work, its "end" (*HSD* 3.10; SC 26, p. 238f.). Basil's comment on the "living creatures" the earth brings forth (Gen 1:24) makes the point and summarizes his view as a whole (*HSD* 9.2; SC 26, p. 482f.):

> Consider the word of God that runs through creation; it began then; it is active up to the present time; and it continues to the end, when the world will be consummated. It is like a ball that, when someone pushes it, rolls downhill and is carried downwards by its own shape and the character of the place, not stopping until it finds itself on level ground. So, too, the nature of existing things, set in motion by one command, moves through creation by birth and corruption on an even path, preserving the sequences of species by likeness, until it arrives at its own end.

The destination of the ball is what interests Basil. The initial push sends the ball toward its goal. So God's initiation of creation sets the universe moving toward its ultimate destination.

The sovereignty of God over nature appears most clearly at the beginning and the end of the process. Even though we cannot speak of freedom, the natural creation has a kind of independence. God allows it to grow, just as the ball is allowed to roll because of its own shape. From this point of view miracles must be regarded as part of the growth of the created order. Our wonder springs solely from the unusual character of the growth. We shall be able to see how this idea is worked out when we turn to the early Augustine. But one other point needs to be made in conclusion. Not only does Basil's account of nature leave room for human freedom, it also presents the natural creation as the setting for human moral and spiritual growth. The Christian Platonism I have been examining is carefully elaborated in order to give pride of place to the human quest for virtue, a quest in which our freedom finds help in God's grace, not least his grace expressed in creation itself. It is with this party platform that Augustine begins. But his radical transformation of it leads to a new theology, and one that is far more congruent with a view of God as active in performing particular miracles in a sovereign fashion.

AUGUSTINE AND THE "NEW THEOLOGY"

Two passages in Augustine's early writings reflect the Christian Platonism I have been examining and also imply that miracles are a thing of the past. The first of these occurs in his treatise *Of True Religion*, written in 390 for his patron Romanianus. Augustine himself describes the context in which his remarks about miracles occur as follows (*OTR* xxiv, 45; LCC 6, p. 247):

> The treatment of the soul, which God's providence and ineffable loving-kindness administers, is most beautiful in its steps and stages. There are two different methods, authority and reason. Authority demands belief and prepares man for reason. Reason leads to understanding and knowledge.

The pattern is as old as Clement of Alexandria. Faith represents a preliminary stage that yields to knowledge. To be sure, Augustine tends to redefine faith as the Catholic faith rather than as a fundamental human capacity that is ours because we are created in the image of God. But the basic transition from faith to knowledge remains the same. The authority that produces faith is, according to Augustine, chiefly "handed down through history and prophecy" (*OTR* xxv, 46; LCC 6, p. 247). Presumably, it is primarily Scripture that represents the authority that faith embraces.

It is in this context that Augustine turns to the question of miracles (*OTR* xxv, 47; LCC 6, p. 248):

> We have heard that our predecessors, at a stage in faith on the way from temporal things up to eternal things, followed visible miracles. They could do nothing else. And they did so in such a way that it should not be necessary for those who came after them. When the Catholic Church had been founded and diffused throughout the whole world, on the one hand miracles were not allowed to continue till our time, lest the mind should always seek visible things, and the human race should grow cold by becoming accustomed to things which when they were novelties kindled its faith. On the other hand we must not doubt that those are to be believed who proclaimed miracles, which only a few had actually seen, and yet were able to persuade whole peoples to follow them. At that time the problem was to get people to believe before anyone was fit to reason about divine and invisible things. No human authority is set

over the reason of a purified soul, for it is able to arrive at clear truth.

Miracles are a secondary concern for Augustine. What he wants to show is that they are no longer necessary because they served their function by establishing the authority of the Catholic Faith. He gives two further reasons for the cessation of miracles. They run the risk of holding the mind to visible things and so preventing its ascent to truth; and, had they continued, they would have become commonplace and so have lost their power as miracles. The point of view is very like that of Chrysostom, and it represents a concern that a preoccupation with miracles might hinder the quest for truth and virtue.

In his *Retractions*, written at the end of his life, Augustine looks back on this passage and is clearly embarrassed by it. He argues that he had said "*these* miracles were not permitted to last till our times," and says that what he meant to do was to make a distinction between miracles in Christ's and the apostles' times, not to assert that "to-day no miracles are to be believed to happen in the name of Christ" (LLC 6, p. 220). At first Augustine appears to be merely attempting to extricate himself from a hopeless contradiction between his earlier and later views. But he goes on in the *Retractions* to point out that he had himself just witnessed in Milan the healing of a blind man "beside the bodies of the Milanese martyrs, Protasius and Gervasius." This observation does tend to justify Augustine's insistence that he had not meant to deny contemporary miracles altogether. But it is difficult to see that the Augustine who wrote *Of True Religion* is in any real way concerned or interested in miracles. His commitment to the mind's quest for knowledge and virtue blocks from his consciousness even the miracles he has witnessed for himself.[24]

A second passage occurs in *The Usefulness of Belief*, written in 391 shortly after Augustine became a presbyter in Hippo. The purpose of the treatise is to persuade Honoratus, whom Augustine had known in his Manichaean days in Carthage, to embrace the Catholic Faith. One of the major stumbling blocks for Honoratus is the necessity of faith. Augustine confesses that he owes his own faith to the universal observance of "the mysteries of the Catholic Church." His belief is grounded on "a report confirmed by its ubiquity, by its antiquity, and by the general consent of mankind" (*UB* xiv, 31; LCC 6, p. 316f.). He goes on to argue that Christ himself "demanded faith above everything else." His miracles were "done for no other purpose than that men should believe in him." Would Christ have performed the miracle at Cana of Galilee if he had been able to gain followers by his teaching alone? Augustine concludes this part of his argument by saying (*UB* xiv, 32; LCC 6, p. 318):

> Christ, therefore, bringing a medicine to heal corrupt morals, by his miracles gained authority, by his authority deserved faith, by faith drew together a multitude, thereby secured permanence of the tradition, which in time corroborated religion.

It need scarcely be said that Augustine is simply repeating the view found in *Of True Religion*. Christ's miracles establish his authority and produce faith. Once this has happened so as to constitute the church, the miracles have fulfilled their function. They belong at a very low and preliminary stage of faith and have value only because they help support Christ's aim in "bringing a medicine to heal corrupt morals."[25]

Augustine's chief concern is not with miracles but with faith and authority, yet his argument continues with two *obiter dicta* that define miracles and explain why they no longer happen. The definition is: "something strange and difficult which exceeds the expectation and capacity of him who marvels at it." Most marvels appeal to the senses, and miracles may be divided into those "which merely cause wonder" and those which "produce great gratitude and good will." The difference is that between a man flying and the healing of a disease (*UB* xvi, 34; LCC 6, p. 320). What is most interesting is that Augustine's definition focuses attention on our perception of the marvelous. Miracles are in the eye of the beholder. His explanation of why miracles do not happen now reflects the same view. His answer is because "they would not affect us unless they were marvellous, and they would not be marvellous if they were familiar." He goes on to appeal to the order of nature—"the alternation of day and night, the unvarying order of the heavenly bodies, the annual return of the four seasons, . . . the beauty of light, colour, sounds, odours, the varieties of flavours." The only reason we do not call all these miraculous is that "we are continually aware of them" (*UB* xvi, 34; LCC 6, p. 320).

What Augustine particularly means is that if Christ's miracles had become familiar and ordinary, they would have lost their miraculous character. But he can say this because he defines miracles from the point of view of our perception. The obvious implication is that, properly speaking, miracles are to be assimilated to nature. They simply represent aspects of nature we cannot understand or predict. There need be no appeal to any particular and sovereign act of God, only to his general providence which oversees nature in all its aspects. Once again we are on familiar Christian Platonist ground. And once again the mature Augustine looks back on his earlier thoughts with embarrassment. In the *Retractions* he is content to say that, in replying as he did to the question why miracles do not happen now, "I meant that such great miracles do not happen now, not that no miracles happen even today" (LCC 6, p. 286).

Augustine's later view of miracles is, however, not so much a repudiation of his earlier one as its transformation. Both his insistence upon the relation of miracles to God's creative power and his tendency to define the miraculous in terms of our perception find expression in his later writings. One important discussion of miracles occurs in Book 3 of *On the Trinity*, which was probably written about ten years after *Of True Religion*. Augustine's main concern in this book is to explain the appearances of God in the Old Testament as angelic meditations directed by God's power. The general principle he establishes is that "the will of God is the first and the highest cause of all corporeal appearance and motions." (*OT* 3.4; *NPNF* 1.3, p. 59). Chapters 5 through 9 are concerned to show that the principle also applies to miracles.

Augustine's first step is to argue that God's working of miracles is no more than a special operation of his creative power. God ordinarily sends rain upon the earth; but when he does so in answer to Elijah's prayer (1 Kings 18:41ff.), "the divine power was apparent in the great and rapid showers that followed, and by which that miracle was granted and dispensed." Similarly, God sent thunder and lightning upon Mount Sinai (Ex 19:6) "in an unusual manner." And when Christ turned water to wine at Cana, it was the "extraordinary quickness" of the change that constituted the miracle, since water ordinarily is drawn up through the root of the vine to the grapes so as to produce wine (*OT* 3.5; *NPNF* 1.3, p. 59). These and other examples suggest that the distinction between the "natural" and the "miraculous" is that between things happening "in a continuous kind of river of everflowing succession . . . by a regular and beaten track" and things happening by being "thrust in by an unusual changeableness" (*OT* 3.6; *NPNF* 1.3, p. 60). We are dealing with two different modes of God's creative activity.

Augustine takes a further step by arguing that the creator's power is not exercised directly. There are "some hidden seeds of all things that are born corporeally and visibly . . . concealed in the corporeal elements of this world" (*OT* 3.8; *NPNF* 1.3, p. 60).[26] The "world itself is pregnant with the causes of things that are born." These causes God has implanted in Creation, and they function to produce growth and change. But we must also consider (*OT* 3.9; *NPNF* 1.3, p. 62)

> . . . the applying from without of adventitious causes, which, although they are not natural, yet are to be applied according to nature, in order that those things which are contained and hidden in the secret bosom of nature may break forth and be outwardly created in some way by the unfolding of the proper measures and numbers and weights which they have received in secret from [God].

The angels, good and evil, are able to introduce these "adventitious causes." Moreover, human beings can be held responsible when they employ angels for their purposes. Obviously, miracles occur when God uses the blessed angels for his own purposes; magic, when wicked people use the evil angels for their own purposes.

Augustine expounds much the same view in the earlier books of the *City of God.* In Book 7.30 he speaks of God as the source of "the vital force of seeds" and as the one who "knows and orders all causes, primary and secondary alike." We cannot parcel out different natural operations to different gods, as Varro does. Rather (*CG* 7.30; PC, p. 292),

> . . . it is the one true God who is active and operative in all those things, but always acting as God, that is, present everywhere in his totality, free from all spatial confinement, . . . filling heaven and earth with his ubiquitous power which is independent of anything in the natural order. He directs the whole of his creation, while allowing to his creatures the freedom to initiate and accomplish activities which are their own; for although their being completely depends on him, they have a certain independence. He often acts through the medium of his angels, but he is himself the sole source of the angels' blessedness.

The Christian Platonist orientation of Augustine's view leads him to treat the natural order as subject to God's providence, but at the same time in some degree independent of God. Moreover, his tendency is to argue for the organic harmony and even uniformity of nature. The unusual and special are not entirely severed from his basic view, and his tendency is to argue that in the long run what is miraculous is really natural.

The early chapters of Book 10 of the *City of God* repeat the themes I have listed, but in chapter 12 Augustine adds to the picture the issue of our perception. True miracles "are effected by divine power, whether by means of angels or in any other manner, so as to commend to us the worship and religion of the one God, in whom alone is the life of blessedness." Moreover, these miracles are simply part of a larger whole (*CG* 10.12; PC, p. 390):

> And so although the miracles of the visible world of nature have lost their value for us because we see them continually, still, if we observe them wisely they will be found to be greater miracles than the most extraordinary and unusual events. For man is a greater miracle than any miracle effected by man's agency.

Even though Augustine can distinguish between two modes of God's creative power, the natural and the miraculous, the two modes tend to fuse together. He shifts the ground to our perception of God's creative work, and a new sort of distinction emerges. What we are accustomed to is natural; what we find unusual is miraculous.

There are probably conceptual difficulties in Augustine's view as I have so far outlined it, but my major point is that his tendency is to locate the miraculous in the larger context of God's providential ordering of Creation. His Christian Platonist roots are evident, and in many ways he simply reproduces the sort of view we have encountered throughout this chapter. The only possible peculiarity in what he says has to do with an apparent emphasis upon God's power and sovereignty. And even this emphasis does not prepare us for what we find in the last two books of the *City of God*. Augustine wrote *City of God* 6–10 in 415–17, while Books 18–22 appeared in 425–427.[27] In Books 21 and 22 we find an understanding of the miraculous that is, paradoxically, both the same as and radically different from his earlier teaching. By pressing the importance of God's sovereignty and by radicalizing our faulty perceptions of nature, Augustine virtually turns a Christian Platonist theology inside out.

Let me begin with the first ten chapters of *City of God* 21. Augustine wants to prove that the eternal fire with which the wicked are to be punished is not an impossibility. He appeals, for example, to the salamander, who lives in fire, and to "mountains in Sicily which are a seething mass of flames and yet remain entire" (*CG* 21.4; PC, p. 968). He plays upon a long list of natural marvels to argue that our inability to give a rational explanation of things in the future should not produce disbelief, since "there are things in the present which are equally insusceptible of rational explanation" (*CG* 21.5; PC, p. 971). Many things in nature defeat "the feeble reasoning powers of mortal minds" (*CG* 21.5; PC, p. 973):

> And yet we should have maintained that our rational belief was unshaken, that the Almighty does not act irrationally in cases where the feeble human mind cannot give a rational explanation; and that in many matters, certainly, we are uncertain of God's will; and yet one thing is utterly certain, that nothing he wills is impossible for him, for we cannot believe that God is impotent, or that God is a liar.

Both our ignorance and God's sovereignty are painted in more vivid colors in this passage. But Augustine goes on to speak of things that "*seem* to contradict the rational order of nature." And so we might suppose that he has not abandoned his fundamental notion that in the long run miracles are somehow part of nature.

In chapters 7 and 8, however, Augustine takes the final step that transforms his view. We may accept miracles not merely because of the radical character of our own ignorance, but because we must bow to the absolute sovereignty of God (CG 21.7; PC, p. 977):

> But since God is the author of all natures, why do they object to our supplying a stronger reason? For when they refuse to believe something, alleging its impossibility, and demand that we supply a rational explanation, we reply that the explanation is the will of Almighty God.

Somewhat later Augustine goes even further. Portents are not really contrary to nature. "For how can an event be contrary to nature when it happens by the will of God, since the will of the great Creator assuredly *is* the nature of every created thing" (CG 21.8; PC, p. 980). This astonishing statement sweeps away the whole of the elaborate conceptualization we have been examining. It even presses beyond an appeal to human ignorance and beyond any location of the problem at the level of perception rather than at that of God's nature. God's will is all that remains, and it is difficult to see that "nature" remains in any sense a meaningful concept. The pieces of the puzzle are the same, but they have been rearranged. No longer are miracles natural; nature is itself miraculous.[28]

It is, I think, Augustine's increasing emphasis upon the sovereignty of God that explains the sea change he imposes upon the Christian Platonist theology that represents the majority opinion of his day.[29] I should not wish to argue that it is the cult of the saints or his sudden interest in miracles toward the end of his life that explains Augustine's radicalization of God's sovereignty. Other factors are probably more important—his deep sense of his own inability to find perfect spiritual healing, deeply ingrained sensibilities of North African Christianity, the issues of the Pelagian controversy. But I should suggest that his insistence upon God's omnipotence produces a theology that accords far more readily with the miraculous than the Christian Platonist theology out of which it grows and which it transforms. The theological platform of Book 21 sets the stage for Augustine's enthusiastic account of contemporary miracles in *City of God* 22.8–10. The supposition that miracles no longer occur is possible only because modern miracles have not been sufficiently advertised (CG 22.8). And so Augustine has instituted the practice of publishing authenticated pamphlets describing the miracles that take place. Seventy such documents have already been produced at the shrine of St. Stephen in Hippo (*CG* 22.8; PC, p. 1043).

It is difficult to escape the conclusion that Augustine's mature thought is the "new theology" of his day. The controversy over his writings began during the last years of his life and remained a bitter one, particularly in Gaul, until the death of John Cassian in about 435. In one way or another the controversy persisted. Even the council of Orange in 529 should probably not be regarded as the last word. Of course, the "new theology" in a somewhat modified form eventually triumphed. But to trace the controversy and the establishment of an "Augustinian" theology in the West takes me beyond my more limited purpose, which is simply to argue that with Augustine a new view emerges that binds theology more closely to the social dimension of Christianity. That is, his theology of the sovereignty of grace correlates with the cult of the saints and its emphasis upon divine power.

A few words about Prosper of Aquitaine will enable me to draw together my conclusions. Prosper was a staunch advocate of Augustine and an opponent of the so-called semi-Pelagians, the best known of whom was John Cassian. In his writings in defense of Augustine we find a clear recognition that two theologies are in conflict. In his *Against Cassian* Prosper characterizes Cassian's views as "the dogmas of the new teachers who, in order to corrupt the faith in Catholic minds, spread calumnies against the defenders of grace" (*AC* 21.1; ACW 32, p. 133). What he characterizes as "new" is really the old theology. And while he may well be wrong in his assessment of the whole of that theology as Pelagian, he does rightly see that it places a premium upon freedom and virtue.

Prosper characterizes the Pelagian view as follows (*LR* 1; ACW 32, p. 21f):

> The Pelagians first wished to say that human nature is perfectly sound and able to attain the kingdom of God by its unaided free will, the reason being that nature finds help enough in the very gift of creation. Being naturally endowed with reason and intellect, it can easily choose what is good and avoid what is evil.

Grace, for the Pelagians, becomes no more than "some sort of teacher of man's free will"; and even miracles have only the purpose of instructing "the mind from outside" (*LR* 2; ACW 32, p. 22). This is why the Pelagians attack Augustine for abolishing free will and upholding fatalism "under cover of grace" (*LR* 3; ACW 32, p. 23). But Prosper does recognize that the Pelagians "have run into danger because of their very zeal for virtue, into peril because of the integrity of their lives" (*LR* 4; ACW 32, p. 24). In other words, Prosper rightly understands that what I should call the old theology gives a central place to human freedom and the quest for virtue. What he fails to understand is that the old theology has its own way of talking about God's grace.

In contrast, Prosper's new theology starts with God's grace as what causes "what is good in man" (*LR* 2; ACW 32, p. 22). Like Augustine, Prosper constantly underlines human weakness and sinfulness. Even free will is no longer a natural human capacity. It was lost in Adam's fall, and God gives it to the elect by setting them free from original sin.[30] This new sort of freedom is not so much a power of choosing as a reconciliation with God. True freedom, as Augustine says, is cleaving to the good. The paradox, of course, is that freedom is really servitude to God. And only God can bestow this freedom upon us. Just as freedom is something caused by God rather than a capacity exercised by human beings, so miracles are effective rather than merely instructive. Miracles cohere better with the grace of the new theology than with the freedom of the old. And yet grace and miracles provide a new kind of freedom.

CONCLUSION

The predominant theology of the fourth century is Christian Platonist in character, and it focuses attention upon human freedom and our natural capacity for virtue. God's gift to us is his image, and that gift enables us to discern good and evil. Moreover, we have the power to act upon that discernment. Choosing the good, in the first instance, means the difficult struggle involved in taming the passions and establishing the mind as the governing principle over the body and its passions. The moral virtue thus achieved enables us to move toward the full contemplation of God. Virtue, then, is both moral and spiritual. It represents human destiny. At the same time, we do not accomplish this destiny apart from God. He has made us for himself and implanted in us a natural yearning for our proper goal. In baptism the Spirit awakens this free capacity, and the Christian life progresses as an education in which God always remains the beneficent teacher.

The Christian Platonists of the fourth century seek to place this basic perception in relation to a commitment to the Christian community and an understanding of the corporate character of human nature. And they refuse to regard it as in any way contradictory of the resurrection of the body. Human destiny involves not only the perfection of our contemplation of God but also the transfiguration of our physical nature. Moreover, the implications of this theology for doctrines of God and of the created order are carefully drawn. God's goodness, at least by implication, takes precedence over his sovereignty. And God will be omnipotent in the full sense of the word only when he has finally persuaded all things to be subject to him, in other words in the age to come. The created order, in turn, is really an organic process that has its own independence. Its growth supplies the arena in which human freedom receives its training and education.

Christian Platonism finds it easier to treat the martyrs and the saints as examples meant to encourage and challenge the Christian than as sources of power. This is why Athanasius is, I think, somewhat embarrassed and puzzled by Antony's miracles. The wonders performed by the martyrs and saints tend to supply them with authentic credentials, but what is important is their virtue. As a result, a gap begins to appear between the predominant theology and the social dimension of Roman imperial Christianity. Both the cult of the saints and the rise of the holy person result in a shift of attention. The martyrs are no longer so much examples as sources of power, and the saint is less someone to be imitated than a source of extraordinary patronage. The gap is not one between official and popular piety, nor can it be explained by an expelled paganism entering the back door of the church. Rather, it appears within the religious sensibilities of a single figure like Gregory of Nyssa. Gregory is equally committed to Christian Platonism and to the cult of the saints. The gap, then, is between the theological interpretation of the Gospel and the life of Christian communities. And it is not, I think, as evident to Christians in the fourth century as it is to us.

The mature Augustine bridges the gap somewhat. His "new theology" revolves around a highly pessimistic assessment of humanity and its capacities and a radical insistence upon God's absolute sovereignty. I do not suppose that this new theology is in any sense a direct response to the social dimension of late fourth-century Christianity or that it represents any conscious attempt on Augustine's part to bridge the gap. Nevertheless, we cannot discount the impact of the life of the church on Augustine's thinking. It is surely one factor among others. More important, the new theology functions far more harmoniously with the miraculous and with the cult of the saints than the old. A sovereign God, whose purposes are absolutely inscrutable, can restore a blind man's sight as easily as he can rescue an individual from a doomed humanity by election. With Augustine's theology we find the end of the kind of freedom that made sense to late antiquity. But we also find a new definition of freedom. If Augustine feared a freedom that was purely human, he placed his hope in a freedom that was God's gift.

Epilogue

 I have sought to argue that the Constantinian revolution altered the character of Christianity by seeking to establish a sacral commonwealth that would bring heaven to earth. In addition, central to that enterprise were the saints, dead and living, who acted as conduits of power, giving those on earth access to heavenly power. Chapters 4 and 5 are largely concerned with painting this picture. But, as should be clear from the first three chapters, the theological and homiletical articulation of the Gospel that predominated in the fourth and fifth centuries betrays a very different sensibility. Christianity primarily means the victory of Christ and Christians over Satan. Part of this is promise and grace; but part of it is a challenge to individual Christians to embark upon the pursuit of a moral and spiritual virtue that represents their destiny. The roots of this understanding of Christianity are to be found in the Christian Platonism of the second and third centuries. As a result, in the Roman imperial church we find a tension, if not a contradiction, between the Christian message which revolved around virtue and the individual, and a corporate piety, in some degree novel, that focused upon the empowering of the people of God.

I have argued in chapter 6 that with Augustine we find Christian Platonism transformed into a "new theology" far more congruent with the corporate piety that had by then developed. An emphasis upon grace and upon God's sovereignty fits a preoccupation with miracles better than the old emphasis upon human freedom and virtue. Moreover, the stage is set for the Western Middle Ages. The cult of the saints, organized and made central to Christian piety, is what I have in mind. It also looks as though the West remained suspicious of the holy man. Living saints as a source of power have the possibility of undermining the authority of the church. Indeed, one could argue that the living saint, problematic because elite, represents a natural development of the individualism that represented a danger in the Christian Platonism largely definitive of asceticism. Perhaps these ideas would be better presented as hypotheses to be tested by a study of the Western church in the sixth and seventh centuries. I suspect that my conclusions would have to be qualified somewhat, but that they would stand as generalizations.

In any case, what I think we discover from a study of Roman imperial Christianity before the collapse of the West is the tendency to substitute one kind of freedom for another. Freedom as the capacity of human beings to choose the good does not, of course, disappear. But, on the whole, it is made subordinate to notions of God's sovereign grace and even to an insistence upon the authority of the church. It is impossible not to think of Dostoyevsky's Grand Inquisitor. His argument against Christ, who appears to him, is that freedom is incompatible with happiness:

> There are three forces, the only three forces that are able to conquer and hold captive for ever the conscience of these weak rebels for their own happiness—these forces are: miracle, mystery, and authority. You [Christ] rejected all three and yourself set the example for doing so.[1]

Freedom, in the Grand Inquisitor's view, is our fundamental problem because it can bring only suffering. We neither want freedom nor can benefit by it. Augustine saw the problem. Our freedom to choose means not only that we are obliged to choose between good and evil but that we must constantly choose between goods. As a result, the will is constantly divided; and the only healing of that division is a new kind of freedom in which, to use Dante's words, we find our peace in God's will.

If we can argue that the repression or subordination of human freedom as choosing found in the cult of the saints and in Augustine's theology represents a loss, we can also argue that it represents a gain. For example, Peter Brown assesses the function of the cult of the saints as follows:

> In late-Roman conditions, *potentia* had a more gentle reverse side. Patronage and dependence, even the exigencies of aristocratic *amicitia*, might seem hard, binding relations to us; but it was

> through these that late-Roman men hoped to gain that freedom of
> action from which the miracle of justice, mercy, and a sense of
> solidarity with their fellow humans might spring.[2]

The new sort of freedom, then, need not exclude our pursuit of virtue.
Perhaps the two alternatives are not exclusive of one another. The fear of
human freedom as the choosing required of moral agents may up to a
point be legitimate, and the substitution of freedom as God's service need
not exclude the importance of our moral agency. But there remains a
tension not only at a theological level but also at a practical one. How do
we balance the individual's importance as a moral agent with the power
of the community and God's gracious working through the community?
The tension has complex implications and may not be finally resolvable. A
large part of the fascination in studying church history is discerning ways
in which the tension plays itself out. Were the tension capable of resolution, there would be the danger of stagnation. We need not, then, decide
whether the fear of freedom is good or bad. Instead, we can see it as
having the possibility of a catalyst, transforming and renewing the ways in
which Christians seek to understand the Gospel.

Notes

INTRODUCTION

1. See, for example, Robin Lane Fox, *Pagans and Christians* (New York: Alfred A. Knopf, 1987). Fox studies the problem of the triumph of Christianity under Constantine and challenges some of the usual assumptions of scholars about the period. For example, he wants to insist upon the vitality of the paganism that Christianity replaced (see Part One) and to argue that the Constantinian revolution was religious in character (see chapters 12 and 13). He sees no "rise in credulity" in the third century (p. 250).

2. See Mary Hesse's excellent discussion, "Miracles and the Laws of Nature," in *Miracles*, ed. C. F. D. Moule. The first part of her discussion leads her to say: ". . . it is tempting to draw the conclusion that on any view of scientific laws other than the Laplacian, which is in any case discredited, no events can positively be shown to be violations of generally accepted laws" (p. 39f.). But Hesse regards the temptation as one to be avoided and argues: "There is finally, however, a much more difficult question which is related to the problem of miracles, but is more general and less specifically related to the scientific world-view. This is the sense in which the acts of God can be distinguished *at all* in special and providential events as distinct from the ordinary course of nature and history" (p. 41).

3. See R. A. Markus's view in *The Cambridge History of Later Greek and Early Medieval Philosophy*, p. 400: "Augustine is feeling his way towards the later scholastic distinction between a 'first cause' and the whole order of 'second causes'. . . . But how far he was from really holding a view of nature on such lines appears from what he has to say about miracles."

4. Cited by Thomas Gilby in *St. Thomas Aquinas: Theological Texts* (London: Oxford University Press, 1955), pp. 102 and 106 (Disputations, vi *de Potentia*, 1 and 2).

5. Pausanias, *Guide to Greece* 1.21.5 (Penguin Classics, English trans. and ed. Peter Levi [Harmondsworth: Penguin Books, 1971]), volume 1, p. 59.

6. See, for example, Clare Stancliffe's discussion of St. Martin's miracles in *St. Martin and His Hagiographer*, especially chapter 18. "The real stumbling-blocks for a twentieth-century reader are the nature miracles. Some of these are explicable in non-miraculous terms, or at least could have been due to chance. . . . Others may be due to Sulpicius' heightening of the miraculous. . . . At other times, the miracles told by Sulpicius may have been described in language which was originally intended metaphorically, not literally. There are a few nature miracles, however, for which we are unlikely to be able to find any underlying rationale" (p. 255). Without denying the value and interest of this approach, I should question whether we can ever be sure which category to invoke. The risk, I should think, is that our modern explanation may really be an explaining away of the ancient story.

7. Robert N. Bellah et al., *Habits of the Heart: Individualism and Commitment in American Life* (New York: Harper & Row, 1985), p. 254. The Founding Fathers did not agree with Montesquieu that reconciling the private and the public was incompatible with democracy.

8. Bellah, *Habits of the Heart*, p. 48.

9. *Letters of E. B. White*, ed. Dorothy L. Guth (New York: Harper & Row, 1976), p. 376f. For his reactions in 1942, see pp. 221–26 and 228–29.

CHAPTER 1

1. See, for example, the discussion in Richard Krautheimer, *Rome: Profile of a City, 312–1308*, p. 40ff. The figures of the *ecclesia ex synagoga* and the *ecclesia ex gentibus* are apparently found only in the West. We need to understand the apse mosaic of S. Pudenziana in relation to the traditional iconography of the *traditio legis*. Christ is flanked by Peter and Paul, and the law is delivered to Peter. It is important to note that Paul is on the right hand of Christ, and this may be a way of giving him equal time with Peter. I am indebted to Graydon Snyder for this suggestion. In any case, the iconography is related to the complicated question of the development of the veneration of Peter and Paul in Rome. They seem to become the Christian substitute for Romulus and Remus.

2. See Jean Doignon's introduction to his Sources chrétiennes edition and his book, *Hilaire de Poitiers avant l'Exil*.

3. See J. Doignon, SC 254, p. 20, note 8.

4. It is worth pointing out that Hilary's Christological exegesis dominates his discussion of Peter's confession in Mt 16. Christ is teaching the disciples who he is. Peter is correct in perceiving that he is the Son of God, but fails at first to see that he is Son of man, despite the fact that Christ includes the title in his question at Mt 16:13. Hilary also interprets Mt 16:23 to mean "Go, Satan; as for you, Peter, follow after me" (HM 16,6ff.; SC 258, p. 52ff.). What I am driving at is that Hilary does not associate the apostles Peter and Paul with the churches from the synagogue and from the Gentiles.

5. See also HM 12,20; SC 254, p. 289.

6. Let me refer the reader to Doignon's discussion in the works cited above. In particular, he says on page 28 of his introduction to SC 254: "Cette forme de composition débouche sur les *ordines narrationis*, où la succession des faits est

structurée par une unité de sens indiquée dans une *propositio*, véritable exposé des motifs. C'est le cas en particulier des scènes de *miracula*, dont la plus représentative est celle de la première multiplication des pains."

7. The two blind men in Mt 20:30 stand for the Gentiles, Ham and Japheth (HM 20,13; SC 258, p. 118).

8. See Robert Evans, *One and Holy*.

9. Here I find myself in some disagreement with Bonnard, who wishes to speak of "un exposé cohérent" (SC 242, p. 23ff.). I should agree that Jerome does more than simply supply a set of random notes, organized verse by verse. But it seems to me that he is less successful than Hilary in conveying a unified overview of the Gospel.

10. See, for example, his discussion of the citation of Ps 78 in Mt 13:35 (SC 242, p. 284).

11. Jerome distinguishes between the narrative meaning (*historice*) and the spiritual meaning (*secundum anagogen*). See JM 10,9–10; SC 242, p. 192.

12. Jerome also appeals to Jeremiah 51:25 in order to describe the "mountain" as one that "corrupts the whole earth." The parallel passage in Mt 21:21 elicits a parallel comment from Jerome (JM 21,21; SC 259, p. 122).

13. See also Jerome's comments on the healing of the two blind men in Mt 20:29ff. (JM 20,29–31; SC 259, p. 98f.). Whether the two are the Pharisees and the Sadducees and the crowd is the Gentiles or the two are the Jews and the Gentiles, the story refers to the pattern of the tame and wild olive trees Paul speaks of in Rom 11.

14. *Theodori Mopsuesteni Commentarius in Evangelium Iohannis Apostoli*, ed. and Latin trans. J.-M. Vosté, CSCO 115–16, Louvain, 1940.

15. M. F. Wiles, following Vosté, suggests the first decade of the fifth century (*The Spiritual Gospel*, p. 5).

16. For a fuller discussion, see Wiles, *The Spiritual Gospel*, p. 16ff.

17. See Wiles' discussion in *The Spiritual Gospel*, chaper IV. His preoccupation in the chapter is with the meaning of the Johannine signs, and this obliges him virtually to ignore Theodore. For example, with regard to the miracle at the wedding in Cana, "Theodore discusses the details of the miracle at some length, but makes no attempt to give any spiritual interpretation of the sign as a whole" (p. 44). It seems to me that Wiles is quite correct in seeing that Theodore confines himself to the narrative meaning of the text.

18. See the standard accounts of Theodore's Christology in Kelly, Grillmeier, and Norris.

19. See Wiles, *The Spiritual Gospel*, p. 6.

20. For Cyril's antipathy to the Jews, see Robert L. Wilken, *Judaism and the Early Christian Mind: A Study of Cyril of Alexandria's Exegesis and Theology*. Wilken persuasively argues that the problem of Judaism is not merely theoretical for Cyril, but that he is obliged to face real conflict between the church and the synagogue.

21. One peculiarity of Cyril's interpretation of the miraculous feeding is that he takes seriously John 6:14 as an expression of faith. This positive judgment is made of those "who dwelt away from Jerusalem." The Jews, on the other hand, who ought to have profited "lost even the power of right judgment" (P 1, p. 421). What is puzzling is that Cyril seems to be contrasting the faithful multitude with the disbelieving Jews, and yet later in the commentary clearly supposes that the disbelieving Jews are part of the multitude that was fed. Perhaps what he thinks is that the multitude included both believers and others whose belief was merely tempo-

rary. The difficulty, of course, is to be found in the text of John as well as in Cyril's commentary.

22. See P 1, pp. 200f., 301, 303, 408, 410, 426; P 2, pp. 271, 281, 285.

23. See Wiles, *The Spiritual Gospel*, p. 2.

24. For further discussion of Cyril's treatment of the Johannine signs, see Wiles, *The Spiritual Gospel*, chapters III and IV.

CHAPTER 2

1. This is the older view. See the discussion in J. Quasten, *Patrology*, volume 4, p. 144ff.

2. For discussion of the problem, see Quasten, *Patrology*, volume 4, p. 164f.; Gabriel Tissot, SC 45, introduction, pp. 9–18.

3. See *Confessions* 5.13–14 where Augustine describes Ambrose's preaching. "I was delighted with his charming delivery, but although he was a more learned speaker than Faustus, he had not the same soothing and gratifying manner." Though he at first pays no attention to the content of Ambrose's sermons, Augustine finds their truth begins to sink into him. "I began to believe that the Catholic faith . . . might fairly be maintained, especially since I had heard one passage after another in the Old Testament figuratively explained" (PC, pp. 107–8).

4. See also AL 4, 46; SC 45, p. 169.

5. The comments of Hilary and Jerome on the visit of the Magi to the Christ child are disappointingly brief. Hilary sees the Magi as indicating that the Gentiles and those alienated from the knowledge of God by *scientia* will come to Christ. The gifts of gold, frankincense, and myrrh symbolize Christ's royalty, divinity, and humanity—and also Christ's judgment as king, his death as man, and his Resurrection as God. That the Magi return another way shows that we must not return to our former life after embracing Christ (HM 1, 5; SC 254, p. 98). Jerome also relates the story to the conversion of the Gentiles. He alludes to Balaam's oracle (Nm 24:17), and he supplies the same interpretation of the gifts. The Magi return another way to avoid the Jews (JM 2, 2ff.; SC 242, p. 82f.).

6. See above, page 14.

7. See above, page 15.

8. See above, page 14.

9. One theoretical framework that holds the ideas together is Ambrose's notion of "three deaths." One is the death of sin; the second, physical death; and the third, death to sin. The last of these prepares the believer for the resurrection of the dead. Ambrose elaborates this schema by commenting on Christ's words, "Leave the dead to bury their own dead" (Lk 9:60; AL 7, 35ff.; SC 52, p. 21).

10. Ambrose uses the same idea to explain why Christ's first miracle in Luke (4:31ff.) took place on a sabbath. "The new creation begins where the old creation stops" (AL 4, 57; SC 45, p. 174). On the other hand, the call of Levi, since it is the sixth of Christ's works, stands for new creation of humanity, which was created on the sixth day (AL 5, 27; SC 45, p. 193).

11. See also AL 8, 83; SC 52, p. 137, where a confession of faith is said to be required before healing can take place.

12. Letter 22, *NPNF* 2.10, p.436ff.

13. The dating is uncertain, but the sermons fall into two collections—1–54 and 55–124. See J. Quasten, *Patrology*, volume 4, p. 395.

14. See also AJ 9.1, 24.1.

15. Let me add that Augustine occasionally understands Christ's power to be operative wherever true miracles are to be found. The miracles of the Old Testament are ones which "no one else did" (John 15:24) because they are works he did in people like Elijah and Elisha (AJ 91). And the "greater works" done by "he who believes in me" (John 14:12) are the miracles done by the apostles (AJ 72,1f.).

16. It is clear that Augustine's sermons presuppose the schema elaborated in *The City of God* and the *Enchiridion*. "When a man is born, he is born already in a state of death; for he inherits sin from Adam" (AJ 49.12; *NPNF* 1.7, p 274). "He knew all the names of His own saints, whom He predestinated before the foundation of the world" (AJ 7.14; *NPNF* 1.7, p. 53). "How many evil men there are in the Church! And one womb carries them until they are separated in the end" (AJ 11.10; *NPNF* 1.7, p. 78). What we inherit by original sin is both the first (spiritual and physical) death and the second death of eternal damnation. The first resurrection takes us out of the "mass of perdition" and prepares us to escape the second death and attain the second resurrection.

17. For the two resurrections, see also AJ 22.12; *NPNF* 1.7, p. 149. For the importance of the soul, see AJ 8.2; *NPNF* 1.7, p. 58. The soul's power is manifested in its ability to govern the body and its capacity for reasoning and understanding, the image of God. Its full powers are reserved for the age to come. "If such is its power, acting through corruptible flesh, what shall be its power through a spiritual body, after the resurrection of the dead?"

18. The exhortation seems to imply that Augustine's hearers can choose grace. It is clear enough that the later Augustine believes that grace chooses us. We must allow him some homiletical license if we are to escape charging him with contradicting his own views.

19. Cf. *Contra litteras Petiliani* 2.203.224: ". . . neither do we say that we are to be believed to be in the Catholic Church because . . . throughout the whole world, in holy places frequented by our communion, so many miracles take place either in the granting of prayers or in miracles of healing. . . . Whatever such like take place in the Catholic Church are therefore to be approved because they take place in the Catholic Church; but it is not manifested to be the Catholic Church by the fact that such things take place therein."

20. See also ChJ 17, 50, 68.

21. See ChM 4.4, 5.2, 25.4. Chrysostom consistently speaks of the miracle of the virgin birth.

22. Chrysostom in this passage also describes Christ's crucifixion as the fulfillment of the type of Abraham's sacrifice of Isaac. He also notes that "some say" Adam died and was buried at Golgotha. Redemption, then, fulfills the types of the Old Testament. For other passages referring to the miracles at the Passion, see ChM 66.1, 67.1, 79.3, 84.1, and ChJ 53, 72.

23. See ChM 26.6 and ChJ 9, 45, 52.

24. See ChM 16.2, 25.2, 27.1, 49.2, and ChJ 22, 24, 64.

25. See ChM 25.1, 62.1, 65.1, 67.1, and ChJ 43.

26. See ChJ 20, 21, 24, 35, 36, 42, 50.

27. For the occasional reference to no faith or an inadequate faith, see ChM 32.2 and ChJ 35, 37. For the faith of others, see ChM 27.1, 57.3. For the display or

unfolding of faith, see ChM 26.1, 26.6, 31.2, 52.3. For the requirement of faith, see ChM 29.1, 32.1, 49.1, 52.3, 57.4, 66.1.

28. For Christ's seeking out those to be healed, see ChM 32.3 and ChJ 56. For his waiting to be called, see ChM 49.1, 53.1.

29. See ChM 50.2 and ChJ 37, 42, 62, 63.

30. See ChM 7.1, 25.1, 39.1, 40.2, 66.3, and ChJ 55, 66. Even Peter and Judas are not benefited by the miracles. See ChM 54.4, 80.3.

31. See ChM 43, 44.1, 53.3, and ChJ 23, 45, 48, 61.

32. See ChM 43.4, 69.1, 76.1, 88.1.

33. See ChM 30.1, 48.1.

34. See ChM 31.1, 32.1.

35. See ChM 8.4, 13.4, 29.1, 68.2.

36. See ChM 54.4, 57.2, 65.2, 85.1, 87.1.

37. See ChM 24.1–2, 32.6, 32.8.

38. See ChM 24.2, 90.4.

39. See ChM 15.1, 27.3, 63.1. The woman who anoints Christ's head (Mt 26.6ff.) also comes to Christ not for the healing of her body but "for the amendment of the soul" (ChM 80.1; NPNF 1.10, p. 480).

40. See ChM 34.4–5, 42.4.

41. See ChM 34.1, 44.4, 59.1.

42. See also ChM 14.4, 27.7, 28.5, 50.3, 67.4, and ChJ 22.

43. For the cessation of miracles, in addition to the passages discussed here, see de sac. 4.3, 6; de Laz. 4.3; de sanct. Pent. 1.3; ad Demetr. 1.8; in Ps. 142, 5; inscr. Acts 2.3; hom. Rom. 8.7; hom. 2 Cor. 7.

44. See ChM 12.3 and ChJ 24, 42.

45. See Robert Wilken, *John Chrysostom and the Jews.*

46. See J. Quasten, *Patrology*, volume 3, p. 123f. I have consulted R. M. Tonneau, *S. Cyrilli Alexandrini Commentarii in Lucam*, CSCO 140, Script. Syri 70, Louvain, 1954 (to be abbreviated T, number of homily, page), which translates the 80 Syriac homilies into Latin, and Joseph Reuss, *Lukas-Kommentare aus der Griechischen Kirche*, TU 130, Berlin; Akademie-Verlag, 1984 (abbreviated R, section, fragment number, page).

47. See, for example, T 37, p. 48ff.; T 80, p. 225f.; R 1.280, p. 191; R 2.40, p. 240; R 2.53, p. 245f.

48. See, for example, T 35, p. 41; R 1.145, p. 128; T 36, pp. 44–46.

49. See, for example, T 35, p. 39; T 80, p. 226; T 43, p. 79f.; R 1.141, p. 126; R 2.27, p. 233; R 2.43, p. 241f.; R 2.44, p. 242; R 2.51, p. 245; R 2.54, p. 246; R 2.88, p. 263; R 2.89, p. 263f.

CHAPTER 3

1. The easiest way to gain access to the scholarship available and to reproductions of the mosaics with which I am primarily concerned is to consult Giuseppe Bovini, *La Vita di Cristo nei Mosaici di S. Apollinare Nuovo di Ravenna*. Also to be consulted is O. G. von Simson, *Sacred Fortress: Byzantine Art and Statecraft in Ravenna*.

2. My colleague John Cook tells me that a similar figure appears in ivory carvings and illuminated manuscripts treating the same stories from the sixth and seventh centuries.

3. This suggestion was made as long ago as 1907 by Beissel. Baumstark adopted the suggestion in 1910 and argued that the lectionary in question was related to Syrian Jacobite usage. In 1953 C. O. Nordstrom revised the theory by arguing that the closest parallels may be found in Latin and even Milanese sources. See Bovini, *La Vita di Cristo*, p. 101f., where the other sources in the secondary literature may also be found.

4. See the discussion by Thomas F. Mathews, *The Early Churches of Constantinople: Architecture and Liturgy*, p. 147ff.

5. I have consulted Juan Mateos, *Le Typicon de la Grande Église, Tome II, Le Cycle des Fêtes Mobiles*. The manuscript Mateos has published, translated, and annotated is from the tenth century.

6. See Thomas J. Talley, *The Origins of the Liturgical Year*, p. 211.

7. F. C. Burkitt, *The Early Syriac Lectionary System*.

8. Burkitt, p. 6.

9. See the discussion in J. Quasten, *Patrology*, volume 3, p. 362ff. The reader should also consult the introduction by William Telfer in *Cyril of Jerusalem and Nemesius of Emesa*, LCC 4.

10. A. Mingana, WS 5 and 6. See also R. Tonneau, *Les Homélies Catéchètiques de Théodore de Mopsueste* (ST 145), Vatican City, 1949.

11. Two homilies were published in Migne. In 1909 A. Papadopulos-Kerameus discovered four, while in 1955 A. Wenger discovered a manuscript at the Stavronikita monastery on Mount Athos that contained eight new baptismal homilies. For full discussion, see Antoine Wenger, Jean Chrysostome, *Huit Catéchèses Baptismales*, SC 50 (Paris: Éditions du cerf, 1957), and Paul W. Harkins, *St. John Chrysostom: Baptismal Instructions*, ACW 31. Harkins's translation has the advantage of including all the extant homilies.

12. For full discussion, see Bernard Botte, SC 25*bis*.

13. For convenience, I shall refer to the author of the mystagogical lectures as Cyril.

14. See Wenger's discussion, SC 50, p. 84ff.

15. See the discussion in Aidan Kavanagh, *The Shape of Baptism: The Rite of Christian Initiation*, p. 47ff. Kavanagh argues that "the ethos of East Syrian baptismal patterns is perhaps more consecratory than initiatory" (p. 48).

16. See WS 6: "Our Lord God made man from dust in His image . . . but he accepted and completed the image of the Devil . . . And from the above sin death entered in" (p. 21); "When this state of our affairs became desperate, our Lord God willed in His mercy to rectify it. With this end in view He assumed a man from us. . . . The Tyrant, however, . . . brought an unjust death upon Him. . . . God, the just judge, . . . pronounced Him not liable to the punishment of death. . . . And He became for ever immune from death. . . . He became a messenger on behalf of all the (human) race so that the rest of mankind might participate with Him in His great change" (p. 22). See also pp. 30–34.

17. I have focused upon Chrysostom's homilies in this part of the argument. Cf., however, Cyril of Jerusalem, *NPNF* 2.7, pp. 7, 82, 118, 121, 133. In these passages the same apotropaic effect is attributed to the baptismal seal and the sign of the cross. The power is a gift of the Spirit.

18. Cf. also the passage on p. 146.

19. Needless to say, the two metaphors occur with considerable frequency. See, e.g., Cyril (*NPNF* 2.7, p. 17); Ambrose (SC 25*bis*, p. 136); Theodore (WS 6, p. 46); Chrysostom (ACW 31, pp. 58–60, 91–92, 140–41, 182–84).

20. Cf. Peter Brown's suggestion: "It may well be the case that the Christian Church effected a *détente* in sorcery beliefs in this period [Late Antiquity]. But it did not do this through its repeated and ineffective injunctions against 'superstitious' practices: rather, the Christian Church offered an explanation of misfortune that both embraced all the phenomena previously ascribed to sorcery, and armed the individual with weapons of satisfying precision and efficacy against its suprahuman agents." He is, of course, referring to demons and to the notion of Christ's victory over Satan. "Sorcery, Demons and the Rise of Christianity: From Late Antiquity into the Middle Ages," in *Religion and Society in the Age of Saint Augustine*, p. 132.

21. The date of the *Demonstration* is something of a problem since some passages appear to be written during a time of persecution (e.g., 2.3.82c; p. 97), while others refer to the peace of the church (e.g., 3.3.103c; p. 119, and 3.7.138b; p. 159). One resolution is to suppose that Eusebius is writing during and immediately after the Diocletian persecution; another is to suppose that the references to persecution refer to the immediate past rather than to the present. In any case we are dealing with a work produced about the time of the Constantinian revolution.

22. See also 3.2.97c, 98c; p. 112f.: 4.10.165a; p. 185.

23. For other passages associating the victory over Satan with the deliverance of many nations from idolatry, see 5.2.218b; p. 237, and 5.5.229c; p. 249.

24. For other references to the equation of demons and idolatry or paganism, see 1.6.20b; p. 37: 3.2.100c; p. 115: 3.3.107b; p. 123: 4.12.167c; p. 187: 6.13.272c; p. 14: 6.13.274a; p. 16.

25. Cf. the parallel passage 9.10.443a; p. 173.

26. See also *OI* 12–14, 43, 46–48; LCC 3, pp. 66ff., 97, 101ff.

27. For chastity, see *OI* 48; LCC 3, p. 102. References to massive conversion are frequent and probably reflect Athanasius's reaction to Constantine's willingness to patronize the church: *OI* 30, 32, 50, 52, 55; LCC 3, pp. 84, 86, 104, 106, 108.

28. See, for example, Rom 3:25, 5:9; Eph 1:7, 2:13; Col 1:14, 20; Heb 9:12, 26, 10:12, 19, 13:12.

CHAPTER 4

1. The story is perhaps best known from Jerome's *Life of Hilarion*, written about 390, when he took up residence at Bethlehem. Jerome treats Hilarion as the founder of Palestinian monasticism and tells of numerous miracles. A charioteer of Gaza, healed by Hilarion of a total paralysis, "rejoiced more in the saving of the soul than in that of the body" (*NPNF* 2.6; p. 306). Italicus, who kept circus horses, found himself opposed by a rival who hired a magician to help him win. Since "no Christian man could employ magic," Italicus successfully sought Hilarion's assistance. "After this the opponents in their rage demanded that Hilarion as a Christian magician should be dragged to execution. This decisive victory and several others which followed in successive games of the circus caused many to turn to the faith" (p. 307). Hilarion was equally successful in thwarting a magical plate used by a local youth to win the love of one of "God's virgins" (p. 307f.). He even expelled a demon from a large Bactrian camel (p. 308).

2. *Life of Constantine* 1.27–31. See the accounts in Soc. 1.2 and Soz. 1.3.

3. There is no need to try to wrestle with the true character of Constantine's conversion. Whatever we say needs to take account of the fact that Constantine

apparently had a similar vision in Gaul, but attributed it to Sol Invictus and of his ambiguous religious policy, which fell short of making the Empire Christian. The point I am making here has to do with Christian perceptions of the story.

4. For the story of Helena's discovery of the true cross, see Soc. 1.17, Soz. 2.1, Sulpicius Severus *HS* 2.33–34, Rufinus *EH* 1.7–8. The accounts, of course, differ with respect to details of the story.

5. See Eusebius's account of Galerius's death as a "punishment from God" (*EH* 8.16; *NPNF* 2.1, p. 338). Cf. Lactantius, *On the Manner in Which the Persecutors Died* 33.

6. See Soc. 3.20, Soz. 5.22, Rufinus *EH* 1.37–39, Theodoret *EH* 3.20, Ammianus Marcellinus 23.1–3. Ammianus mentions only the fire from the foundations of the Temple. As to the crosses miraculously appearing on the clothing, the same phenomenon has occurred in the present in Egypt, resulting in accusations by Muslims against the Coptic Christians. A possible explanation has to do with the way dyes behave on certain kinds of silk.

7. See Robert Wilken, *John Chrysostom and the Jews.*

8. Theodoret (*EH* 3.6–7) and Sozomen (*EH* 5.19–20) tell the story this way. Socrates (3.18) and Rufinus (*EH* 1.36) fail to mention the destruction of the temple of Apollo, while Ammianus (22.13) makes no reference to the transfer of Babylas's relics. He also says that, though Julian suspected the Christians of setting the fire, it was actually caused accidentally by a pagan votary who left candles burning in the temple. See also Chrysostom *On St. Babylas against Julian and the Pagans* and *Homily on St. Babylas*; Gregory Nazianzen, Orations 4–5.

9. The same story is told by Palladius in *Lausiac History* 36. Cf. the story of how Antony learns of Ammon's death in Soz. 1.14, *Lausiac History* 41, *Life of Antony* 60.

10. See, for example, Sozomen's account of how George of Laodicea as bishop of Alexandria destroyed the Mithraeum in Alexandria, exposed its secrets, and suffered assassination at the hands of the pagans at the beginning of Julian's reign (Soz. 5.7; cf. Soc. 3.2). Sozomen's aim is to shift the blame away from Athanasius and his supporters.

11. Cf. Theodoret *EH* 4.16, where the possibility of the miracle is tied to the child's baptism and where the Arians who do baptize the boy "immediately died" (*NPNF* 2.3, p. 120). Gregory of Nyssa describes what is apparently the same confrontation with Valens, but makes no mention of the child (*Against Eunomius* 1.12; *NPNF* 2.5, p. 48f.).

12. Athanasius tells of a miracle that vindicates orthodoxy. The Arians at one point took over the great church in Alexandria, and a "licentious" youth sat himself upon the bishop's throne. When he tried to drag the throne toward him, "he struck it into his own bowels; and instead of carrying out the throne, he brought out by a blow his own entrails." The punishment is that of Judas. Another heretical mocker is struck blind (*History of the Arians* 57; *NPNF* 2.4, p. 291). Cf. Epistle 49, where we read: "Or is it not a great wonder to make a damsel live as a virgin, and a young man live in continence, and an idolator come to know Christ? . . . We know bishops who work wonders, as well as monks who do not" (*NPNF* 2.4, p. 560).

13. Rufinus *EH* 1.9–10, Socrates 1.19, Sozomen 2.24, Theodoret *EH* 1.22.

14. The work survives in a shorter and a longer recension. The shorter is translated from Greek in *NPNF* 2.1. The longer exists only in Greek fragments and in a complete Syriac translation. I will use W. Cureton's translation of the Syriac (London: Williams and Norgate, 1861). See J. Quasten, *Patrology*, volume 3, p. 317f.

15. Cf. Patricia Cox's account of Eusebius's biography of Origen in Book 6 of his *Ecclesiastical History* (*Biography in Late Antiquity*, chapter 4). "Eusebius' picture of the holy man who works within a providential framework helps explain why the hero of his biography is cast in the godlike, rather than the son-of-god, mold" (p. 79). Cox here appeals to her distinction between two sorts of divine sages. "Sons of god work miracles; the godlike types do not" (p. 43). Her discussion helps explain why Eusebius prefers to treat the martyrs as examples of virtue and tends to play down their function as sources of power.

16. See another story in Eusebius that shows he takes the miraculous seriously. Some of the oil that Narcissus, a third-century bishop of Jerusalem, had made miraculously from water was preserved in Jerusalem. Eusebius betrays no doubt and has obviously seen the oil for himself (*EH* 6.9; *NPNF* 2.1, p. 255). The note in the *NPNF* translation fails to understand: "His travels had evidently not taught him to disbelieve every wonderful tale that was told him."

17. For the demons' association with vices, see *SF* 4.51 (anger), *SF* 5.11, 21, 23, 29, 36 (lust). For temptations not to fast or abstain from wine, see *SF* 4.25, 36, 37.

18. Peter Brown makes this point in connection with Theodoret's *History of the Monks in Syria*. See "The Holy Man in Late Antiquity," in *Society and the Holy*, p. 121: "The miracle is felt to be secondary: for it was merely a proof of power—like good coin, summarily minted and passed into circulation to demonstrate the untapped bullion of power at the disposal of the holy man."

19. See also John Cassian, *Institutes* 4.24, and Sulpicius Severus, *Dialogues* 1.19. Cassian omits the miracle.

20. See also Sozomen 3.14 and John Cassian, *Conf.* 15.3.

21. For example, Paul the Simple expels a demon (*LH* 22; ACW 34, p. 80); Innocent heals a paralyzed demoniac by employing the relics of John the Baptist (*LH* 44; ACW 34, p. 121); Benjamin, though monstrously swollen with dropsy and about to die, still heals (*LH* 12; ACW 34, p. 48); Sarapion meets Domninus, one of Origen's disciples, in Rome; after Domninus's death, his bed heals people (*LH* 37; ACW 34, p. 108); Julian has the gift of healing (*LH* 42; ACW 34, p. 119); Macarius of Egypt outwits a pagan sorcerer who has changed a man's wife into a brood mare (*LH* 17; ACW 34, p. 56); and we find two stories of raising people from the dead (*SF* 5.37 and 14.17; LCC 12, pp. 72 and 154).

22. See R. C. Gregg's discussion in CWS, p. 11ff.

23. See *Confessions* 8.6.

24. The role of Scripture in *The Life of Antony* is central. It is hearing the Gospel read in church (Mt 19:21, 6:34) that leads Antony to embark on the ascetic life (*LA* 2–3; CWS, p. 31). Antony learns about the wiles of the devil from Scripture (*LA* 7; CWS, p. 35). He uses actual verses from Scripture to rebuke the demons: Ps 118:7 (*LA* 6; CWS, p. 35), Rom 8:35 and Ps 27:3 (*LA* 9; CWS, p. 38), Ps 68:1–2 and Ps 118:10 (*LA* 13; CWS, p. 41f.), Rom 8:35 (*LA* 40; CWS, p. 61), Ps 20:7 and Ps 38:13 (*LA* 39; CWS, p. 60f.).

25. In addition to the passage cited here, see *LA* 56, 62, 65, 84; CWS, pp. 73, 77, 78, 92.

26. The long discourse is *LA* 16–43; CWS, p. 43ff. It represents more than a third of the text of *The Life of Antony*.

27. See Peter Brown's discussion of the passage in *The Cult of the Saints*, p. 94.

28. Martin Esper has studied this work from the point of view of its rhetorical form: "Enkomiastik und Christianismos in Gregors epideiktischer Rede auf den Heiligen Theodor," in *The Biographical Works of Gregory of Nyssa*.

29. See Monique Alexandre, "Les Nouveaux Martyrs," in *The Biographical Works of Gregory of Nyssa*, p. 36f.

30. The story is almost the same as the one told of Epiphanius. See above, page 95.

31. See Peter Brown's discussion in *The Cult of the Saints*, p. 57f.

32. *GT, PG* 46. 901, 908, 913. For the comparison with Moses, see also 925, 949. Comparisons also occur with Joseph (905), Solomon (925), and Samuel (933). See also Marguerite Harl, "Moïse Figure de l'Évêque dans l'Éloge de Basile de Grégoire de Nysse," in *The Biographical Works of Gregory of Nyssa*, p. 80 ff.

33. See *MS* 21.6–7, 24.4, 27.3, 29.5.

34. See *MS* 7.4, 21.20, 24.2. A counter-theme is that of the monk who seeks to conceal his burial place: *MS* 3.18, 15.5, 21.30.

35. The same story as that told of Gregory Thaumaturgus and of Epiphanius. See above, pages 95, 110.

36. See Peter Brown, "Town, Village and Holy Man: The Case of Syria," in *Society and the Holy in Late Antiquity*, p. 153ff.

37. Here I find myself disagreeing with Pierre Canivet's argument that despite surface appearances Theodoret is not preoccupied with miracles. See especially *Le Monachisme Syrien selon Théodoret de Cyr*, p. 96, and the whole of chapter 6. I should agree that *On Divine Love* represents the framework into which Theodoret wishes to place the lives of his monks, but am doubtful that the framework is quite able to hold its contents.

CHAPTER 5

1. In the 1850 edition, volume 3, pp. 161, 163. (Edward Gibbon, *The History of the Decline and Fall of the Roman Empire*, ed. H. H. Milman [New York: Harper & Brothers, 1850].)

2. I am thinking primarily of Brown's discussion in *The Cult of the Saints*, pp. 13–22.

3. See above, pages 47, 56, 73f., 78f.

4. See A. A. Barb, "The Survival of Magic Arts," in *The Conflict Between Paganism and Christianity in the Fourth Century*, ed. Arnaldo Momigliano, p. 105: "But while the Church consistently and uncompromisingly refused to make any distinction between magic and paganism, the emperors half-heartedly tolerated the old religious institutions which had been part and parcel of Roman public administration, but turned savagely against the prevalence of sorcery."

5. See Charles Joseph Hefele, *A History of the Christian Councils from the Original Documents*, volume 1, p. 131ff.

6. Hefele, volume 1, p. 221.

7. Hefele, volume 2, p. 295ff.

8. Cf. Barb's discussion in "The Survival of Magic Arts," p. 107.

9. Hefele, volume 3, p. 170.

10. Cf. Augustine, Ep. 22. See also Peter Brown, *The Cult of the Saints*, p. 26. The issue does not arise in Augustine's *The Care to be Taken for the Dead*, where he is preoccupied with burial itself and with the function of the buried saints.

11. *Theodosian Code* 9.16.2, see N. Lewis and M. Reinhold, *Roman Civilization, Sourcebook II: The Empire*, p. 607.

12. See Barb, "The Survival of Magic Arts," p. 107: "Contrary to Gibbon's sugges-

tion, repeated by many subsequent historians, there is not, it must be stressed, a single imperial decree before Theodosius at the end of the century which under Christian influence prohibits any institution of the established pagan religion of the Roman state, as far as—and this is important—genuine public institutions, defined and ordered by sacred law, are concerned." The evidence may be found in the Theodosian Codex 9 and 16.

13. See Peter Brown, "Sorcery, Demons and the Rise of Christianity: From Late Antiquity into the Middle Ages," in *Religion and Society in the Age of Saint Augustine*, p. 119ff. See especially p. 122f.: "My thesis, in the first part of this paper, is that a precise *malaise* in the structure of the governing classes of the Roman Empire (especially in its eastern, Greek-speaking half) forced the ubiquitous sorcery beliefs of ancient man to a flash-point of accusations in the mid-fourth century A.D." The *malaise* to which Brown refers is "the problem of the conflict between change and stability in a traditional society" (p. 124).

14. See above, pages 47, 73f., and chapter 4, note 1.

15. See, for example, Michel Meslin, *Le Christianisme dans l'Empire Romain*, p. 168ff. Meslin attempts to distinguish pagan prodigies from Christian miracles as theophanies.

16. Cf. Peter Brown, *The Making of Late Antiquity*: "Men believed in both 'miracles' and 'magic.' This was not because their credulity was boundless. It was rather so that they should feel free to exercise a choice as to which wielder of supernatural power they would acclaim as a holy man and which they would dismiss as a sorcerer" (p. 19). "The sorcerer was merely a paradigm of supernatural power misapplied in society; and the criteria used to judge the source and exercise of such power involved issues that were far from being purely theological" (p. 20). "For the distinction between rational philosophy and irrational magic, though present, was never central to the debate. What was hotly debated was the difference between legitimate and illegitimate forms of supernatural power" (p. 60).

17. See Charles Cochrane, *Christianity and Classical Culture*.

18. See A. H. M. Jones, *The Later Roman Empire*, chapters 22 and 23.

19. See J. Quasten, *Patrology*, volume 3, p. 542ff., and Pierre Canivet, *Histoire d'une entreprise apologétique au Ve siècle*.

20. See above, pages 60, 117, 154, 162ff., 165, 166.

21. Peter Brown, *The Cult of the Saints*, p. 37.

22. See Ammianus Marcellinus 27.3.12–15. The church was then called the basilica of Sicininus. Though they do not give the number of the slain, Socrates (4.29) and Sozomen (6.23) agree with Ammianus's account if not with his interpretation. He digresses from his story to attack bishops like Damasus who are "enriched from the offerings of matrons, ride seated in carriages, wearing clothing chosen with care, and serve banquets so lavish that their entertainments outdo the tables of kings. These men might be truly happy, if they would disregard the greatness of the city behind which they hide their faults, and live after the manner of some provincial bishops, whose moderation in food and drink, plain apparel also, and gaze fixed upon the earth, commend them to the Eternal Deity and to his true servants as pure and reverent men."

23. "Matronarum auriscalpius." See *Collectio Avellana*, Ep. 1 (*CSEL* 35, p. 4).

24. H. P. V. Nunn, *Christian Inscriptions*, p. 49f.

25. Nunn, p. 55.

26. Nunn, p. 65.

27. See also *City of God* 22.8, Sermon 286.

28. Ambrose defends the truth of the miracle of the blind man's healing and compares it to the story in John 9 (*NPNF* 2.10, p. 439).

29. See also Poem 19; ACW 40, pp. 133, 136.

30. See above, pages 130 and 100.

31. See Socrates 7.21–22, Sozomen 9.1, Theodoret *EH* 5.36. Cf. the discussion in J. B. Bury, *History of the Later Roman Empire*, volume 1, p. 212ff.

32. See Elizabeth A. Clark, *The Life of Melania the Younger*.

33. See Bury, *History of the Later Roman Empire*, volume 1, p. 227.

34. See Norman H. Baynes, "The Supernatural Defenders of Constantinople," in *Byzantine Studies and Other Essays*, p. 250ff.

35. See Norman H. Baynes, "The Finding of the Virgin's Robe," in *Byzantine Studies and Other Essays*, p. 240ff.

36. Not only the date but also Egeria's name is uncertain. She is often called Etheria. See the discussion in J. Quasten, *Patrology*, volume 4, p. 558ff., and in Hélène Petré, *Éthérie: Journal de Voyage*, SC 21 (Paris: Éditions du Cerf, 1948), p. 7ff.

37. Cf. Augustine's discussion of purgatory in the *Enchiridion*. Only those who already have Christ as their foundation gain benefit from purgatory and are aided by our prayers.

38. Peter Brown assesses Augustine's attitude from a different, but not, I think, an incompatible point of view. Augustine, "the eloquent exponent of the ideal unity of the Catholic church . . . whose education and later clerical career had enabled him to step aside a little from the aristocratic structures of the Latin West, was lukewarm. He accepted the practice [of *depositio ad sanctos*]; but he paints in distinctly pastel shades the associations of the *memoria* of Saint Felix, which Paulinus and his aristocratic friends had been painting with so rich a palette for over a generation." *The Cult of the Saints*, p. 35.

39. Jerome treats these statements as the words of Vigilantius.

40. See J. N. D. Kelly's discussion, *Jerome*, pp. 286–90.

41. See Henry Chadwick, *Priscillian of Avila*, p. 33. See page 14 for the canons of Saragossa. I should add that I am depending fully upon Chadwick's careful reconstruction of the events and of Priscillian's teaching.

42. See Chadwick, p. 35.

43. Siricius refused to see Paulinus in 395. See Paulinus of Nola, Ep. 5.13–14; ACW 35, p. 62f. Paulinus gives no explanation of the event, but it seems likely enough that Siricius, and Damasus before him, were perplexed about the charismatic leaders of the new asceticism.

44. See J. N. D. Kelly, *Jerome*, p. 314.

45. See Kelly, *Jerome*, chapter 11 ("Triumph and Disgrace"), p. 104ff.

46. See Kelly, *Jerome*, p. 186: "But what is most disappointing is that he nowhere comes to grips with, nowhere seems to understand Jovinian's fundamental thesis, viz. that baptism received with genuine faith really does abolish original sin and effects a total regeneration, creating a unified, holy community in which distinctions based on merit are without meaning."

47. See Owen Chadwick's remarks in *John Cassian*, p. 26.

48. I understand that Elizabeth Clarke is working on a book that will deal fully with the Origenist controversy. Such a volume will fill an important gap in the literature.

49. See my discussion in *Broken Lights and Mended Lives*, p. 180ff.

50. See Peter Brown, "Pelagius and His Supporters: Aims and Environment" and "The Patrons of Pelagius: The Roman Aristocracy between East and West," in *Religion and Society in the Age of Saint Augustine*, p. 183ff.

51. See Peter Brown, *Augustine of Hippo*, p. 346: "Pelagianism had appealed to a universal theme: the need of the individual to define himself, and to feel free to create his own values in the midst of the conventional, second-rate life of society."

52. For an excellent discussion of literary character of the *Life*, see Jacques Fontaine, *Sulpice Sévère: Vie de Saint Martin*, SC 133, p. 59ff.

53. See, for example, the stories in *Dialogues* 2.3, 6, 7; 3.4, 13.

54. For his conversation with saints and angels, see *Dials.* 2.13, *LMar* 21. For demons, see *LMar* 6, 22, 23; Ep. 2; *Dials.* 3.6. For miracles of healing, see *LMar* 16–19; Ep. 3; *Dials.* 2.9, 3.6. For resurrections, see *LMar* 7–8, *Dials.* 2.5.

55. See *LMar* 13, *Dials.* 3.9.

56. See Jacques Fontaine, SC 133, p. 80ff. The opponents of the new asceticism include pagans, Christians like Ausonius who remain committed to classical culture, and those who associate Martin and his followers with Priscillianism. See also Clare Stancliffe's discussion in *St. Martin and His Hagiographer*, chapter 18. Stancliffe points out that doubts about Martin's miraculous powers center upon his visionary claims and not upon his ability to manipulate nature. "Brice's enraged outburst to Martin [*Dials.* 3.15] . . . illustrates the real grounds for contemporaries' mistrust of the claims made about Martin: how were they to know that his so-called visitations by saints, angels, and demons were not mere illusions?" (p. 258).

57. *Dials.* 1.26; *NPNF* 2.11, p. 37. See also *Dials.* 3.5 and *LMar* 25.

58. According to Severus (*SH* 50), Ithacius, the chief foe of Priscillian, brought a formal charge of heresy against Martin, even though Martin's fault was merely that of arguing that excommunication sufficed as a punishment for Priscillian and that he should not be tried or executed by a civil court.

59. In the following passage Severus's chronology appears mistaken. Priscillian seems to have been executed in 386, and Martin died in 397. For other passages regarding the hostility of the bishops to Martin, see *LMar* 27, *Dials.* 1.24. For the chronology, see Chadwick, *Priscillian of Avila*, p. 133.

60. Clare Stancliffe in *St. Martin and His Hagiographer* also recognizes that opposition to Martin springs not only from his association with Priscillianism (p. 260 and chapter 20) but also from animosities stirred up by the Origenist controversy (p. 307). Stancliffe is rather more cautious and careful than I have been, and she might not be willing to follow me in arguing that the problem is not merely the debates over asceticism in the West but more broadly the issue of whether there should be such a thing as a holy man. Nevertheless, her detailed and convincing account of Martin and of Sulpicius Severus drives in the direction I have taken.

61. Cf. Peter Brown, "Eastern and Western Christendom in Late Antiquity: A Parting of the Ways," in *Society and the Holy in Late Antiquity*, p. 166ff. See especially, p. 178f.: "In the West the precise *locus* of the supernatural power associated with the holy was fixed with increasing precision. . . . At the same time, the eastern Church had entered on to what came to strike early medieval western observers as a baffling 'crisis of overproduction' of the holy. More men were accepted as bearers or agents of the supernatural on earth, and in a far greater variety of situations, than came to be tolerated in a Western Europe. As a result, the precise *locus* of spiritual power in Byzantium remained, by western standards, tantalizingly ambiguous."

CHAPTER 6

1. See Geoffrey Faber, *Oxford Apostles: A Character Study of the Oxford Movement* (London: Faber and Faber, 1933/74), p. 19f.

2. The translation is from Werner Jaeger, *Two Rediscovered Works of Ancient Christian Literature*, p. 116. See also discussions of the work in Louis Bouyer, *The Spirituality of the New Testament and the Fathers*, p. 358ff., and Ronald E. Heine, *Perfection in the Virtuous Life*, p. 19ff.

3. The translation is, again, Jaeger's, *Two Rediscovered Works*, p. 50. Jaeger defines the two parts of the treatise as 40, 1–66, 13 and 66, 14–end (p. 51).

4. Cf. Jaeger, *Two Rediscovered Works*, p. 49: "Here . . . Gregory teaches that there is in the soul of man an inborn *eros* of the good, but this divine *eros*, which is part of man's original and true nature, is obscured by the rule of passion over reason; and if it is the goal of man's life to fulfill his true nature (as Plato would put it), he can attain the goal only by setting free this divine *eros* within him."

5. Here Gregory repeats a theme found in Methodius. *Parthenia* (virginity) means nearness to God (*para theo*).

6. See also *Republic* 613 B. Jaeger also points out that the theme approximates Aristotle's definition of human destiny (*Eth. Nic.* X 7, 1177 b 33) as "to live the eternal life so far as is possible for a human being." *Two Rediscovered Works*, p. 103.

7. Gregory's Christianization of the Platonic theme of "likeness to God as far as possible" by no means implies any repudiation of the Platonic themes. Indeed, in many places his language reflects Plato's understanding of love and of the soul. See, for example, *On the Soul and the Resurrection* (*NPNF* 2.5, p. 450): "Whenever the soul, then, having divested itself of the multifarious emotions incident to its nature, gets its Divine form and, mounting above Desire, enters within that towards which it was once incited by that Desire, it offers no harbour within itself for hope or for memory. . . . None of its habits are left to it except that of love, which clings by natural affinity to the Beautiful." Gregory weaves together the theme of Diotima's account of love in the *Symposium* with Paul's panegyric of love in 1 Corinthians 13.

8. See Jaeger, *Two Rediscovered Works*, p. 58.

9. See Heine, *Perfection in the Virtuous Life*, p. 2, and Bouyer, *Spirituality of the New Testament*, p. 355f. The major point to make is that Gregory does not establish any single pattern, even though he sets the stage, through his reworking of Origen, for the distinctions between the purgative, the illuminative, and the unitive stages. He tends to treat the moral life as a preparation for contemplation; but, while he retains the contemplative ideal as one way of speaking of human destiny, he also regards contemplation as what enables the moral life.

10. See the notes in FC 65, p. 60ff., including the reference to P. Courcelle, *Recherches sur les "Confessions" de saint Augustin*, pp. 107–9.

11. See above, pages 41 and 62, for Ambrose's view that punishment is the negative effect of providence that we bring upon ourselves; see page 53 for Chrysostom's use of the sailing-ship metaphor to explain the relation of providence and freedom; page 85 for Gregory's treatment of Satan in the light of providence and freedom.

12. See above, pages 74ff. and 80. See page 107 for Athanasius's treatment of Antony's virtue.

13. See above, pages 83 and 111.

14. Cf. Quasten's judgment of Gregory's *De instituto Christiano* (*Patrology*, volume 3, p. 274): "It is in this admirable form that Gregory's teaching penetrated the monastic world and influenced the educational system of the East. The author's purpose is to harmonize the concept of grace with the Hellenistic ethical tradition and the classical ideal of virtue (*arete*). The roots of his 'Christian philosophy' go back to Platonism and the Stoa, but he forms something entirely new in this intermarriage of Hellenism and Christianity."

15. Chrysostom returns to these themes at *OP* 8.11.

16. See also *On the Incomprehensibility of God* 1; SC 28, p. 80ff.

17. See also *On the Incomprehensibility of God* 1; SC 28, p. 96.

18. See above, page 53.

19. See the discussion of providence and freedom in Louis Meyer, *Saint Jean Chrysostome: Maître de Perfection Chrétienne*, pp. 108–29.

20. The phrase is Jerome's. See above, page 17. See also pages 11, 17, 27, 32, 33, 37, 38, 60.

21. See Robert M. Grant, *Miracle and Natural Law in Graeco-Roman and Early Christian Thought*, chapters 1 and 2. One should also consult Baziel Maes, *La Loi Naturelle selon Ambroise de Milan*, especially Art. II.

22. God's lack of envy almost certainly alludes to Plato, *Timaeus* 28b–30a. In addition to the passage discussed here, see also *HSD* 1.7; SC 26, p. 118.

23. See *HSD* 5.1; SC 26, p. 280. Here Basil actually uses the expression "law of nature" (*nomos tis egeneto physeos*).

24. Peter Brown in *Augustine of Hippo*, p. 413ff. takes essentially the same approach. See, for example, page 415: "Thus, Augustine's sudden decision to give a maximum of publicity to miraculous cures in Africa, should not be regarded as a sudden and unprepared surrender to popular credulity. It is, rather, that, within the immensely complex structure of Augustine's thought, the centre of gravity had shifted; modern miracles, which had once been peripheral, now become urgently important as supports of faith."

25. See also Augustine's words in the very next section (*UB* xv, 33; LCC 6, p. 319): "Miracles must be presented to the eyes, of which fools are much readier to make use than of the mind, so that under the constraint of authority men's lives and morals may first be purified, and they may thus become able to follow reason."

26. See the discussion of Augustine's use of the notion of "rational seeds" by R. A. Markus in *The Cambridge History of Later Greek and Early Medieval Philosophy*, p. 395ff. Markus supplies references to important passages in *De Gen. ad litt.* that I omit from my discussion. Markus's judgment is: "Though primarily exegetical in its purpose, the notion of 'seminal reasons' had far-reaching implications for Augustine's conception of nature. It suggested a conception of nature as a system of processes, subject to their own laws, of things interacting, functioning, and developing according to the primordial principles of their being" (p. 399).

27. I am following Peter Brown in *Augustine of Hippo*, Chronological Tables D and E.

28. I owe this formulation to Grant, *Miracle and Natural Law*, p. 217: "We may say that Augustine's view is not so much that miracles are natural as that nature is miraculous." See the whole of Grant's discussion. He concludes that Augustine's view of miracles "marks the end of ancient science and indeed of ancient civilization" (p. 220). Markus's judgment in *The Cambridge History of Later Greek and Early Medieval Philosophy* (p. 402) is similar: "God's freedom to act in nature is

triumphantly vindicated, but nature itself is dissolved in the freedom of the divine will."

29. My emphasis differs from Peter Brown's. See, for example, *Augustine of Hippo*, p. 417: "To 'heal the eyes of the heart', remained the essence of religion; but Augustine had now made room, also, for the fate of the body." See also *The Cult of the Saints*, p. 77: "The recorded miracles of healing at the shrines show God's power and his abiding concern for the flesh." My impression is that Brown would emphasize the second, while I wish to underline the first.

30. See, for example, *LR* 17; ACW 32, p. 34. *AC* 3; ACW 32, p. 90. *Answer to the Gauls*, Art. 6; ACW 32, p. 144f.

EPILOGUE

1. Fyodor Dostoyevsky, *The Brothers Karamazov* (Baltimore, Md.: Penguin Books, 1958), volume 1, p. 299.

2. Peter Brown, *The Cult of the Saints*, p. 126f.

Selected Bibliography

Armstrong, A. H. *Plotinian and Christian Studies*. London: Variorum Reprints, 1979.
———, ed. *The Cambridge History of Later Greek and Early Medieval Philosophy*. Cambridge: At the University Press, 1970.
Balás, David L. *Metousia Theou: Man's Participation in God's Perfections according to Saint Gregory of Nyssa*. Studia Anselmiana 55. Rome: Libreria Herder, 1966.
Barnes, Timothy D. *Constantine and Eusebius*. Cambridge, Mass.: Harvard University Press, 1981.
Baur, Chrysostomus. *John Chrysostom and His Time*. 2 vols. Westminster, Md.: Newman Press, 1960–61.
Baynes, Norman H. *Constantine the Great and the Christian Church*. London: Oxford University Press, 1929, 1972.
———, *Byzantine Studies and Other Essays*. London: The Athlone Press, 1955.
Bouyer, Louis. *The Spirituality of the New Testament and the Fathers*. New York: Desclée Company, 1963.
Bovini, Guiseppi. *La Vita di Cristo nei Mosaici di S. Apollinare Nuovo di Ravenna*. Ravenna: Edizioni Dante, 1959.
Brown, Peter. *Augustine of Hippo: A Biography*. Berkeley: University of California Press, 1969.
———. *Religion and Society in the Age of St. Augustine*. New York: Harper & Row, 1972.
———. *The Making of Late Antiquity*. Cambridge, Mass.: Harvard University Press, 1978.
———. *The Cult of the Saints*. Chicago: University of Chicago Press, 1981.
———. *Society and the Holy in Late Antiquity*. Berkeley: University of California Press, 1982.

Burkitt, F. C. *The Early Syriac Lectionary System*. London: Proceedings of the British Academy, vol. 11, 1923.

Bury, J. B. *History of the Later Roman Empire: From the Death of Theodosius I to the Death of Justinian*. 2 vols. London: Constable, 1958.

Canivet, Pierre. *Histoire d'une entreprise apologétique au Ve siecle*. Paris: Bloud & Gay, 1957.

———. *Le monachisme syrien selon Théodoret de Cyr*. Paris: Editions Beauchesne, 1977.

Chadwick, Henry. *Priscillian of Avila: The Occult and the Charismatic in the Early Church*. London: Oxford University Press, 1976.

Chadwick, Owen. *John Cassian*. Cambridge: Cambridge University Press, 1950.

Chesnut, Glenn F. *The First Christian Histories: Eusebius, Socrates, Sozomen, Theodoret, and Evagrius*. Paris: Editions Beauchesne, 1977.

Chitty, Derwas J. *The Desert a City: An Introduction to the Study of Egyptian and Palestinian Monasticism under the Christian Empire*. Oxford: Basil Blackwell, 1966.

Clark, Elizabeth A. *Jerome, Chrysostom, and Friends: Essays and Translations*. New York: Edwin Mellen Press, 1979.

Cochrane, Charles N. *Christianity and Classical Culture: A Study of Thought and Action from Augustus to Augustine*. London: Oxford University Press, 1940.

Collectio Avellana. *Corpus Scriptorum Ecclesiasticorum Latinorum 35*, ed. Otto Guenther. Vienna and Prague: F. Tempsky, 1895–98.

Courcelle, Pierre P. *Recherches sur les "Confessions" de Saint Augustin*. Paris: E. de Boccard, 1968.

Cox, Patricia. *Biography in Late Antiquity: A Quest for the Holy Man*. Berkeley: University of California Press, 1983.

Dodds, E. R. *The Greeks and the Irrational*. Berkeley: University of California Press, 1951, 1964.

Doignon, Jean. *Hilaire de Poitiers avant l'Exil*. Paris: Etudes Augustiniennes, 1971.

Evans, Robert F. *One and Holy: The Church in Latin Patristic Thought*. London: S. P. C. K., 1972.

Gallagher, Eugene V. *Divine Man or Magician? Celsus and Origen on Jesus*. SBL Dissertation Series 64. Chico, Calif.: Scholars Press, 1982.

Grant, Robert M. *Miracle and Natural Law in Graeco-Roman and Early Christian Thought*. Amsterdam: North Holland Publishing Company, 1952.

Greer, Rowan A. *Broken Lights and Mended Lives: Theology and Common Life in the Early Church*. University Park and London: Pennsylvania State University Press, 1986.

Grillmeier, Aloys. *Christ in Christian Tradition: From the Apostolic Age to Chalcedon (451)*. Ed. J. S. Bowden. London: A. R. Mowbray & Co., 1965; enlarged & revised 1975.

Hefele, Charles Joseph. *A History of the Christian Councils from the Original Documents*. 4 vols. Ed. W. R. Clark. Edinburgh: T. & T. Clark, 1894.

Heine, Ronald E. *Perfection in the Virtuous Life*. Cambridge, Mass.: The Philadelphia Patristic Foundation, 1975.

Henry, Patrick, ed. *Schools of Thought in the Christian Tradition*. Philadelphia: Fortress Press, 1984. See especially Robert L. Wilken, "Alexandria: A School for Training in Virtue."

Jaeger, Werner. *Early Christianity and Greek Paideia.* Cambridge, Mass.: Harvard University Press, 1962.

———. *Two Rediscovered Works of Ancient Christian Literature: Gregory of Nyssa and Macarius.* Leiden: E. J. Brill, 1965.

Jones, A. H. M. *The Later Roman Empire, 284–602.* 2 vols. Norman: University of Oklahoma Press, 1964.

Kavanagh, Aidan. *The Shape of Baptism: The Rite of Christian Initiation.* New York: Pueblo Publishing Company, 1978.

Kee, Howard Clark. *Miracle in the Early Christian World: A Study in Sociohistorical Method.* New Haven: Yale University Press, 1983.

Kelly, J. N. D. *Early Christian Doctrines.* London: Longmans, Green & Co., 1950.

———. *Jerome: His Life, Writings, and Controversies.* New York: Harper & Row, 1975.

Krautheimer, Richard. *Rome: Profile of a City, 312–1308.* Princeton: Princeton University Press, 1980.

———. *Three Christian Capitals: Topography and Politics.* Berkeley: University of California Press, 1983.

Lewis, N., and M. Reinhold. *Roman Civilization, Sourcebook II: The Empire.* New York: Harper & Row, 1966.

Louth, Andrew. *The Origins of the Christian Mystical Tradition: From Plato to Denys.* Oxford: At the Clarendon Press, 1981.

MacMullen, Ramsay. *Christianizing the Roman Empire: A.D. 100–400.* New Haven: Yale University Press, 1984.

Maes, Baziel. *La Loi Naturelle selon Ambroise de Milan.* Rome: Presses de l'Université Gregorienne, 1967.

Markus, R. A. *Saeculum: History and Society in the Theology of St. Augustine.* Cambridge: Cambridge University Press, 1970.

Mateos, Juan. *Le Typikon de la Grande Eglise, Tome II, Le Cycle des Fêtes Mobiles.* Orientalia Christiana Analecta 166. Rome: Pont. Inst. Orient. Stud., 1963.

Mathews, Thomas F. *The Early Churches of Constantinople: Architecture and Liturgy.* University Park and London: Pennsylvania State University Press, 1971.

Meslin, Michel. *Le Christianisme dans l'Empire Romain.* Paris: presses Universitaires de France, 1970.

Meyer, Louis. *Saint Jean Chrysostome: Maître de Perfection Chrétienne.* Paris: Gabriel Beauchesne et ses fils, 1933.

Momigliano, Arnaldo, ed. *The Conflict Between Paganism and Christianity in the Fourth Century.* Oxford: At the University Press, 1963.

Moule, C. F. D., ed. *Miracles: Cambridge Studies in their Philosophy and History.* London: A. R. Mowbray & Co., 1965.

Norris, Richard A. *Manhood and Christ: A Study in the Christology of Theodore of Mopsuestia.* Oxford: At the Clarendon Press, 1963.

Nunn, H. P. V. *Christian Inscriptions.* New York: Philosophical Library, 1952.

Osborn, Eric. *Ethical Patterns in Early Christian Thought.* Cambridge: Cambridge University Press, 1976.

Quasten, Johannes. *Patrology.* 4 vols. Westminster, Md.: Christian Classics, 1986. (The new edition includes a fourth volume.)

Remus, Harold. *Pagan-Christian Conflict over Miracle in the Second Century.* Cambridge, Mass.: Philadelphia Patristic Foundation, 1983.

Rist, John M. *Eros and Psyche: Studies in Plato, Plotinus, and Origen.* Toronto: University of Toronto Press, 1964.

Rousseau, Philip. *Ascetics, Authority, and the Church in the Age of Jerome and Cassian.* London: Oxford University Press, 1978.

Spira, Andreas, ed. *The Biographical Works of Gregory of Nyssa.* Cambridge, Mass.: Philadelphia Patristic Foundation, 1984.

Stancliffe, Clare. *St. Martin and His Hagiographer: History and Miracle in Sulpicius Severus.* Oxford: At the Clarendon Press, 1983.

Talley, Thomas J. *The Origins of the Liturgical Year.* New York: Pueblo Publishing Company, 1986.

TeSelle, Eugene. *Augustine the Theologian.* London: Burns & Oates, 1970.

Tiede, David L. *The Charismatic Figure as Miracle Worker.* SBL Dissertation Series 1. Missoula, Mont.: The Society of Biblical Literature, 1972.

von Simson, O. G. *Sacred Fortress: Byzantine Art and Statecraft in Ravenna.* Chicago: University of Chicago Press, 1948.

Voöbus, Arthur. *History of Asceticism in the Syrian Orient.* CSCO Subsidia 14 and 17. Louvain: CSCO, 1958, 1960.

Wiles, Maurice. *The Spiritual Gospel: The Interpretation of the Fourth Gospel in the Early Church.* Cambridge: At the University Press, 1960.

Wilken, Robert L. *Judaism and the Early Christian Mind: A Study of Cyril of Alexandria's Exegesis and Theology.* New Haven: Yale University Press, 1971.

———. *John Chrysostom and the Jews: Rhetoric and Reality in the Late Fourth Century.* Berkeley: University of California Press, 1984.

Winslow, Donald F. *The Dynamics of Salvation: A Study in Gregory of Nazianzus.* Cambridge, Mass.: Philadelphia Patristic Foundation, 1979.

Young, Frances. *From Nicaea to Chalcedon.* Philadelphia: Fortress Press, 1983.

Index

Adam, 13, 14, 21, 41, 45, 51, 69, 71ff., 82,
  84f., 178
  and Eve, 41, 72, 84, 110, 141, 157, 159
  new Adam, 21, 41, 71ff., 75, 82
Ambrose, 138
  and Christian Platonism, 156–61
  and cult of saints, 125, 127–28, 138
  and Priscillian, 139
  catechetical works, 68ff.
  homilies on Luke, 36–42
amulets. *See* magic
Arianism, 10, 17, 29, 43, 63, 76, 94, 104,
  122, 128
astrology. *See* magic
Athanasius, 93, 96
  Life of Antony, 91, 104–7, 110, 113, 179
  On the Incarnation, 82–84, 107
Augustine, 2, 36, 104, 119, 129, 138
  and miracles, 170–77, 179, 180
  and Pelagianism, 143
  and Platonism, 150–51, 169ff.
  homilies on John, 43–48
  On the Care to be Taken for the Dead,
  135ff.

baptism, 40, 62–76, 156, 157–58, 160
  catechetical homilies, 67ff.
  Christ's, 49, 50, 70

meaning of, 70ff.
  rites of, 68ff., 75
Basil the Great, 94, 100, 148
  Homilies on the Six Days of Creation,
  166–70
Brown, Peter, 3, 118–19, 125, 127, 181–82

church,
  context for miracles, 2–3, 5, 6, 87, 103,
  115–16, 117ff., 123–24, 128ff., 148–49
  miracles establish, 10, 17, 49, 50, 51, 52,
  53, 56, 57, 60, 79, 171ff.
  miracles signify, 10, 13–16, 21ff., 31, 33,
  38ff., 57–58, 60
  ship of, 14, 15, 16, 31, 46
Constantine, 2–3, 6, 8–9, 91ff., 121, 126,
  131, 132, 137, 148
Constantinian revolution, 2–3, 8–9, 125,
  180
  and Christian commonwealth, 10, 51,
  78–79, 91–92, 115–16, 129, 147ff.
  and sacralizing the Empire, 5, 33, 124,
  125, 148–49, 180–81
contemplation, 111, 114, 151, 152, 153,
  155–56, 158ff., 160, 161. *See also* Platonism, Christian
cult of saints, 2–3, 5, 73, 97, 117ff., 124–38,
  147, 176–77, 181

organization of, 125ff., 129ff., 132–33,
    135. *See also* martyrs; relics
Cyril of Alexandria, 119
    commentary on John, 29–32
    homilies on Luke, 57–60
Cyril of Jerusalem,
    and true cross, 132ff.
    catechetical homilies, 67ff.

Damasus, 126–27, 139, 140
Didymus the Blind, 90, 93

Eucharist, 31, 40, 54, 62, 64, 73, 75, 156
Eusebius of Caesarea, 88, 89, 90, 119, 148
    Demonstration, 76–81
    Life of Constantine, 8–9, 91ff.
    Martyrs of Palestine, 97–99
Evagrius Ponticus, 90, 102, 138, 142
evil, problem of, 161ff., 168. *See also* free-
    dom and providence

freedom, 1ff., 5, 6, 60, 69, 70, 74–75, 80,
    84, 86, 151, 154, 156, 157–58, 160, 161,
    177, 178, 179, 181–82
    and providence, 41, 42, 53, 61–62, 73,
        84–85, 87, 92, 154, 155–56, 160, 161ff.,
        164ff., 167, 172
    and virtue, 2, 3, 5–6, 7, 53, 54–55, 58, 76,
        82, 83, 86, 101, 106ff., 110–11, 112,
        114, 119, 135, 151–53, 156–57, 160,
        161, 165, 171, 176. *See also* Platonism,
        Christian; Satan, warfare with; sover-
        eignty of God

Gregory of Nyssa, 3, 6, 81, 113, 179
    Address on Religious Instruction, 84–85
    and miracles, 91, 108–11
    and Platonism, 151–56
    dream of 40 Martyrs, 109
    On Pilgrimages, 135

Hilary of Poitiers, 16, 21, 31, 38ff., 144
    commentary on Matthew, 10–16

image of God, 83–84, 141, 151, 153–54,
    161, 170, 178. *See also* Platonism,
    Christian

Jerome, 90, 129, 143
    and Jovinian, 140ff.
    and Origenist controversy, 141ff.

and Priscillian, 139–40
and Vigilantius, 136ff.
commentary on Matthew, 16–23
John Cassian, 100, 103, 138, 142–43, 177
John Chrysostom, 27, 90, 95, 100, 119, 142,
    148, 171
    and Origenist controversy, 142–43
    catechetical homilies, 67ff.
    homilies on Matthew and John, 48–56
    homilies *On Providence*, 161–66

magic, 12, 19–20, 46–47, 50, 56, 61, 73–74,
    78, 82, 119ff., 139
    amulets, 47, 73, 78, 79, 119, 120, 122,
        123, 124
    and Ammianus Marcellinus's history,
        121–22
    and church controversy, 122–23
    astrology, 47, 50, 73, 82, 119, 120, 122,
        161
    canons against, 119–20
    Jews as magicians, 53, 56, 73
    legislation against, 120–21
    oracles, 73, 79, 82, 93
Martin of Tours, 138, 139, 144ff.
martyrs, 5, 42, 73, 82, 89, 95, 97ff., 99,
    108ff., 116, 127, 128ff., 131, 171
    and monks, 97, 105, 145
    as examples, 82, 97–98, 179
    as patrons, 5, 97, 100, 103, 108ff., 116,
        125, 127, 128, 129ff., 135–36, 137, 138,
        147. *See also* cult of saints; relics
Melania the Younger, 131ff., 143
mind as governing body and passions, 58,
    83–84, 86, 106–7, 152–53, 156ff., 158,
    160–61, 178. *See also* Platonism, Chris-
    tian
miracles of Christ,
    described as absent in infancy, 38, 50, 77
    described as attending Christ, 37, 38, 49–
        50, 60, 77, 84
    described as contrasting to vainglory, 11,
        25, 53
    described as greater than prophets', 25–
        26, 28, 32
    described as not magical, 30, 47, 78–79
    described as problematic, 35, 41–42, 44–
        45, 55–56, 58–59, 87
    described as related to Jews' rejection of
        Christ, 26, 29–30, 31, 52–53, 57

described as related to meaning of scripture, 13–14, 21, 23–24, 26, 30, 34, 36–37, 41, 46, 51ff.

described as related to passion and humility, 44, 53, 60, 64–65, 78, 103, 147

described as relatively unimportant, 16–17, 18, 30, 32, 33, 41, 43ff., 46ff., 51, 53, 77–78

described as undoubted, 16, 34, 49–50, 53, 78, 86

function to educate and give faith, 12, 16, 17, 21, 24, 25, 26, 30, 45, 50, 52–53, 57, 60

function to educate if faith present, 11–13, 19–20, 21–22, 23, 33, 52, 53

function to effect faith but fail to do so, 12, 18–19, 26, 29–30, 33, 44, 51, 53, 57, 60

function to give moral example, 25–26, 30, 33, 58

function to give the simple and grosser people knowledge, 24–25, 29, 49, 52

function to reveal Christ as God and creator, 11, 13, 16, 27, 31–32, 33, 37, 43, 50, 51, 57, 60, 77, 82, 166, 173

function to reveal Christ's person as incarnate Lord, 10, 11, 12, 13, 16, 17, 23, 26ff., 29, 31ff., 33, 37–38, 43–44, 57, 60, 65, 77

function to supply authority for Christ and church, 10, 17, 49, 50, 51, 52, 53, 56, 57, 60, 79, 171ff.

signify the church, 10, 13–16, 21ff., 31, 33, 38ff., 57–58, 60

signify redemption, 13, 33, 40ff., 44ff., 57, 60, 86–87

signify resurrection, 44–45, 60, 126

signify spiritual and moral meaning of redemption, 20, 40ff., 45, 54–55, 58, 60, 77, 80, 86

miracles in the church,

ancient view of miracles, 3–4

apostles' and prophets' miracles, 12, 13, 17, 19–20, 52, 58, 113

described as associated with community, 2–3, 5, 6, 87, 103, 115–16, 118ff., 123, 128ff., 148–49

described as ceasing after Christ, 52, 56, 115, 170ff.

described as important, 2–3, 6, 90, 111, 114–15, 125, 148

described as producing vainglory, 51, 54, 59, 103

described as relatively unimportant, 3, 47, 51, 54, 55ff., 61, 81, 87, 103, 106–7, 111, 117, 171, 180

described in contrast to demonic and false miracles, 12, 19, 26, 33, 47, 51, 53, 147

described in relation to Christ's, 106, 113, 115, 145–46

described in relation to church and theology, 9, 42, 48, 60

described in relation to nature, 3–4, 17, 37, 43, 61, 166ff., 170ff.

described in tension with Christian message, 2–3, 5, 61, 103, 105–6, 107, 111–12, 114–15, 116, 117–18, 148, 171, 179, 180

function to convert, 96–97, 109–10

function to establish authority, 97–98, 102

function to refute heresy, 94, 95, 96, 112

function to refute paganism, 52, 56, 91ff., 93–94, 99, 109, 145

take form of benefactions, 89, 94–95, 95–96, 97, 101–2, 102–3, 105, 108, 110–11, 112–13, 130–31, 145

take form of exorcisms, 89, 95, 101, 102, 105ff., 110, 112, 131, 145, 179

take form of healings, 89, 92, 95, 96, 101, 102, 105ff., 108, 110–11, 112–13, 127, 128, 130, 131, 132, 145

take form of moral benefits, 100, 101, 102, 111, 112, 128

take form of raising the dead, 102, 145–46. *See also* martyrs; monks

monks (and holy people), 2, 5, 89–90, 100ff., 116, 138–47, 141, 142, 152, 156, 181

as examples, 54, 58, 59, 104ff., 106, 111, 113, 144

as patrons, 5, 97, 102ff., 105ff., 109ff., 113ff., 114–15, 116, 125, 138, 145, 147

problem of holy people, 104, 138, 140–41, 142, 144, 148, 181

relation to martyrs, 97, 105, 145

Nestorian controversy, 29, 57, 90

oracles. *See* magic

Origen, 5, 6, 11, 30, 35, 83, 89, 155, 156, 159, 161

Origenist controversy, 90, 138, 140, 141–42, 147

paganism, 8, 19, 52, 58, 76, 84, 89, 91ff., 92–93, 96, 100–101, 105, 109, 117, 119ff., 125, 129, 145
Palladius, 88, 90, 94–95, 100ff.
patron. *See* martyrs; monks
Paulinus of Nola, 129ff., 131, 134, 135, 136, 139, 143, 144
Pelagius and Pelagian controversy, 138, 139, 143ff., 177ff.
piety, popular, 3, 9, 117ff.
Plato and Platonism, 153–54, 156, 160, 161, 162, 167
Platonism, Christian, 2–3, 5ff., 42, 83, 150–70, 180–82. *See also* contemplation, freedom; image of God; mind; sovereignty of God
Priscillian, 138ff., 146–47
Prosper of Aquitaine, 177ff.
providence. *See* freedom
Prudentius, 128ff.

relics, 3, 63, 92, 97ff., 99–100, 108–9, 110, 112, 116–17, 118, 124, 125, 126, 127, 128, 130, 131, 132, 134, 136, 137, 147–48
of St. Peter's chains, 132
of true cross, 92, 132–34
private ownership of, 100, 116, 125, 131–32
relation of saints to, 129–30, 135–36. *See also* cult of saints; martyrs
Rufinus, 88, 90, 91, 93, 96, 129, 131, 141ff.

San Apollinare Nuovo, 62ff.
Santa Pudenziana, 9–10, 16, 33
Satan,
and idolatry, 79, 80, 98, 100–101, 105, 109
and Jews, 15, 39
and persecution, 80
as death, 72–73, 82
as sin, 73, 74, 79, 82, 100–101
Christ's victory over, 12, 17, 41, 49, 50, 57ff., 60, 65, 72–73, 76, 77, 78, 79, 80, 81, 82, 83, 84, 85ff., 86, 105, 110, 157, 180
battle with and Christian victory over, 13, 21, 54, 55, 57ff., 60–61, 69–70, 72ff., 74ff., 76, 77, 79, 95, 98, 100–101, 105, 106–7, 110, 113, 147, 161, 180
ransom to, 21, 82–83, 84–85, 157
redemption of, 85, 141
renunciation of, 68ff., 73
scripture, 9ff., 13ff., 15, 20, 21, 23, 24, 29, 30ff., 35, 36–37, 41–42, 49, 62, 65ff., 90, 105, 141, 151, 153, 160, 166, 170
Socrates Scholasticus, 88, 89–90, 94, 95, 96, 97
sovereignty of God,
emphasis upon, 175, 176, 179, 181
qualification of, 161–66, 169–70, 179. *See also* freedom and providence; Platonism, Christian
Sozomen, 88, 89–90, 91–92, 93, 94, 95, 96, 99ff.
Sulpicius Severus, 129, 134, 136, 138–39, 144ff.

Theodore of Mopsuestia, 31
catechetical homilies, 67ff.
commentary on John, 23–28
Theodoret, 88, 90, 93, 94, 96
and cult of saints, 124–25
History of the Monks in Syria, 91, 112–15, 138, 144, 146

virtue. *See* freedom

Index of Biblical Citations

Genesis 1:1, 167
1:5, 167
1:9, 167
1:20, 167
1:24, 168, 169
1:26, 83
1:27, 154
1:31, 162
2:7, 27
3:16, 31
3:21, 159
22, 163
49, 158
Exodus 19:6, 173
Leviticus 19:19, 153
Deuteronomy 6:16, 55
22:10, 153
1 Kings 17:14, 25
17:16, 40
18:41ff., 173
2 Kings 4:1–7, 26
5:14, 40
6:16, 128
Job 9:8, 81
38:16f., 81
Psalm 2, 24
8, 24, 51
19:1, 127

45, 24
68:31, 21
69:2, 81
69:9, 24
74:13, 81
103:11ff., 162
103:13, 162
110, 24
133:2, 69
145:3, 151
145:5, 151
Ecclesiastes 2:14, 69
Song of Solomon 1:2f., 69
5:3, 159
8:6, 160
Isaiah 7, 80
7:4, 80
8:4, 80
30:3–4, 68
35:1–7, 81
49:14f., 162
61:1, 80
62:5, 162
Daniel 3, 54
7, 77
Jonah 4, 163
Zechariah 11:12f., 77
Malachi, 24

Matthew 1:1–17, 46
2:9, 50
3:3, 12
4:18ff., 64
5:3, 80
5:19, 20
7:9ff., 162
7:22, 12
7:22–23, 19
8, 14
8:1–13, 13, 17
8:5ff., 22
8:7, 20
8:10, 20
8:15, 17
8:20, 20
8:23ff., 11
8:26, 16
8:28, 39
8:28–9:8, 14
9:1ff., 20
9:2, 75
9:2ff., 13
9:18–34, 14, 21
9:20ff., 20
9:22, 50
9:23ff., 39
9:27, 15

9:27ff., 12
9:32, 15
9:35, 15, 17
10:1ff., 13
10:5ff., 17
10:8, 19
11:3, 12
11:20–24, 19
11:22, 23
11:28, 80
12:9ff., 11, 15
12:14, 11
12:22, 15
12:24ff., 15
12:43ff., 15
13:58, 18
14, 15
14:13, 15
14:13ff., 11
14:14–22, 66
14:16, 18
14:25ff., 81
14:29, 51, 75
14:33, 17
14:36, 20
15:21ff., 15, 20, 22
15:30–31, 20
15:34ff., 15
16:1, 12, 18
17:1ff., 18
17:15, 21
17:20, 13, 21
17:24ff., 21
17:27, 51
19:16ff., 53
20:29–34, 66
20:30, 39
20:34, 17
21:15ff., 51
21:18ff., 22
21:21, 19
21:28ff., 12
27:45, 50
28:2, 13
28:11, 19

Mark 2:1–12, 66
2:5, 37
2:7, 37
5:21–43, 66

6:5f., 18
7:31ff., 75
8:5ff., 22
9:24, 75
11:13, 22
13:22, 48
Luke 1:1, 42
2:1ff., 40
4:1ff., 41
4:21, 80
4:25ff., 38
4:27, 41
5:13, 37
5:14, 42
5:17ff., 41, 66
5:25, 37
6:6ff., 41
6:17, 37
7:1–17, 38
7:3ff., 57
7:11–17, 66
7:14, 58
7:18ff., 40
8:22ff., 37
8:26ff., 58
8:27, 39
8:27ff., 66
8:39, 39
8:40–56, 39
8:41–56, 66
8:42, 21
8:45, 26
9:1–5, 58
9:17, 58
9:49f., 59
10:18, 58
10:20, 48, 56, 59, 107
11:13, 58
11:21f., 58
11:24ff., 39
13:10ff., 39
13:18f., 40
18:35, 39
19:13ff., 154
23:46, 77
24:13ff., 46
John 1:11, 26, 51
2:1–11, 30, 43, 45, 65, 75, 171, 173

2:4, 44, 47
2:6ff., 41
2:9, 37
2:11, 44
2:17, 24
2:23, 24
2:23–25, 24
2:24, 29
3:2, 24
3:16, 164
4, 64
4:46ff., 24
4:48, 24, 44
4:50, 25
4:53, 25
5, 26
5:1, 30
5:1ff., 26, 66, 75
5:5, 31
5:6, 25
5:10, 26, 30
5:17, 27
5:18, 26
5:19, 27
5:20, 45
5:22, 28
5:25, 27, 45
5:30, 28
5:43, 26
6, 31
6:5–14, 66
6:10, 24
6:11, 25
6:12, 26
6:16ff., 46
6:17ff., 31
6:30, 26
6:33, 40
6:36, 30, 51
6:62, 32
7–9, 25
7:31, 51
7:38, 51
8:28, 32
8:41, 74
8:59, 25
9, 25, 26
9:6, 27, 37
9:16, 26
9:33, 43

9:39, 25
10:33, 26
10:41, 32, 55
11, 27, 32, 37, 45, 66
11:14ff., 75
11:33, 26
11:35, 25
11:43, 28
11:52, 58
12:24, 40
12:37, 26
14:6, 22
20:29, 56
20:30, 49
20:30–31, 24
21:25, 19, 49

Acts   3:12, 53
8:19, 20
Romans   1:20, 37

6:1ff., 70
8:35ff., 99
9–11, 16, 22, 164
9:11, 39
9:20, 164
9:25, 39
11:16ff., 22
11:25f., 22
11:33, 164
12:2, 154
13, 43

1 Corinthians   13, 56, 153
13:2, 48
13:12, 164
14:22, 49,
56, 137

2 Corinthians   3:14ff., 46
5:10, 135
5:14f., 82

5:17, 153
8:9, 40
Galatians   6:15, 153
Ephesians   2:14, 82
4:13ff., 154
6:13ff., 114
Colossians   1:15, 154
2 Timothy   4:7f., 110
Titus   2:13, 46
Hebrews   1:2, 28
2:14f., 82
1 Peter   2:9, 69
2:22, 21
5:5, 151
2 Peter   1:4, 37
Wisdom of Solomon   2:23f.,
72,
82
Baruch   3:37, 29